Modern Judgements

PASTERNAK

PG Davie
3476 Pasternak
.P27
Z66
1970

Oakland Community College
Orchard Ridge Campus Library
27055 Orchard Lake Road
Farmington Hills, MI 48018

MODERN JUDGEMENTS
General Editor: P. N. FURBANK

Dickens   A. E. Dyson
Henry James   Tony Tanner
Milton   Alan Rudrum
Sean O'Casey   Ronald Ayling
Pasternak   Donald Davie and Angela Livingstone
Walter Scott   D. D. Devlin
Shelley   R. B. Woodings
Swift   A. Norman Jeffares

IN PREPARATION

Matthew Arnold   P. A. W. Collins
Ford Madox Ford   Richard A. Cassell
Freud   F. Cioffi
Marvell   M. Wilding
Pope   Graham Martin
Racine   R. C. Knight

PASTERNAK

MODERN JUDGEMENTS

edited by
Donald Davie and Angela Livingstone
with verse translations by Donald Davie

Aurora Publishers Incorporated

NASHVILLE/LONDON

FIRST PUBLISHED 1969 BY
MACMILLAN AND COMPANY LIMITED
LONDON, ENGLAND

COPYRIGHT © 1970 BY
AURORA PUBLISHERS INCORPORATED
NASHVILLE, TENNESSEE 37219
LIBRARY OF CONGRESS CATALOG CARD NUMBER: 75-127562
STANDARD BOOK NUMBER: 87695-096-9
MANUFACTURED IN THE UNITED STATES OF AMERICA

Contents

Acknowledgements	7
Note on Translations	7
General Editor's Preface	9
Introduction, by Donald Davie	11
Chronology	35
ILYA EHRENBURG Boris Leonidovich Pasternak	39
MARINA TSVETAYEVA A Downpour of Light	42
OSIP MANDEL'SHTAM Notes on Poetry	67
NIKOLAI ASEEV Melody or Intonation	73
A. LEZHNEV The Poetry of Boris Pasternak	85
WLADIMIR WEIDLE The Poetry and Prose of Boris Pasternak	108
YURI TYNYANOV Pasternak's 'Mission'	126
ROMAN JAKOBSON The Prose of the Poet Pasternak	135
ANNA AKHMATOVA Boris Pasternak	152
ANDREI SINYAVSKY Boris Pasternak	154
MICHEL AUCOUTURIER The Legend of the Poet in the Short Stories	220
NICOLA CHIAROMONTE Pasternak's Message	231
ISAAC DEUTSCHER Pasternak and the Calendar of the Revolution	240

IRVING HOWE Freedom and the Ashcan of History   259

Select Bibliography   269
Notes on Contributors   273
Index   275

Acknowledgements

Nicola Chiaromonte, 'Pasternak's Message', in *Partisan Review*, xxv (Winter 1958) i 127-34 (© *Partisan Review*, 1958); Isaac Deutscher, 'Pasternak and the Calendar of the Revolution', in *The Ironies of History* (Oxford University Press); Irving Howe, 'Freedom and the Ashcan of History', in *Partisan Review* (Spring 1959) pp. 266-75.

We wish to express our thanks to Mrs Valentina S. Coe for her help with this book; the translations both of the critical prose and of the quoted verse would have been very much the poorer had she not generously put at our service her sensitive and deep understanding of literary Russian.

We should also like to thank Mr John Rignall for doing most of the work of translating Roman Jakobson's article from the German.

Finally thanks are due to Mrs Marjorie McGlashan and Mrs Jean Budd for their assistance in typing out the many versions of the manuscripts.

Note on Translations

Responsibility for the translations in the present volume is as follows:

Translation from the Russian of articles by Ehrenburg, Tsvetayeva, Mandel'shtam, Aseev, Lezhnev, Weidle, Tynyanov and Sinyavsky – Angela Livingstone; translation from the Russian of poem by Akhmatova – Donald Davie; translation from the German of article by Jakobson – John Rignall and Angela Livingstone; translation of verse quotations from Pasternak throughout the volume – Donald Davie.

Footnotes to each article that is translated from Russian are provided by the translator, except where it is indicated that they are by the author of the article.

General Editor's Preface

LITERARY criticism has only recently come of age as an academic discipline, and the intellectual activity that, a hundred years ago, went into theological discussion, now finds its most natural outlet in the critical essay. Amid a good deal that is dull or silly or pretentious, every year now produces a crop of critical essays which are brilliant and profound not only as contributions to the understanding of a particular author but as statements of an original way of looking at literature and the world. Hence, it often seems that the most useful undertaking for an academic publisher might be, not so much to commission new books of literary criticism or scholarship, as to make the best of what exists easily available. This at least is the purpose of the present series of anthologies, each of which is devoted to a single major writer.

The guiding principle of selection is to assemble the best *modern* criticism – broadly speaking, that of the last twenty or thirty years – and to include historic and classic essays, however famous, only when they are still influential and represent the best statements of their particular point of view. It will, however, be one of the functions of the editor's Introduction to sketch in the earlier history of criticism in regard to the author concerned.

Each volume will attempt to strike a balance between general essays and ones on specialised aspects, or particular works, of the writer in question. And though in many instances the bulk of the articles will come from British and American sources, certain of the volumes will draw heavily on material in other European languages – most of it being translated for the first time.

P. N. FURBANK

Introduction

IT would be presumptuous and contradictory for us, having collected what we judge to be the best critical essays on Pasternak, to preface our selection by a critical essay of our own. That would suggest that having mastered what Tynyanov and Jakobson and Sinyavsky have to say, we can supplement, correct and synthesize them; as if we were schoolmasters and they our class of talented but still immature pupils.

What may be useful on the other hand is to take their insights, which they have expressed naturally and properly in the perspective of the Russian poetic tradition, and try to find whatever analogies there may be between that tradition as Pasternak inherited and augmented it, and the tradition of Anglo-American poetry as it was inherited and enriched by the British and American poets who were Pasternak's contemporaries. This is a sufficiently hazardous undertaking. But since there would be no point to this publication if we did not believe that Pasternak is important to readers who have no Russian, it must be true that there are bridges, if only we can find them, by which we may grope uncertainly from the poetry we know in our own language to the poetry in the unknown language of Pasternak.

Pasternak: the Early Collections[1]

At first sight, however, one is dismayed by the extent to which all the bridges are down. In respect of the early collections by which Pasternak made his name, there are in particular three areas in which misunderstanding is very likely, and yet may be avoided; three bridges which

---

[1] *Twin in the Clouds* (1914); *Over the Barriers* (written 1914-16; published 1917); *My Sister Life* (written 1917; published 1922); and *Themes and Variations* (written 1916-22; published 1923).

need to be repaired. They may be labelled as Sound, Symbolism and Syntax. And we may briefly consider these in turn.

It is Tynyanov in particular who shows how appreciative readers of early Pasternak were enthralled by his compositions considered as textures of sheer sound. This is at once a large stumbling-block for Anglo-American readers. It is not that this feature is peculiarly untranslatable, for in fact it is often possible for the translator to create equivalent harmonies. The trouble is that in the present century many of us have been schooled either to disregard this dimension of poetry altogether, or else, more grievously, to suspect it. We have been told to beware of poets who work upon us particularly by means of euphony, onomatopoeia, alliteration, assonance. Ever since I. A. Richards's *Principles of Literary Criticism* there have been influential critics warning us that the semantic aspect of poetry must be primary, and that the musicality of poetry can legitimately be exploited only so as to point up and emphasize the play of meanings. Only very lately have we begun to realize that the interplay of sound and sense in poetry is too subtle to be schematized in this way. And investigations of this interplay, such investigations as Tynyanov's, still seem to us very risky:

> THE RISK: to suggest that the conquest of babble by the ear – to distinguish and organize, to make significant, to relate as experience, to name – is the origin of speech and emotion. Speech at this level articulates internal sensations. 'The inner voice' as a counterpart of the inner light. The recurrence of vowels and consonants, the tonal structure, is related to heart and alimentary tract in its rhythmic organization; it is expressive. It is 'moving' – melopoeia is the passionate system of the poem.[1]

In Pasternak's lifetime, Joyce's *Finnegans Wake* is the one ambitious work of the English-speaking world which explores this region in which sense grows out of sound, as much as sound grows out of sense. The young Pasternak, on the other hand, explored this possibility constantly. In many of his early poems he dramatized 'the conquest of babble by the ear' in search of meanings. And an American scholar, Dale L. Plank, has lately most valuably dotted the *is* and crossed the *t*s of Tynyanov's observations to this effect.[2]

---

[1] Robert Duncan, 'Notes on Poetics, Regarding Olson's Maximus', in *Agenda*, III (Dec. 1964) vi 32.

[2] Dale L. Plank, *Pasternak's Lyric: A Study of Sound and Imagery* (The Hague, 1966).

Perhaps the poet in English who comes nearest to emulating Pasternak in this respect is Hart Crane. At any rate Hart Crane, for instance in *White Buildings*, orchestrates his verses very voluptuously. And not many English-speaking critics have been ready to trust Crane's 'music' as the Russian critics in this volume have trusted the music, the luxuriant clash and crackle of sheer sound, in Pasternak. In Pasternak as in Crane the rich orchestration often goes along with synaesthesia, the mingling or deliberate muddling of appeals to the five senses. This is what Louis Zukofsky, when he writes of Crane, refers to as 'the Wagnerian ideal'.[1] And Zukofsky quotes Ezra Pound's description of this method of proceeding: 'You confuse the spectator by smacking as many of his senses as possible at every possible moment, this prevents his noting anything with unusual lucidity, but you may fluster or excite him to the point of making him receptive.' Some of Pasternak's poems seem to fluster or excite the reader into receptivity, rather than presenting him with one image at a time sharply edged and lucid. An example is 'Margarita', a poem from *Themes and Variations* (1918), which is quoted in full and approvingly by Wladimir Weidle (below, p. 116). British and American readers in our time are more suspicious of being flustered in this way than are for instance French-speakers and Spanish-speakers, if only because the French and the Spanish poetic traditions have come to terms with surrealism, as the Anglo-American tradition has not.

But 'the Wagnerian ideal', as Zukofsky and Pound define it, does not account for more than a few of Pasternak's poems in which the texture of sound counts for a great deal. Apart from anything else many such poems, particularly in *My Sister Life*, are notable for sharply edged and immediately lucid images, particularly of landscape and weather. Dale L. Plank, in painstaking analysis of several such poems, discovers that many of them 'are more densely, more consciously ... organized in their sounds at first, less so as the poem progresses'.[2] In other words 'the conquest of babble by the ear' is something that happens in the course of the poem, as we move through it from first to last; the poem begins in 'babble' and ends in 'conquest'. And this brings us to the second of our broken bridges, that of 'Symbolism', specifically, of Pasternak's relation to the French *symboliste* poets. For Plank points out very justly that in the case of poems which progress in this way,

[1] Louis Zukofsky, 'American Poetry 1920-1930' (1930), in *Prepositions* (1967) p. 131.
[2] Plank, op. cit. p. 26.

We may assume that the poem's composition proceeded according to the plan described as follows by Valéry:

> If I am questioned; if anyone wonders (as happens sometimes quite peremptorily) what I 'wanted to say' in a certain poem, I reply that I did not *want to say* but *wanted to make*, and that it was the intention of *making* which *wanted* what I said....
>
> As for the *Cimetière marin*, this intention was at first no more than a rhythmic figure, empty, or filled with meaningless syllables, which obsessed me for some time....

Russia had had its own Symbolist school of poets. For that matter Valeri Bryusov, himself an ex-Symbolist, recorded that as late as 1922 self-styled 'Symbolists' were advertising public readings of their poems, as were acmeists, futurists, expressionists, neo-classicists, realists, and neo-realists, neo-romantics, and comically many others.[1] And the Russian Symbolists were aware of having some intentions in common with the French *symbolistes*, though the Russian school and the French came to stand for such different things that the common title 'Symbolist' is misleading. Pasternak, however, if we except an early and not very decisive connection with Centrifuga, a group of moderate Futurists, never aligned himself with any consciously instituted school, and the things he has in common with French *symboliste* poets (Mr Plank convincingly finds parallels with Mallarmé and Verlaine as well as Valéry) are to be thought of as 'parallels', not in terms of derivations, allegiances or influences. Certainly Pasternak could never have subscribed to Valéry's categorical insistence that Art is superior to Nature. Quite the contrary, indeed, as we shall see. On the other hand in his autobiography *Safe Conduct* (1931) he declared something that Valéry would have subscribed to, when he wrote: 'The clearest, most memorable and most important thing in art is its coming into being, and the world's best works, while telling of the most diverse things, are in fact narrating their own birth.' And Plank shows how poem after poem by Pasternak is like Valéry's *Cimetière Marin* or Mallarmé's *Prose pour Des Esseintes* in having for subject nothing but its own way of coming to birth, sustaining itself, and drawing to a close.

Unless I misunderstand T. S. Eliot's 'Love Song of J. Alfred Prufrock', that poem is another of the same kind, as are the *Four*

---

[1] Valeri Bryusov, 'Vchera, sevodnya i zavtra v russkoi poezii', in *Pechat' i Revolyutsiya*, VII (1922) 38–67.

Quartets also. And indeed Eliot was so explicit about his kinship with the French *symbolistes* – Laforgue in his youth, Valéry in his maturity – that there is no excuse for Anglo-American readers when they find the *symboliste* poetic bizarre and sterile. Unfortunately, 'aestheticism' is a word of such ill omen in modern English usage, and a term which cloudily comprehends so much, that we commonly dismiss out of hand any poem which is related to 'life' so indirectly, so far below the surface, as are the poems written in the *symboliste* tradition. In order to save Eliot from the imputation of Art for Art's Sake, our philistinism has distorted him by insisting on looking for help with his poems anywhere but where he pointed, to France. And it is likely enough that we shall try to do the same with Pasternak. Accordingly it needs to be said that in Pasternak's poetry, no less in his theory of poetry as we find it in Section VII of *Safe Conduct*, there is a marked strain of what the English-speaking reader will take to be haughty aestheticism.

The musicality of *symboliste* poetry is not always a matter of what I have called 'orchestration'. Valéry mocks any attempt to define *symbolisme* by pressing the notion of 'symbol', and declares instead that what defines it is 'the common intention of several groups of poets (otherwise mutually inimical) to "reclaim their own from Music"'.[1] And the context makes clear that Valéry has in mind far more than patternings of sound, important as that is to *symboliste* poetry and to all poetry. Even Verlaine, when he declared 'De la musique avant toute chose', may have intended to stress, along with orchestration of sounds, the *continuity* of music, its way of never stopping but to start again. In this way *symboliste* poetry, notably in Valéry as earlier in Baudelaire, is as much concerned with the unsounded rhythms of syntax, the swerving and coiling and unwinding of the poetic sentence, as with the sounded rhythms that are governed by prosody. And this is the third of the bridges that need to be built or rebuilt if we are to cross from the world of our poetry to the world of Pasternak. To Mayakovsky, according to Ehrenburg in his memoirs, it seemed in 1923 that Pasternak's poetry manifested 'application of a dynamic syntax to the revolutionary task'. And to Yevgeni Zamyatin writing in the same year on Pasternak's stories in prose (*Russkoye Iskusstvo*, II–III) it appeared that 'The shift he has made, the new thing he has given, that which is his own, is not in his plots (he has no plots) and not in his vocabulary,

[1] Paul Valéry, 'A Foreword' (1920), in *The Art of Poetry*, trans. Denise Folliot (1958), p. 42.

but on a plane where hardly any one else but he is working: in syntax.'
However, the fullest and most valuable statement of this, again in 1923,
came from Mandel'shtam:

> In poetry the truly creative age is not the age of invention but the age of
> imitation. When the prayer-books have been written then it is time for the
> service to be held. The last Poetic Breviary to have been issued for general
> use in Russia is Pasternak's *My Sister Life*. Not since the time of Batyushkov
> has such a mature new harmony been heard in Russian poetry. Pasternak is
> no mere thinker-up of novelties, no conjuror; he is the begetter of a new
> way of writing, a new structure for Russian verse, which corresponds to the
> virile maturity attained by the language. In this new harmony everything
> can be expressed, and every one, whether they want to or not, will use it,
> because from now on it is the common achievement of all Russian poets.
> Hitherto the logical structure of the sentence has been growing weaker,
> along with the weakening of the poem itself, i.e. it was but the shortest
> way to express a poetic idea. Frequent poetic use wears down the customary
> path of logic until it becomes – as such – unnoticeable. Syntax, which is
> poetry's circulatory system, is attacked by sclerosis. Then there comes a poet
> who resurrects the virgin vigour of the logical sentence-structure. This was
> what Pushkin was amazed by in Batyushkov; and now Pasternak awaits
> his Pushkin.[1]

To be sure, the concern for syntax which produced in Pasternak's
poetry the effects that Mayakovsky and Mandel'shtam respond to need
not be the sort of concern for syntax that we find in Valéry. Indeed
Mayakovsky's word 'dynamic' and Mandel'shtam's 'virgin vigour'
suggest something rather different. And it may be in fact that there is a
much nearer parallel to be found in English than in French. I have in
mind a well-known letter of 1926 written by W. B. Yeats to H. J. C.
Grierson. Here Yeats declares:

> The over childish or over pretty or feminine element in some good
> Wordsworth and in much poetry up to our date comes from the lack of
> natural momentum in the syntax. This momentum underlies almost every
> Elizabethan and Jacobean lyric and is far more important than simplicity of
> vocabulary. If Wordsworth had found it he could have carried any amount
> of elaborate English. Byron, unlike the Elizabethans though he always
> tries for it, constantly allows it to die out in some mind-created construc-

[1] *Russkoye Iskusstvo* (1923) 182.

tion, but is I think the one great English poet – though one can hardly call him great except in purpose and manhood – who sought it constantly.[1]

This concern remained with Yeats until his last years, when it crops up in his letters to Dorothy Wellesley, and the effect of this preoccupation is to be seen in the poems which he wrote from 1916 onwards. His reference to 'Elizabethan and Jacobean lyric' is significant in a letter to Grierson, the editor of John Donne. For the syntax that has 'natural momentum' appears in Yeats's poems whenever we are aware of the presence of Donne. If his 'momentum' corresponds to Mayakovsky's 'dynamic' and Mandel'shtam's 'virgin vigour', it may be that in Pasternak as in Yeats we encounter a syntax that has to do, not with *symboliste* 'music', but with the dramatic or histrionic illusion of a man's presence and his impassioned speech.

Unfortunately, the grammatical structures of Russian and of English are so different that the translator despairs of producing any equivalent to this feature of his style which Mandel'shtam and Mayakovsky thought so important. Five polysyllabic words can be ranged in two lines of Pasternak as massively as blocks of masonry – an effect available only in a highly inflected language, something that English, with its clutter of prepositions and particles, can hardly attain to.

Pasternak and the Formalists

By 1922 Pasternak's reputation in Russia was already assured. What is striking, among Russian critics who respond to him in 1922 and 1923 (the first years after the Revolution when reliable publication of books and journals was resumed), is the stress on Pasternak's originality, his 'newness'. And there was no particular strangeness or difficulty, in those years, about acknowledging Pasternak's remoteness from political activity and at the same time seeing a profound affinity between the Revolution of 1917 and this poet's revolutionary attitude to his art, and his revolutionary handling of his medium.

For Bryusov in his 'Yesterday, Today and Tomorrow of Russian Poetry', yesterday was represented by Symbolism, today by Futurism, and tomorrow by 'proletarian poetry'; and when poetry emerged which expressed the 'new world-view' of the proletariat, then (Bryusov

[1] *The Letters of W. B. Yeats*, ed. Allan Wade (New York, 1955) p. 710.

believes) Pasternak would be left behind as a 'poet of the intelligentsia':

> To the same extent that Mayakovsky, in the moods of his poetry, is close to the proletarian poets, Pasternak is without doubt a poet of the intelligentsia. In part, this leads to a breadth of creative range: history and the present age, the data of science and the talk of the day, books and life – all these things on equal terms get into Pasternak's poems and there, in accord with his special sense of what the world is, they are all set out as it were on one level. In part, though, this excessive intellectuality makes his poetry anaemic, pushing it towards anti-poetic reflections, turning some poems into philosophic discussions, sometimes substituting witty paradoxes for living images.

Bryusov, apparently concerned in this article to deny his Symbolist past and prove himself a supporter of the most modern, the Bolshevik cause, none the less acknowledges:

> Pasternak's poems have had an honour, accorded to almost no works of poetry (except those that were prohibited by the Tsarist censorship) since about the time of Pushkin: they have circulated in manuscript. Young poets have known by heart poems by Pasternak that have not yet anywhere appeared in print, and they have imitated him more entirely than they have imitated Mayakovsky....

And accordingly Bryusov is eager to enlist Pasternak as a poet of the Revolution *à son insu*:

> Pasternak has not written any poems specifically about the Revolution but, perhaps even without his knowing it, his poems are steeped in the spirit of the present; his psychology is not borrowed from books of the past, it is an expression of his own being and could have been formed only in the conditions of our life.[1]

Very strikingly Bryusov agrees with the resolutely a-political Mandel'shtam (with Tynyanov also) in seeing Pasternak as pathfinder and trail-blazer, as pioneer and innovator, not as the 'classic' master, Pushkin to his Batyushkov, who characteristically takes over and consummates the innovations of others; an Ezra Pound, we may say, rather than a Yeats.

However, the twenties in Russia were the years of a school of gifted

---

[1] Bryusov, op. cit.

Introduction

critics who were not, like Bryusov, mainly concerned with the significance of the Revolution nor yet, like Mandel'shtam, creative writers concerned to understand their contemporaries so as to find their own way forward. These were the Formalists. It is no accident, for instance, though to the English-speaking reader it is very unexpected, that in the very years of the Revolution, immediately after Pasternak's experiments with orchestration of sounds in poetry, there should have appeared 'the pioneer study directed at the discernment of patterns in sounds in poetry and their classification',[1] Osip Brik's 'Zvukovye povtory'.[2] Brik's studies are a contribution to a revolution in poetic theory and critical method which parallels Pasternak's revolution in poetic method, as that in turn parallels the Bolsheviks' revolution in political method and political structure. And this is the revolution which called itself 'Formalism'.

The Formalist critics are represented in our selection by Tynyanov and by Roman Jakobson. Formalist criticism as a whole gave no specially prominent place to Pasternak's writing, yet there are illuminating parallels between Pasternak's theory and practice and Formalist doctrine. In the first place, according to Formalist doctrine what art does is *ostranenie*, making strange. Art by the distortions it effects makes the world strange and novel, restoring to the reader, who is blinkered and dulled by habit and linguistic cliché, a child-like vision. In the words of Viktor Shklovsky: 'Thus in order to restore to us the perception of life, to make a stone stony, there exists that which we call art.'[3] There has to be some connection between this and Pasternak, the poet who was acclaimed in the twenties by critics and reviewers in Russia as above all a man who sees the world as if 'for the first time'. And in his poems Pasternak is constantly fascinated by this capacity of poetry for renewing and refreshing perception – yet with this crucial difference, that for him it is poetry that does this, not the poet; that it is the world which thus renews itself, through the poet and his poem, but not at the poet's behest. Equally the distortions, deformations or displacements by which reality refreshes itself in poems are for Pasternak something that happens in the world, something that the poet notices and records, whereas to the Formalists the displacements are effected by the poet. To this end, as they understand it, the poet may

[1] Plank, op. cit. p. 19.
[2] In Osip Brik, *Sborniki po teorii poeticheskovo yazyka* (Petrograd, 1916-17).
[3] Quoted in Victor Erlich, *Russian Formalism* (The Hague, 1965) p. 76.

employ certain devices. And indeed the notion of 'device' is central to Formalist criticism. For them subject-matter is unimportant. And by taking the work as device, or as a structure of devices, they proclaim their indifference to the work in its aspect as a reflection of biographical circumstances, psychological or social. There are closely related attitudes to be found in Pasternak, and it is these indeed which can mislead the English-speaking reader into thinking him an aesthete. Not that Pasternak busies himself with detailed study of this or that poetic device. But like the Formalists he declares himself to be centrally concerned, in any work, with the presence of Art in it; not at all with the overt subject-matter, still less with the personality of the author, or with his representativeness:

> When we suppose that in *Tristan, Romeo and Juliet*, and other great works a powerful passion is portrayed, we under-estimate their content. Their theme is wider than this powerful theme. Their theme is the theme of power.
>
> And it is from this theme that art is born. Art is more one-sided than people think. It cannot be directed at will, wherever you wish, like a telescope. Focused upon a reality that has been displaced by feeling, art is a record of this displacement. It copies it from nature. How then does nature become displaced? Details gain in sharpness, each losing its independent meaning. Each one of them could be replaced by another. Any one of them is precious. Any one, chosen at random, will serve as evidence of the state which envelops the whole of transposed reality. (*Safe Conduct*)

Tynyanov similarly notes how any one of Pasternak's images by itself is fortuitous (random, and replaceable), yet the whole which they make up (the 'theme') is obligatory. This obligatoriness (*obyazatel'nost'*) is, however, in Pasternak's understanding total. For art 'is a record', it 'copies from nature'.

This humility at the heart of what looks like arrogance is what sharply distinguishes Pasternak not only from the Formalists but also from other gifted Russian poets of his time, from Blok, Mayakovsky and Yesenin. This is what he means in *Safe Conduct* when he records that, as early as *Over the Barriers*, 'I abandoned the Romantic manner':

> But a whole conception of life lay concealed under the Romantic manner which I was to forbid myself from henceforth. This was the conception of

life as the life of the poet. It had come to us from the Symbolists and had been adopted by them from the Romantics, principally the Germans.

This idea had taken possession of Blok but only during a short period. In the form in which it came naturally to him it was incapable of satisfying him. He had either to heighten it or abandon it altogether. He abandoned the idea, Mayakovsky and Yesenin heightened it.

In this poet who sets himself up as the measure of life and pays for this with his life, the Romantic conception is disarmingly vivid and indisputable in its symbols, that is in everything that figuratively touches upon Orphism and Christianity. In this sense something not transient was incarnate both in the life of Mayakovsky and in the fate of Yesenin, a fate which defies all epithets, self-destructively begging to become myth and receding into it.

But outside the legend, the Romantic scheme is false. The poet, who is its foundation, is inconceivable without the non-poets to bring him into relief, because this poet is not a living personality absorbed in moral cognition, but a visual-biographical 'emblem', demanding a background to make his contours visible. In contra-distinction to the Passion Plays which needed a Heaven if they were to be heard, this drama needs the evil of mediocrity in order to be seen, as Romanticism always needs philistinism and with the disappearance of the petty bourgeoisie loses half its content.

The notion of biography as spectacle was inherent in my time. I shared this notion with everyone else. I abandoned it while it was still flexible and non-obligatory with the Symbolists, before it bore any implication of heroism and before it smelt of blood. And in the first place, I freed myself from it unconsciously, abandoning the Romantic devices for which it served as basis. In the second place, I shunned it consciously also, considering its brilliance unsuited to me, because, confining myself to my craft, I feared any kind of poeticizing which would place me in a false and incongruous position.

With this crucial passage (which incidentally brings out some of the ways in which Russian Symbolism was radically different from French *symbolisme*) we come at last to something which the Anglo-American reader should be able to respond to eagerly. For what Pasternak here sets his face against is that which Louis Zukofsky in 1930 called, with obvious distaste, 'overweening autobiographies of the heart'.[1] And our poetry ever since 1920 has been marked generally by a revulsion against Romanticism conceived in this way, on the grounds that it is 'overweening'.

[1] Zukofsky, loc. cit. p. 141.

It is important to get this clear. For Pasternak's writing, early and late, is full of the lyrical 'I', and he has not shared the reluctance of Zukofsky and of our poets in the Imagist tradition, to reflect upon the experience which he renders, even as he renders it. Moreover Pasternak dedicated *My Sister Life* to an arch-Romantic, Lermontov. What does this mean, in view of the anti-Romantic stance declared in *Safe Conduct*? George Reavey records how, in Cambridge in 1927, he graduated to Pasternak from Yesenin:

> Pasternak, when I discovered him, seemed to have no public face ... he was all contained in the movement of his own verse, in the rhythm of the creative act, and this very act of apparently spontaneous creation, and the resulting chain of his images, were what seemed to absorb him wholly.[1]

This may be taken in several ways. One way of mistaking it would be to envisage Pasternak as self-absorbed in a tiresomely self-regarding and egocentric way, with no interests outside the rarefied ecstasies of his own sensibility and the drama of his personal, vocational destiny. And an unsympathetic reader of Lermontov might recognize him in this description.

The apparent contradiction was removed in one way by Renato Poggioli when he observed, 'The raw material of Pasternak's poetry is introspection. Yet Pasternak treats the self as object rather than as subject.' But this is still cryptic. Victor Erlich glosses it more helpfully:

> His work does not so much project a coherent and dramatically effective image of the poet as dramatize what Edgar Allan Poe calls the poetic principle – the power which brings the poem into being.[2]

In other words, the 'autobiography' is not of the poet's heart, but of the heart of poetry. And it is against this background, with these weighty qualifications, that one must understand Pasternak's dedication of *My Sister Life* to the most confessional of Russian poets, Lermontov; his poem to the same effect, 'In Memory of the Demon'; and his explanation of this to Eugene Kayden.[3] But in any case Pasternak was quite explicit, not only in *Safe Conduct* but elsewhere:

[1] George Reavey, *The Poetry of Boris Pasternak, 1917-1959* (New York, 1959) p. 45.
[2] Victor Erlich, *The Double Image* (Baltimore, 1964) p. 140.
[3] Eugene Kayden, *Poems by Boris Pasternak* (Ann Arbor, 1959) p. ix.

Introduction

> People nowadays imagine that art is like a fountain, whereas it is a sponge. They think art has to flow forth, whereas what it has to do is absorb and become saturated. They suppose that it can be divided up into means of depiction, whereas it is made up of the organs of perception. Its job is to be always a spectator and to look more purely, more receptively, more faithfully than anyone else; but in our age it has come to know pomade and the make-up room, and it displays itself from a stage...[1]

In this statement of the early 1920s, we see Pasternak once again implying that the poet is 'a living personality absorbed in moral cognition', and not 'a visual-biographical "emblem"'. This represents a deliberate turning away by Pasternak from the precedents of Blok, Mayakovsky and Yesenin, who all projected an image of the poet or of themselves as poets. Much more than any of these Pasternak eschews 'overweening autobiographies of the heart', and this marks him off from Hart Crane or W. B. Yeats by just so much as it aligns him rather with Pound, William Carlos Williams or Zukofsky.

Pasternak: the Middle Period

In the 1920s Pasternak made several attempts to compose long poems. *The Lofty Malady* consists of two sustained passages which appeared in periodicals, the first in 1923, the second in 1928. The long poem *Nineteen Hundred and Five*, consisting of six sections with a prologue, was published as a book in 1927; and bound up with it was *Lieutenant Schmidt*, a poem in three parts about the revolt of the Black Sea Fleet in 1905. *Spektorsky*, consisting of nine parts with a prologue, was published as a book in 1931.

Nineteen Hundred and Five, with its public theme (the abortive revolution of that year), was welcomed by many who had found the earlier lyrics too difficult. Gorky probably spoke for many Russian readers when he wrote to Pasternak in 1927:

> To be frank, before this book I have always read your poems with a certain effort, for they are excessively saturated with imagery, and the images are not always clear to me; my *imagination* found it difficult to contain your images, wilfully complicated as they are and often incompletely drawn. You know yourself... that their abundance often makes you speak – or

---

[1] 'Neskol'ko polozhenii' ('Some Theses'), 1922; see *Sochineniya* (*Works*) (Michigan, 1961) III 152.

paint – too sketchily. In *Nineteen Hundred and Five* you are simpler and more chary of words, you're more classical in this book, which is filled with a pathos that infects me, as a reader, very quickly, easily, and powerfully. Yes, it is an excellent book. This is the voice of a genuine poet, and of a social poet, social in the best and profoundest sense of the word.

Even so, Gorky wrote again the next day to tell Pasternak that

the 'imagery' is often too small for the theme, and still more often it capriciously fails to agree with it; thus you make the theme unclear.[1]

The émigré D. S. Mirsky, on the other hand, had responded readily to *My Sister Life* and *Themes and Variations*.[2] And yet it is hard not to see the welcome which Mirsky gave to *Lieutenant Schmidt* as a stage in Mirsky's reconciliation with the régime, a reconciliation which in 1928 was almost complete. For, when he calls Pasternak 'a great revolutionary and transformer of Russian poetry', Mirsky goes further than anyone before in identifying Pasternak with the Revolution. Mirsky thought that in *Lieutenant Schmidt* Pasternak had 'given to the whole old tradition of Russian sacrificial revolutionariness its creative fulfilment'. That tradition, he thought, had culminated in Pasternak, or rather in this work of Pasternak's; and Pasternak was 'the starting-point of all future Russian traditions'.[3]

There is no way of knowing how far some of these poems represent a deliberate attempt by Pasternak to graduate from lyric to epic, nor how far, if this was the case, he was swayed by exhortations to this effect from Gorky or others. It was in any case a very arduous task that he set himself. For as some of the early reviewers had recognized, Pasternak's talent was lyrical in an absolute sense. Of *My Sister Life* one reviewer exclaimed:

Reality represented solely by lyrical means! Contemporaneity lives in this book as a scent, as a rhythm, as an unexpected epithet, as an apt definition, as a structure....[4]

And Dale L. Plank notes in Pasternak's lyrics 'the effort to overcome

[1] Gorky's correspondence with Pasternak in *Literaturnoye Nasledstvo* (1963) LXX 300, 301.
[2] D. S. Mirsky, *A History of Russian Literature* (1949) p. 502.
[3] D. S. Mirsky, *Versty*, III (1928) 150–4.
[4] Ya. Chernyak, in *Pechat' i Revolyutsiya*, VI (1922) 303–4.

the temporal successiveness of the poem itself by squeezing in as much action as possible in the shortest possible space, the fascination for things caught in flight, the constant preoccupation with images of water, storm, the seasons, anything that represents change and evanescence'. Plank comments:

> To the lyrical imagination chronology is chaos and is opposed to the order of the world's metaphorism. Pasternak's historical and biographical poems of the twenties..., as well as his prose, illustrate throughout the displacement of the narrative and sequential by the momentary; the scraps of days and hours that refuse to cohere.[1]

Thus in these poems, Pasternak does not abandon his lyrical procedures but on the contrary attempts to build larger structures, and to compass the rhythm and shape of whole lifetimes, by pressing his lyricism further. It may be that the nearest parallel in Anglo-American poetry is once again Hart Crane, who in *The Bridge* similarly tried to build a structure of epic scope by lyrical means. Sinyavsky's comments on *Spektorsky* show something of what this means in practice.

Nineteen Hundred and Five awaits a translator. For of recent years, since the appearance of Robert Lowell's *Life Studies*, poetry in English provides an idiom equivalent in many ways to Pasternak's idiom in his poem. This is true for instance of the curt and abrupt metre which Pasternak finds. Up to this point in his career Pasternak had been comparatively unadventurous in his metres. One of the exceptions, however, is a particularly splendid one, a sequence of lyrics in *Themes and Variations* called 'Razryv' ('The Break'), of which Mirsky wrote that 'For emotional and rhythmical force, these nine lyrics have no rivals in modern Russian poetry.'[2] Aseev (below, pp. 73–84) remarks of this work:

> The lines are all fastened to one another by knots of intonation which carry the voice without pause for breath from one line to the next. The stops are conditioned solely by the taking of new breaths. Who will assert after this that a stanza thus constructed observes the principle of rhythm but not that of intonation?

This represents a recognition by a Russian critic as early as 1929 of

---

[1] Plank, op. cit. pp. 85–6.
[2] Mirsky, *History of Russian Literature*, p. 502.

something that our criticism came to securely only in the 1950s, with Charles Olson's *Projective Verse*: the recognition that the distinction between metrical verse and free verse does not take us far enough to be useful. On the other hand intonational verse, in the sense that Aseev gives to that term, was certainly being written in English at the same time as Pasternak was writing 'Razryv'. Different as it is in every other respect, Pound's *Homage to Sextus Propertius* (1917) is structured upon intonations.

Accordingly Plank is a little misleading when he says of the new collection of lyrics which appeared in 1932:

> Although the tone of the poems of *Second Birth* is strikingly different from that of Pasternak's earlier books – it is now reflective, even elegiacal – the sounds are, if anything, more intensely organized in their patterns and, especially, as metaphors. The illusion of spontaneity that distinguished the earlier books is now almost absent; but in its place we have, not a new poetics, but an application of the old poetics, perfected and even enriched, to the needs of a man speaking.[1]

For as we have seen 'the needs of a man speaking' determine the structure of 'Razryv' in *Themes and Variations*. And indeed if we take seriously Pasternak's tribute to Verlaine, we must suppose that Pasternak was concerned for the cadence of the speaking voice from the start, for Verlaine stands behind some poems that Pasternak wrote as early as 1912. Pasternak says of Verlaine:

> He gave to the language in which he wrote that boundless freedom which was his own lyrical discovery and which is found only in the masters of prose dialogue in the novel and the drama. The Parisian phrase in all its virginal and bewitching accuracy flew in from the street and lay down entire in his lines, not in the least cramped, as the melodic material for the whole of the subsequent composition. Verlaine's greatest charm lies in this directness and spontaneity. For him the idioms of the French language were indivisible. He wrote not in words but in whole phrases, neither breaking them into separate units, nor rearranging them.

Pasternak's reference here to 'prose dialogue in the novel and the drama' is interestingly near to that admonition which Ford Madox Ford gave to Pound, and transmitted through him to Eliot: the

---

[1] Plank, op. cit. p. 112.

Introduction

warning that in the twentieth century poets are in competition not only with poets of the past but also with the great realistic novelists of the previous century. Equally, one of the things that Wladimir Weidle objected to, in his intelligently hostile response to Pasternak (see below, pp. 108–25), is the way in which Pasternak's verse is densely furnished with workaday *things* in all their weightiness and angularity. And this may be just what Pound, true to his Flaubertian allegiance, aimed for in some of his *Cantos*, and what he admired in a pre-Flaubertian realist, George Crabbe. The novelist that Pasternak had chiefly in mind may have been Tolstoy. Or if it was a French novelist, it is less likely to have been Flaubert than Balzac. However, Pasternak's specifying *dialogue* in the novel doubtless means that he might not have thought, with Eliot, that 'Poetry must be at least as well-written as good prose'; but only that it must be as well-written as good *speech*.

With this exception, however, Plank's characterizing of *Second Birth* is very just. In particular 'the illusion of spontaneity' which at this point tends to disappear from Pasternak's lyrics is not anything that we need grieve for; for this illusion sometimes gave the earlier poems a flurried air and a raucous tone. It is the more important to realize with Plank that habits of luxuriance and daring wantonness, in imagery and orchestration alike, survive from the earlier poems into *Second Birth*, although there is seldom by this stage any question of synaesthesia, still less of surrealism. An example is a poem on the death of Mayakovsky, which is quoted almost in its entirety by Sinyavsky:

> They would not credit it, dismissed it as
> So much wild talk – then two advised them, three,
> Then all the world. There aligned themselves in the series
> Of a term run out and halted
> The houses of Mistress Clerk, of Mistress Huckster,
> Yards of those houses, trees, and on the trees
> The dulled rook, stupefied in the sun's eye, screamed
> His inflamed curses after Mistress Rook
> That, what the deuce, henceforward boobies should not
> Obtrude their offices, bad cess to them.
> Only upon the faces came a damp
> Subsidence, as a tattered fishnet crumples.
>
> A day there was, a blameless day, still more
> Blameless than a dozen you have lived through.

> They crowded in, they dressed their ranks in the forecourt
> Like a shot, as if a shot had dressed them,
>
> As if, though razed, there fountained out of channels
> Pike and bream, as when a mine explodes,
> So from the fire-squib charged and laid in the sedges
> Was this exhaled as from sediments still ungelded.
>
> You slept, you pressed the pillow with your cheek.
> You slept, and with clean heels, with raking strides,
> Now with one turn of speed, now with another, you
> Entered the constellation of young legends.
> And among these you burst so much the more
> Notably that you made it in one jump.
> The detonation of your shot was Etna's
> Upon its foothills, Craven and Mistress Craven.

Here the luxuriance is not a matter of logically incompatible similitudes colliding and jarring against each other, but of extraordinarily rapid as it were cinematographic 'cutting' from one similitude to the next. The flow of association, from urban scenes to nursery-rhyme to geological to sporting metaphors and back to the geological volcanic metaphor of Etna in the last lines, is not, as in surrealist writing, the uncontrolled association of the unconscious in dreams. It may seem so, but this is an illusion brought about by the copiousness of the poet's invention, the rapidity and impetuosity of his transitions. It is the quality we associate with Shakespeare above all, and in a later poet such as Dryden only when we detect a Shakespearean note in him. An example of the wanton or arbitrary image might be the unannounced swerve into a metaphor from fishing 'as a tattered fishnet crumples'. Yet this too, in thoroughly Shakespearean fashion, is taken up into the poem as it were retrospectively when we reach (in the original version which Sinyavsky quotes) the later image of fishing by depth-charges:

> As if, though razed, there fountained out of channels
> Pike and bream, as when a mine explodes. . . .

Pasternak and Mayakovsky had been close friends. And the tact of their relationship is beautifully preserved in the way in which the shot by which Mayakovsky killed himself, though it is central to the metaphors of Pasternak's poem, is nowhere brutally stated. Those who know how affectingly Pasternak wrote of Mayakovsky's death in his prose memoirs may not notice how in the poem Pasternak writes not in the first place as a friend nor as a member of the same circle, but publicly, seeing the poet's death as impinging upon his society in the widest sense, affecting people not normally affected by poetry at all. This, at least, is how I read the 'sediments still ungelded', as levels of Russian society which Pasternak had thought of as brutalized into spiritual inertia, which yet show themselves still capable of fructification by virtue of the response they make (however muddled – the rook's response of irrationally alarmed irritation) to the death of the laureate poet. The rook's injunction to his wife not to meddle is perhaps the finest stroke in the poem; it is true to life as we know it, yet true also to the idea of *noli me tangere*, of the poet as tabu because sacred.

It is the public quality of this poem which allows us momentarily to think of that most public of English poets, Dryden. Yet, of course, in Pasternak's case this is the exception that proves the rule. Pasternak as a whole is challenging to the Russian reader because, by writing for the most part so insistently as a private person, he flies in the face of the traditional Russian emphasis (much older than the Revolution) on how the writer has civic responsibilities. *Doctor Zhivago* was to explore the paradox that, in certain states of society, such an insistence on the rights of the private life may itself be a civic duty of a particularly exacting and dangerous kind. And the tumult which surrounded the awarding of the Nobel prize to Pasternak was to show, from the poet's own life, how fulfilling this duty can have momentous and explosive consequences in the public domain. There is no analogue to this in the Anglo-American tradition in the present century. For British and American poets are, as it were, condemned to the private life; and many of them have worried, so far to no purpose, about how to break into the public realm, to take on that civic responsibility which their societies indulgently deny them. The only partial exception among greatly gifted poets in English has been W. B. Yeats, whose society, because it was Irish, permitted him for a while civic responsibility, and the public oratorical style which befits a public rôle. The word 'huckster' in our translation is a Yeatsian word, and may be allowed to hint at the Yeatsian parallel.

From 1934 to the end

The first All-Union Congress of Soviet Writers in August 1934 inaugurated a period when the tension between the private life and public responsibility was, for many Russian writers, stretched to breaking and beyond. A main theme of the Congress was that of the speech in which Maxim Gorky declared that the creative impotence of twentieth-century literature in Europe was to be explained by the fact that man had turned out to be 'a social unit, not a cosmic one', and that 'individualism, which turns into egocentrism, breeds "superfluous people"'. One speaker who spoke at some length about Pasternak was Nikolai Bukharin, whose words are interesting because they define the category – of exquisite but valetudinarian minor talent – which was the most indulgent that official spokesmen could find for Pasternak to the day of his death:

> Boris Pasternak is a poet most remote from current affairs, even in the broadest sense of the term ... a singer of the old intelligentsia, which has now become a Soviet intelligentsia. He unquestionably accepts the Revolution but he is far removed from the peculiar technicism of the period, from the din of battle, from the passions of the struggle. As early as at the time of the imperialist war, he had intellectually broken away from the old world ... and had consciously risen 'above the barriers'. The bloody hash, the huckstering barter of the bourgeois world were profoundly loathsome to him, and he 'seceded', retired from the world, shut himself up in the mother-of-pearl shell of individual experiences, delicate and subtle, of the frail trepidations of a wounded and easily vulnerable soul. He is the embodiment of chaste but self-absorbed laboratory craftsmanship, persistent and painstaking labour over verbal form, the material for which is afforded by the precious things of the 'heritage of the past', by profoundly personal – and hence, of necessity, constricted – associations, interwoven with inward stirrings of the mind.[1]

The tone is plainly apologetic.

Pasternak's life during the thirties can be reconstructed from partial and fragmentary evidence, as has been done for instance by Robert Conquest.[2] But neither Conquest nor any other has yet explained why

---

[1] Nikolai Bukharin, 'Poetry, Poetics and the Problems of Poetry in the U.S.S.R.', in *Problems of Soviet Literature (Reports and Speeches at the First Soviet Writers' Congress)* (Moscow, 1935) p. 233.

[2] Robert Conquest, *Courage of Genius* (1961) pp. 36–40.

Pasternak escaped the purges which carried off so many of his friends and colleagues, especially since from time to time he spoke out rashly. In his literary career the late 1930s are the years of his work as a translator. In 1935 appeared a volume of lyrics translated from the Georgian, which was praised in a review by Mirsky; and this was followed by another collection of Georgian lyrics in 1937. A volume of Selected Translations in 1940 included versions by Pasternak from Shakespeare, Ralegh, Keats and Byron. Translations of *Hamlet*, of *Romeo and Juliet*, *Antony and Cleopatra* and *Othello* appeared during the war. It is clear now that already in the 1930s Pasternak was at work on what was to become *Doctor Zhivago*, and that this was no secret within the circle of his friends. The playwright Afinogenov, for instance, wrote in his diary under 21 September 1937:

> Conversations I have with Pasternak are unforgettable. He comes in and at once starts to talk of something that is important, interesting and real. For him the main thing is art, and nothing but art. That is why he doesn't care to go into town but chooses to live here the whole time, going for walks by himself or reading Macaulay's *History of England*, sitting by the window and looking out at the starry night, sorting out his thoughts, or else, finally, writing his novel. But all of this is inside art and for the sake of art. He is not even interested in the end-product. The main thing is the work at it, the enthusiasm for it; as for what will come of it – well, let's see many years from now. His wife has a hard time, they have to find money and live somehow, but he knows nothing about it, only sometimes when the money problem gets really acute, he gets down to work translating. 'But I'd do just as well being a commercial traveller....' Set him down anywhere you like, he'll still keep his open gaze on nature and people – like the great and rare verbal artist that he is.
>   It's just the same when you go to see him, he leaves behind everything that's petty and he hurls at you subjects, judgments, conclusions – with him everything gets delineated in a real and meaningful way. He doesn't read the newspapers – and this is queer for me, who can't get through a day without the news. But he would never spend all his time up to 2 o'clock in the afternoon, as I did today, doing nothing. He's always taken up with his work, with books, with himself.... And if he should ever find himself in a palace or on the plank-bed of a prison cell, he'll still be taken up like this, perhaps even more than he is here – at least then he wouldn't have to think about money and worries, but could give the whole of his time to thinking and creating....
>   A man of rare integrity, rare interest. And your heart goes out to him

because he can find wonderful human words of comfort, not out of pity but out of his conviction that better things are on the way: 'And these better things will come very shortly – as soon as you put all of yourself into your work, and you start to work and forget about everything else....'[1]

The 'work' which so much mattered to Pasternak, at the time Afinogenov writes of, certainly was not his translations. It may have been some of the poems subsequently printed in *On Early Trains*, in 1943. But more probably it was work directed towards the novel that was not to appear until twenty years later. And *Literaturnaya Gazeta* published in December 1938 a piece of prose by Pasternak under the title, 'Two Excerpts from a Chapter of a Novel: A District behind the Front'.[2]

In his *Essay in Autobiography*, Pasternak declared that all his verse before 1940 was written in a style no longer to his liking. And this is one among many pronouncements to similar effect. The most enlightening of them appears at a point in *An Essay in Autobiography*[3] where Pasternak says that it was his reading of the poems of Marina Tsvetayeva which crystallized his dissatisfaction with his own early verse; and he expresses that dissatisfaction by saying that, in the work he had come to dislike, 'I wasn't looking for the point of things, only for their incidental sharpness.' This is accurate self-criticism. *Ars est celare artem*; and in Pasternak's early poetry the art seldom conceals itself. Knowing itself to be brilliantly resourceful and brilliantly perceptive, it makes no attempt to seem otherwise. Why should it? However this unashamedness consorts rather uncomfortably at times with the illusion of spontaneity which these poems set out to create; for then the poem can seem to be self-congratulating at times quite raucously.

This set aside, however, the matter of Pasternak's revulsion from his earlier styles has been given too much prominence. It is common and indeed inevitable før an artist who keeps moving throughout his life, to regard his own youthful self as a stranger to the man he has become, and to resent it irritably if fame and esteem is given to that stranger too exclusively. Thus Thomas Gray in his later years was impatient with admirers of his *Elegy in a Country Churchyard*, and Yeats came to hate 'The Lake Isle of Innisfree'. Thus Pound, looking back in 1934, felt that

[1] A. N. Afinogenov, *Stat'i, Dnevniki, Pis'ma. Vospominaniya* (Moscow, 1957) pp. 152-3.
[2] Other prose fictions by Pasternak are *Il Tratto di Apelle* (1915); *The Childhood of Luvers* and *Letters from Tula* (1918); *Aerial Ways* (1924) and *A Tale* (published in 1934).
[3] *An Essay in Autobiography* trans. Manya Harari (1959) p. 105.

his own poetry to that date counted for next to nothing when set beside Thomas Hardy's.[1] We are sure Pound was mistaken, though we like him for making the mistake; and this surely ought to be our attitude to Pasternak also. Certainly we must resist any suggestion, basing itself on these pronouncements by Pasternak, to the effect that the poems written since 1940 are superior to those before; that in *Doctor Zhivago* and the poems of his last years Pasternak at last found the ways of writing which he had been groping for unsuccessfully throughout his earlier years. *Doctor Zhivago*, and the poems which Pasternak gives to Yuri Zhivago, are no doubt the crown and consummation of Pasternak's artistic career, but not in any way that supersedes the earlier writing. To regard *My Sister Life* as in this way 'prentice work would be absurd. Equally, though those who can approach *Doctor Zhivago* down the perspective afforded by Pasternak's earlier writings will almost certainly think that this is the way to see *Doctor Zhivago* most accurately; yet, of course, this perspective is not open to the vast majority of those who read Pasternak's novel, and our selection from critics of *Doctor Zhivago* shows that valuable insights can be achieved by looking at it down quite different vistas, for instance in the context of the nineteenth-century realistic novel.

As for the latest poems, it was Yuri Zhivago who claimed to have worked all his life for 'an unnoticeable style'. Boris Pasternak could not have claimed this, and did not claim it. Moreover, it is not in any writer's power to decide whether his style should be 'noticeable' or not. For this is all in the eye of the beholder, it depends upon the prepossessions as well as the attentiveness of the reader. In any case the talented translator of Pasternak's last collection, *When the Weather Clears*, was on the wrong tack when, after recalling Zhivago's wish for an unnoticeable style, he confessed, 'A major criticism of these translations is their failure to be as un-literary as the originals.'[2] For a perky or jaunty colloquialism, such as we encounter in many versions from Pasternak, makes a style even more 'noticeable' than literary stiltedness does. And it would be a bitter irony if the man of whom Afinogenov said 'For him the main thing is art, and nothing but art' were to be called to testify, on the score of certain late pronouncements taken out of context, in the cause of those who believe that art and literature are

[1] Ezra Pound, *Guide to Kulchur*, ch. 52.
[2] Pasternak, *Poems 1955–1959*, trans. Michael Harari (1960), prefatory note.

always guilty until proved innocent, and that they can prove their innocence best by going in disguise.

DONALD DAVIE

Chronology

1890   Born in Moscow.
1903   Meets the composer Scriabin and begins a serious study of music.
1907   Joins a literary group called Serdarda.
1908   Leaves school. Works as tutor.
1909   Enters Moscow University as a student of law.
        Changes to philosophy (on the advice of Scriabin).
1910   Gives a talk on 'Symbolism and Immortality'.
1911   Joins Centrifuga, a group of moderate Futurist writers.
1912   Spends a semester studying philosophy under Hermann Cohen and Nicholai Hartmann at Marburg University.
1912   Visits Italy.
1913   Passes his state exam at Moscow University.
1913   Works as a tutor in Moscow.
1914   Meets Mayakovsky.
1914   Works as tutor in the family of the Lithuanian poet Baltrushaitis.
1914   Publication of his first volume of poetry, *Bliznets v tuchakh* (*Twin in the Clouds*).
1915   Travels, working in the management of chemical factories in the Urals.
1917   Returns from the Urals to Moscow.
1917   Publication of volume of poems, *Poverkh bar'erov* (*Over the Barriers*).
1918   Works as a librarian in *Narkompros* (People's Commissariat of Education).
1921   His parents emigrate to Germany.
1922   Travels to Marburg and Berlin.
1922   Publication of volume of poems: *Sestra moya – zhizn'* (*My Sister Life*).
1922   Marries Yevgeniya Lourié.

1923	Publication of volume of poems: *Temy i variatsii* (*Themes and Variations*).
1923	Birth of his son Yevgeni.
1924	Publication of the long poem *Vysokaya bolezn'* (*The Lofty Malady*) and the story *Detstvo Lyuvers* (*The Childhood of Luvers*).
1925	Publication of a collection of four short stories under the title of one of them, *Vozdushnye puti* (*Aerial Ways*).
1926	Publication of the verse epic *Lieutenant Schmidt*.
1927	Publication of the verse epic *1905-y god* (*The Year 1905*).
1931	Is divorced from his first wife. Travels to Tiflis with his future second wife, Zinaida Neuhaus.
1931	Publication of the autobiographical work *Okhrannaya gramota* (*Safe Conduct*) and the epic poem *Spektorsky*.
1932	Publication of volume of verse, *Vtoroye rozhdeniye* (*Second Birth*).
1934	Speaks at the First All-Union Congress of Soviet Writers, in Moscow.
1934	Publication of the story *Povest'* (*A Tale*).
1934	Marries for the second time. Moves into a house in Peredelkino.
1934–43	Works at translations.
1935	Goes to Paris, though ill, as a member of the Soviet delegation to the International Congress of Writers in the Defence of Culture.
1936	Speaks at the Congress of Soviet Writers in Minsk.
1936	Second trip to the Caucasus.
1938	Birth of his son Leonid.
1943	Publication of volume of verse, *Na rannikh poyezdakh* (*On Early Trains*).
1944	Publication of volume of poems, *Zemnoi prostor* (*Earth's Vastness*).
1946	Attacked by Fadeev, First Secretary of the Writers' Union.
1947	Speaks at literary meetings in Moscow.
1954	Publication of *Ten poems from Doctor Zhivago*.
1956	Publication of two more 'Doctor Zhivago' poems and of eight from *Kogda razgulyayetsa* (*When the Weather Clears*).
1956	*Novy Mir* refuses to publish the novel *Doctor Zhivago*.
1957	Publication of *Doctor Zhivago* in Italy.
1958	Is awarded the Nobel prize, but refuses it 'because of the significance given to this award in the society to which I belong'. Press campaign against him in Russia.
1958	Publication of his *Biograficheski ocherk* (*Essay in Autobiography*) outside Russia.

1959 Publication of volume of verse, *Kogda razgulyayetsa* (*When the Weather Clears*) in Paris.
1960 Dies in Moscow.

ILYA EHRENBURG

Boris Leonidovich Pasternak (1922)

ON the twenty-eighth of December in the year 1920, in the city of Moscow, towards evening, there came into my room a poet. I could not make out his face very well in the dusk. All I could see clearly was a swarthy darkness and large sad eyes. He was wrapped in a big scarf. I was struck by his shy and challenging manner, by the touchiness of his outward pride, and by the infinite bashfulness of all his inner gestures. After long and painful introductions he began to read a poem about the scourged wings of the Demon. Then I realized who it was that had come to me. Yes, on the twenty-eighth of December at five o'clock in the evening, after finishing my copy of the *News*, I found myself chatting with Mikhail Lermontov: and these are not any theosophical *petits laits*[1] – I am simply describing an ordinary meeting with Boris Pasternak, best-loved of all my brothers in the craft.

So my portrait begins with genealogy. I don't mean, of course, the inheriting of a malady, but the vitality of a certain structure of feeling which, though buried by the gravediggers, or simply by the historians of literature, rises again at the most unexpected moments. Will anyone contend, after Pasternak, that romanticism is just a literary school? True, it is very easy to be tempted by historical parallels to make utterances about the outcome of the post-revolutionary period, and so on and so forth, but this befits only those critics who wrote in the 'thick' journals which now, thank goodness, are extinct. The construction of another world by extraordinary combinations of the ordinary forms of this one, with a desperate disregard for proportion, all scales and standards gone crazy: this is an eternal human need.

For all the traditionalness of such concerns, Pasternak is not archaic, nor retrospective, but alive, healthy, young and contemporary. Not

[1] The meaning of this phrase is not completely clear.

one of his poems could have been written before him. There is in him the rapture of amazement, a piling up of new feelings, the vigour of seeing things for the first time: in brief, the world after the flood or after a week spent in a cellar protected from shellfire. In order to convey this novelty of sensations, he set out not to invent words but to arrange them. Pasternak's magic is in his syntax. One of his poems is called 'The Urals for the First Time'; all his books could be called 'The World for the First Time', for they are one huge exclamation, 'Oh!' – more splendid and persuasive than any dithyrambs.

It's hard work talking to Pasternak. His speech is a combination of tongue-twisting, a desperate straining to drag out a needed word from within, and a stormy cascade of unexpected comparisons, complex associations and frank confessions in what is evidently a foreign language. He would be unintelligible were not all this chaos illumined by the singleness and clarity of his voice. Thus his poems, which are sometimes hieroglyphic, go all the way to an anthological simplicity, to a naïve and childish tale about the spring. Certainly, Bunin is easier to understand, and it's easier to get fire from Swedish matches than from stone. But hearts are kindled by sparks of flint; while only cigarettes are lit by matches.

Pasternak's rhythm is the rhythm of our day, violent and wild in its speed. Who would have thought that these good old solid-rumped iambs could leap over the barriers like Arab steeds?

I don't even understand how he has time, as he dashes by so fast in express trains, to distinguish all the flowers of the meadows, to indulge in philosophy, and to love, as tenderly and circumstantially as they used to love 'in the good old days'.

This link, apparently natural in Romantic hemispheres, between titanic perceptions and microscopic objects, is an amazing thing. A love not a whit inferior to the love described in the classics is here given a setting that is far from classical – a pool of oil, some seeds, the wallpaper in a tiny room for humble inhabitants, and the forelock of Pasternak himself that the barber hasn't trimmed. But he transforms all these lowly details into the truly sacred objects of a new mythology.

Pasternak has not, of course, turned himself into a heavenly being; he is subject to the various human ailments. Fortunately for him and for Russian poetry, there are quick effective remedies to hand. He has honourably survived the children's disease of measles, which in his case was called Centrifuga.

He could easily have fallen into the sentimentality of Lenau, but is saved, like Heine before him, by a considerable dose of irony. At times the musicality of his line tends to become Severyaninish; but he is rescued by his intelligence, and perhaps by his philosophical studies at Marburg University. From such studies it is easy to slip into a sinewless philosophizing, but here his lyrical feelings come to his aid – and so on.

Often I doubt the viability of the lyrical. However lovely the poems of Anna Akhmatova may be, they are inscribed on the last page of a closing book. But in Pasternak there are no autumns, sunsets or other sweet inconsolable things. He has shown that the lyrical exists and can go on existing, outside the question of social environment.

Perhaps the whole earth will one day be covered with asphalt, yet still, somewhere in Iceland or Patagonia, one crack will be left. Through it a blade of grass will come up, and scholars and lovers will start making pilgrimages to this wondrous phenomenon. Perhaps, too, lyrical poetry will be abolished for its redundancy, but somewhere the grandson of Pasternak and great-great-grandson of Lermontov will open his mouth in sudden astonishment and will utter – painful for himself but clear and bright for others – the cry, 'Oh!...'

SOURCE: from *Portreti russkikh poetov* (Berlin, 1922).

MARINA TSVETAYEVA

A Downpour of Light: Poetry of Eternal Courage (1922)

BEFORE me is Pasternak's book *My Sister Life*. In its protective binding that recalls both the free distributions of the South and the scantier alms of the North, it's a bleak and boorish-looking book, covered with some sort of black mournful stains – could be an undertaker's catalogue or the last throw of the die by some dying publisher. But I only saw it once this way: in the very first moment when I got it, before I'd had time to open it. Since then it's not been closed. My companion of two days, I carry it with me through all the spaces of Berlin: the classic Linden, the magic Underground (no accidents, while I carry it with me!), I've taken it to the zoo (to make friends), I take it to dinner at my *pension*, and – eventually – I wake at the first ray of the sun, with it lying wide open on my chest. Not two days – two years! I've a prescriptive right to say something about it.

Pasternak. Who is this Pasternak? ('Son of the artist' – I'll omit that.) Not quite an Imagist, not quite... at any rate, one of the new ones.... Ah yes, Ehrenburg is strenuously proclaiming him. Yes, but you know what Ehrenburg is, with his hither and thither rebellion!... And it seems he hasn't even any books to his name....

Yes, ladies and gentlemen, this is his first book (1917) – and is it not significant that in our time, when a book that might have been ripe for writing in 1927 is squandered prematurely in 1917, Pasternak's book, written in 1917, arrives five years late. And what a book! It's as if on purpose he has let all the others say what they had to say first, then at the very last moment, with a gesture of surprise, he takes his notebook out of his pocket: 'As a matter of fact I... though I can't vouch for it....' Pasternak, let me be your guarantor to the West – for a while – till your 'Life' appears here. I declare I'll vouch for it with all my non-demonstrable assets. And not because you need it, but from sheer cupidity: it's a precious thing to participate in such a destiny.

I'm reading Pasternak's poems for the first time. (I have heard them, orally, from Ehrenburg, but thanks to the rebellion that is in me too – alas, the gods forgot to drop into my cradle the gift of all-embracing love! – thanks to an age-old jealousy, the inability to love more than one at a time, I quietly dug my heels in: 'May be works of genius, but I can do without them.') With Pasternak himself I've just about a nodding acquaintance: three or four fleeting encounters – almost wordless ones, because I never want anything new. I heard him once, with other poets, in the Polytechnic Museum.[1] He spoke in a toneless voice and forgot nearly all the lines. The way he seemed out of his element on the platform reminded me strongly of Blok. An impression of painful concentration: one wanted to give him a push, like a carriage that won't go – 'Come on, get a *move* on . . .'; and, as not one of his words came across (a sort of mumbling, like a bear waking up), one thought impatiently: 'Lord, why does he torment himself and us like this!'

Pasternak's physical presence is magnificent: there is something in his face both of the Arab and the Arab's horse – a watchful, tense alertness and, at any moment, utter readiness for flight! And the enormous, also horse-like, wild and timid sideways glance of his eyes. (An orb, not an eye.) As if he were always listening to something, incessantly watching; then, all of a sudden, he'll burst into speech – generally with something primordial, as if a rock had spoken or an oak. His speech (in conversation) is like the rupture of a silence kept from time immemorial. And not only in conversation. I can say just the same – and with much more experience to back me – of his verse. Pasternak doesn't live in his words, as a tree doesn't live in its obvious foliage, but lives from its root (a secret). Underneath the whole book – like some vast passage beneath the Kremlin – is a silence.

> Тишина, ты лучшее
> Из всего, что слышал. . . .
>
> Silence, you are the best thing
> Of all that I have heard. . . .

[1] In the years just after the Revolution many public readings of poetry took place; often they were held in the Polytechnic Museum in Moscow.

As much a book of silences as of chirpings.

Now before I speak of his book (this series of blows and rebounds) a word about the wires that carry the voice – his poetic gift. I believe it's an enormous gift, for his essence, which is enormous, comes over whole. A gift that's clearly equal to its essence – this is very rare, a miracle, for don't we sigh over almost every book by a poet: 'With such talent...' or (immeasurably less often) 'Anyway, *something* gets across....' No, God spared Pasternak this, and Pasternak has spared us. He is unique and indivisible. His verse is the formula of his essence. Divinely apt: 'no other words would do'. Wherever 'form' predominates over 'content', or 'content' over 'form', there no essence ever even set foot. And you cannot copy him: only the garments can be copied. To be like him you must be born again.

Others will speak, in their turn, of the demonstrable treasures in Pasternak (rhythms, metres, and so on) – and probably with no less feeling than I speak of the non-demonstrable ones.

That is the job of poetry specialists. *My* speciality is Life.

My Sister Life! The first thing I did, when I'd borne it all, from the first blow to the last, was spread my arms out wide, so that the joints all cracked. I was caught in it, as in a downpour.

Downpour: the whole sky straight onto my head, plumb-down, vertically pouring and slantingly pouring – drenched through, blown through, and the quarrel of rays of light with rays of rain – and *you* don't count here: once you are caught in it – grow!

A downpour of light.

Pasternak is an important poet: now more important than any. Most present poets *have been*, some *are*, he alone *will be*. For really he isn't yet: a babbling, a chirping, a clashing – he is all Tomorrow! The choking cry of a baby, and this baby is the World. A breathless choking. A suffocating by inspiration. Pasternak doesn't speak, hasn't time to finish speaking, he's all bursting – as if there weren't room in his chest: a-ah! He doesn't yet know our words; his speech seems to come from a desert-island, from childhood, from the Garden of Eden: it doesn't quite make sense, and it knocks you over. At three this is common and is called 'a child'. At twenty-three it is uncommon and is called 'a poet'. (Oh equality, equality! How many God had to rob, even to the seventh generation, so as to create one Pasternak like this!)

Out of his mind, unmindful of himself, he sometimes wakes up suddenly and then, thrusting his head through the little window (onto life – with a small *l*) – yet, O wonder! instead of the transfigured three-year-old's domed head isn't it the rather eccentric cap of the Marburg philosopher?[1] – in a sleepy voice, from his garret heights, he calls down into the courtyard, to the children:

> Какое, милые, у нас
> Тысячелетье на дворе?
>
> Tell me, my dears, what
> Millennium is it out there?

You can be sure he will not hear the answer. Let me return to Pasternak's childishness. It isn't that Pasternak is himself a child (for then he would grow up not into daybreaks, but into a forty-year-old repose – the lot of all earthborn children!), not that Pasternak is an infant, but that the world is an infant within him. Pasternak himself I'd rather relate to the very first days of creation – the first rivers, first dawns, first storms. He is created *before* Adam.

I'm afraid, too, that only one thing may be conveyed by my helpless effusions – the gaiety of Pasternak. Gaiety. Let me think. Yes, the gaiety of an explosion, an avalanche, a stab, the sheerest discharging of all vital fibres and forces, a kind of white-heat which you might – from a distance – take to be just a white page.

Let me think on: what is *not* in Pasternak? (For if everything were in him he would be life, and so he himself *would* not *be*. Only through a no can we fix the existence of a yes, its separateness.) I listen, an answer comes: the sense of weight. Weight is for him only another form of action, it's to be thrown off. You're more likely to see him hurling an avalanche down than sitting somewhere in a snowbound hut awaiting its deadly thud. He will never wait for death: much too impatient and eager – he'll throw himself into it, head-first, chest-first, everything first that is stubborn and can outstrip. Pasternak cannot be robbed. This is Beethoven's 'Durch Leiden – Freuden'.[2]

The book is dedicated to Lermontov (as to a brother?). The illumined to the darkened. It's a natural gravitation: the general pull to the gulf, to be engulfed. Pasternak and Lermontov. Akin, yet thrusting apart, like two wings.

[1] Pasternak spent a semester studying philosophy at Marburg University.
[2] 'Through sufferings – joys.'

Pasternak is the most penetrable poet, and hence the most penetrating. Everything beats right into him (clearly there's justice even in inequality: thanks to you, sole poet, more than one human dome is delivered from celestial thunders!). A blow – a rebound. And the lightning speed of this rebound, its thousandfold speed – this is the thousandmoundedness of all his Caucasuses. No time to understand! (And so, especially in the first moment, but often at the last too, we are bewildered: what? what's this about ?– nothing! It's gone!)

Pasternak is all wide-open – eyes, nostrils, ears, lips, arms. Before him there was nothing. All doors from their hinges: out into Life! And yet more than anyone else he needs to be revealed. (A poetry of plottings.) So that you understand Pasternak in spite of himself, going along some fresh – the freshest – trail. Lightning-like, he is lightning to all experience-burdened skies. A storm is the sky's only expiration, just as the sky is to the storm its only possibility of being, its sole arena!)

Sometimes he is knocked right down: the pressure of life through the suddenly flung-open door is stronger than his stubborn brow. Then he falls – blissfully – on his back, and is more effective in his prostration than all those jockeys and couriers from Poetry, who at this very moment are panting at full gallop over the barriers.[1]

And an illumination: why, he's simply the beloved of the gods! No – a still more clear-sighted illumination – not simply, and not the beloved! The *unbeloved*, one of those youths who once heaped Pelion on Ossa.

Pasternak is wholly spendthrift. An outflow of light. An inexhaustible outflow of light. In him is made manifest the law of the year of famine: only don't spare and you won't want. So we are not anxious on his account but we may well reflect, on our own, being confronted by his essence: 'he that is able to receive it, let him receive it'.

Enough of these chokings. Now for a sober and sensible attempt (no anxiety: he will still be there in the clearest light of day!). By the way, a word on the element of light in Pasternak's poetry. Photo-graphy: light-writing, I would call it. A poet of lightness (as others may be

---

[1] The following two facts turned up at the last moment: (1) *My Sister Life* is *not* his first book; (2) the title of his first book is neither more nor less than *Over the Barriers*. In any event, this barrier has been taken in *My Sister Life*. M.TS.

A Downpour of Light: Poetry of Eternal Courage

poets of darkness). Light. Eternal courage. Light in space, light in movement, openings (draughts) and explosions of light – a sort of feast and revelry of light. He is flooded and whelmed. And not only with the sun but with everything that radiates, and for Pasternak *everything* radiates.

Now at last, having worked my way out of the dreamy eddies of interpretation – out into wakeful reality, out on the sober shoal of definitions and quotations!

1. Pasternak and everyday life.
2. Pasternak and the day.
3. Pasternak and rain.

Pasternak and Everyday Life

Byt ['everyday life']. A heavy word. It's almost like *byk* ['a bull']. I can only bear it when it's followed by 'of nomads'. *Byt* is an oak tree, and under the oak tree (encircling it) a bench, and on the bench a grandfather who was yesterday a grandson, and a grandson who will be a grandfather tomorrow. The everyday oak, the oaken everyday. Good and solid, stifling, ineluctable. You almost forget that the oak, as a tree sacred to Zeus, is honoured more often than others by Zeus's favour, lightning. And it's just when we have quite forgotten this that there come to the rescue, at the very last second, like lightning striking our oaken brows, Byron, Heine, Pasternak.

What first surprises us in Pasternak's verse, which is an unbroken chain of first things, is everyday life. Its abundance, its detail and – its 'prosiness'. Not just the tokens of the day, but of the hour! I fling the book open – 'To the Memory of the Demon'.

> ... От окна на аршин,
> Пробирая шерстинки бурнуса
> Клялся льдами вершин:
> – Спи, подруга, лавиной вернуся!

A yard or so from the window,
Plucking the woollen threads of a burnous,
He swore by the ice of steep places:
Sleep on, my girl, but I ... return as avalanche!

Further, in the poem 'My Sister Life':

> ... Что в грóзу лиловы глаза и газоны,
> И пахнет сырой резедой горизонт.
> Что в мае, когда поездов росписанье
> Камышинской веткой читаешь в купе. ...

> That in the thunder eyes and lawns are lilac,
> And the horizon breathes moist mignonette,
> Or that in May when you in transit scan
> Timetables on a branch-line to Kamyshin. ...

(I'm giving the accompanying lines on purpose, to establish the context.) Further, about a fence:

> Он незабвенен тем еще,
> Что пылью припухал,
> Что ветер лускал семечки,
> Сорил по лопухам. ...

> Unforgettable the more
> For dust distending it,
> For wind uncasing spore
> To cast abroad on burdocks.

About the wind:

> Ветер розу пробует
> Приподнять по просьбе
> Губ, волос и обуви,
> Подолов и прозвищ ...

> Wind attempts to raise
> The rose's head, requested
> Thereto by lips, hair, shoes,
> Familiar names and hemlines.

About a house in the country:

> Все еще нам лес — передней,
> Лунный жар за елью — печью,
> Все, как стиранный передник,
> Туча сохнет и лепечет.

A Downpour of Light: Poetry of Eternal Courage

> Still the woods are ours, for porch;
> Moon's fire behind the pines, for stove;
> And like an apron hanging out, fresh laundered,
> A thundercloud that mutters, drying out.

About the steppe:

> Туман отовсюду нас морем обстиг,
> В волчцах волочась за чулками . . .

> Mist from all quarters is a sea about us
> As thistle-patches check us, catch at socks. . . .

Just a moment! The choice of words – it's all for the sake of repeating the *ch*. . . . But ladies and gentlemen, has none of you ever had burrs biting into your socks? Especially in childhood when we're still in short clothes. True, it isn't 'burr' here, but 'thistle'. But isn't 'thistle' better? (For its rapacity, tenacity and wolfish thistliness?)
Further:

> На желобах,
> Как рукава сырых рубах,
> Мертвели ветки . . .

> In the gutters
> Like sleeves of damp shirts
> Branches went limp. . . .

From the same poem:

> В запорошенной тишине,
> Намокшей, как шинель . . .

> In the powdery stillness
> Sodden, like an overcoat. . . .

(This poem is 'A Still More Sultry Dawn' – my fingers itch to quote it here in full, just as they do to tear up altogether these meditations on the subject and send *My Sister Life* herself around the bookstalls of the West – Alas, I've not enough hands!)
Further:

> У мельниц – вид села рыбачьего:
> Седые сети и корветы. . . .

> The mills have the look of a fishing-village:
> Grizzled nets, corvettes....

Then, in the tea-room:

> Но текут и по ночам
> Мухи с дюжин, пар и порций,
> С крученого паныча,
> С мутной книжки стихотворца,
> Будто это бред с пера....

>> Even in the nights they flow,
>> Flies off dozens, pairs and portions,
>> Off the wild convolvulus,
>> Off the poet's turbid book,
>> Like delirium from the pen....

Approaching Kiev by train:

> Под Киевом - пески
> И выплеснутый чай,
> Присохший к жарким лбам,
> Пылающим по классам....

>> Approaching Kiev – sands
>> And spattered tea
>> Dried on to hot temples
>> Burning through all the classes....

(Tea that has already turned into sweat and dried. A poetry of plottings! 'Burning through all the classes' – the third-class carriages are hottest of all! In this quatrain is the whole of the Soviet 'hunt for bread'.)[1]

'At Home':

> С солнца спадает чалма:
> Время менять полотенце,
> (– Мокнет на днище ведра).
>
> В городе – говор мембран,
> Шарканье клумб и кукол....

---

[1] Many people, in the Civil War years, travelled by train to the south of Russia, in search of bread or flour.

The turban slips from the sun:
Time for renewing towels
(One soaks in the pit of a pail).

In town – the discoursing of membranes,
Shuffle of flowerbeds and dolls....

Then, on the eyelids of a sleeping woman:

> Милый, мертвый фартук
> И висок пульсирующий...
> Спи, Царица Спарты,
> Рано еще, сыро еще.

> Dear and deathly apron,
> And the pulsating temple...
> Sleep on, Queen of Sparta,
> It is early still, still damp....

(The eyelid: an apron to protect a banquet from dust, the magnificent banquet of the eye!)

> Топтался дождик у дверей,
> И пахло винной пробкой.
> Так пахла пыль. Так пах бурьян.
> И, если разобраться,
> Так пахли прописи дворян
> О равенстве и братстве....

The small rain stamped its feet at the doors.
There came up a smell of wine-corks.
So smelled the dust. And such was the smell of the weeds.
And if you look into it closely
That was the smell of all the gentry's screeds
About equality and brotherhood.

(Smell of young wine: of thunder! Is not the whole of the 'Serment du jeu de paume' in this?[1])

And now, ladies and gentlemen, the final quotation, one that seems

---

[1] The oath sworn in the *Salle du Jeu de Paume* at Versailles by members of the newly self-proclaimed *Assemblée Nationale* on 17 June 1789. (They swore 'ne jamais se séparer et de se rassembler partout où les circonstances l'exigeront jusqu'à ce que la constitution du royaume soit établie et affermie sur des fondements solides'.) Tsvetayeva perhaps has in mind the painting entitled 'Serment du Jeu de Paume' by David.

to contain the whole solution to the question of Pasternak and everyday life:

> И когда к колодцу рвется
> Смерч тоски, то-мимоходом
> Буря хвалит домоводство.
> -Что тебе еще угодно?

> When towards the well-head rushes
> The whirlwind, anguish, pausing in mid-passage
> The storm applauds our household management,
> - What more do you ask for?

Why nothing! Surely not even God has the right to ask more than this from a storm!

Now let us think it over. I think we've proved the presence of everyday life. Now – what shall we do with it? Or rather, what does Pasternak do with it and what does it do with him? First of all, he sees it clearly: he'll grasp it and let it go. Everyday life is for Pasternak as the earth is to the footstep: a moment's restraint and a flying off. For him (check this in the quotations) it is nearly always in movement: a windmill, a carriage, the vagrant smell of fermenting wine, the discourse of membranes, the shuffling of flower-beds, spattered tea – I'm taking examples at random! Check for yourselves: even sleep is in movement for him – the pulsing temple!

Everyday life as inertia, as furniture, as an oak (a dining-room of oak, as advertised, so often repanelled by poets in Paul and Catherine rosewood), everyday life as oaken won't be found here at all. His everyday life is in the open air. Not settled, but in the saddle.

Now about his prosaic quality. Much could be said about this – it bursts out – but I'll yield to one who bursts out of me still more strongly: Pasternak himself.

> ... Он видит, как свадьбы справляют вокруг,
> Как спаивают, просыпаются,
> Как общелягушечью эту икру
> Зовут, обрядив ее, -паюсной.

> Как жизнь, как жемчужную шутку Ватто
> Умеют обнять табакеркою,
> И мстят ему, может быть, только за то,
> Что там, где кривят и коверкают,

> Где лжет и кадит, ухмыляясь, комфорт,
> Где трутнями трутся и ползают ...

> He sees his neighbours celebrating weddings,
> How they get roaring drunk and sleep it off
> How they call common roe – that pickled frogspawn –
> Once ritually treated, caviare.
>
> And how life like the pearl of a jest by Watteau
> They can contrive to cram into a snuffbox
> And are a scourge to him, perhaps, because
> All the time that they contort and crook,
>
> Through the lickspittle lies of sniggering comfort
> While, like the drones they are, they creep and crawl ...

Pasternak's prosaic quality, apart from being his native clearsightedness, is the divine rebuff that Life gives to aestheticism – the axe to the snuffbox. Most valuable of all. Where, in all these 136 pages, will you find a single aestheticist comma? He makes no more use of the common stock of poetical 'moons' and 'swoons' than he does of the 'ever so distinctive' tooth-picks of aestheticism. This double vulgarity misses him by a loop of a hundred miles. He is human – through and through. Nothing but life, and any means is the best. And it is not the Watteau snuffbox that he stamps on, this infant Titan of everyday life, but the kind of life that will fit into a snuffbox.

Pasternak and Mayakovsky. No, Pasternak is more formidable. His 'Afterword' alone utterly eclipses all of Mayakovsky's 150 millions.[1]

Look at the end:

> И всем, чем дышалось оврагам века,
> Всей тьмой ботанической ризницы,
> Пахнет по тифозной тоске тюфяка
> И хаосом зарослей брызнется.

> And all that was breathed to the age's ravines,
> All the dark of the botanic vestry,
> Wafts over the typhoid yearning of a mattress,
> Thrusts out, chaos of herbage, spurting.

This is it – Retribution! Chaos of herbage smothers the rotting mattress, aestheticism!

[1] '150 Millions' is the title of a poem by Mayakovsky.

What's a decree and a bayonet to the Ganges!

For Pasternak everyday life is a curb, but not more than the earth is a token (a tie) of holding back (holding out).

For since time immemorial the temptation of such souls, undoubtedly, in all their haloed brightness, is Death.

Pasternak and the Day

Not the cosmic day, heralded by the dawn, and not the broad daylight in which everything is clear, but the element of day (light).

There is another day – evil (because blind), effective (because blind), irresponsible (because blind); a tribute to our transience, the day of tribute: today. Endurable only because yesterday it was tomorrow and tomorrow it will be yesterday: from now to forever: eyes shut.

The summer day of 'seventeen is hot: aglare – under the tramp of the stumbling front. How then did Pasternak meet this avalanche of avalanches – Revolution?

There are few incontrovertible signs of 1917 in the book: listen very vigilantly, consider the quietest hints – there are some three, four, or five such signs.

Let's start. (With the poem 'The Sample'):

> ... Былые годы за́ пояс
> Один такой заткнет.
>
> Все жили в сушь и впроголодь,
> В борьбе ожесточась.
> И никого не трогало,
> Что чудо жизни – с час.

> All years that were erewhile
> One year like this outdoes.
>
> All lived it dry, half-starved,
> And in the struggle hardened.
> And none cared that the prodigy
> Of life was one hour long.

Then, in the poem 'Break up':[1]

> ... И где привык сдаваться глаз
> На милость засухи степной,
> Она, туманная, взвилась
> Революционною копной ...

> It, where the eye was used to yield
> To the small mercies of the droughty steppe,
> Now, muffled in mist, arose,
> Haystack of revolution!

Further, in the same poem:

> ... И воздух степи всполошен:
> Он чует, он впивает дух
> Солдатских бунтов и зарниц,
> Он замер, обращаясь в слух,
> Ложится – слышит: обернись!

> And the air of the steppe is stirred.
> It takes the scent, it drinks the air
> Of soldiers' mutinies and summer lightnings.
> It freezes in its tracks, it is become all ears.
> It lies full length, then hears the summons: Turn!

(Doesn't he mean himself?)

Again, in the poem 'The Militiaman's Whistle' (needless to say, leaving the militiaman out):

> ... за оградою
> Север злодейств сереет ....

> ... behind the fence
> The north of villainy grows grey ....

Three more lines from the poem 'A Sultry Night':

> ... В осиротелой и бессонной
> Сырой, всемирной широте
> С постов спасались бегством стоны ...

[1] 'Break-up' is the name of a railway station. 'It' refers to this.

> In the unparented, insomniac
> Damp and universal vast
> A volley of groans broke loose from standing posts...

The poem to Kerensky, 'Spring Rain', with these amazing lines:

> В чьем это сердце вся кровь его – быстро
> Хлынула к славе, схлынув со щек....
>
> In whom was that heart where all the blood in him fast
> Gushed to glory, sucked back out of the cheeks....

I'd read this as a magic spell worked on the youth of the word Enthusiasm – and certainly not as any political preference.

And that's all!

One thing is clear from the above divinations: Pasternak did not hide from the Revolution in any of the available intellectual cellars. (Not a cellar in the Revolution, only an area in a field!) An encounter did take place. He saw it for the first time – somewhere far off, in a mirage – as a haystack rearing wildly in the wind, and heard it in the headlong moan of roads. It gave itself to him (reached him), like everything in his life, through nature.

What Pasternak has to say about the Revolution, no less than what the Revolution has to say about itself, is still to come. In the summer of 1917 he walked in step with it; carefully listening.

Pasternak and Rain

Dozhd' ['rain']. What first of all springs to mind, in the fellowship of like sounds? *Dazhd'* ['grant']. And with 'grant' – naturally – 'God'.

God grant – what? – Rain! In the very name of the Slavonic sun there is already a prayer for rain.[1] Moreover, rain is somehow already granted in it. How amicable! How succinct! (Your teachers, Pasternak!) And now with a turn of the head, into the last decade. Who, in Russia, ever wrote nature? I do not wish to stir up names (to tear myself away and think about others) but – at a lightning glance – no one, ladies and gentlemen. We have written much and excellently (Akhma-

---

[1] In the religion of the Eastern and Baltic Slavs the god of the sun and of fire bore the name 'Dazhbog' which, its two parts being translated, means 'God grant' or 'grant God'. (He later became the god of goodness and abundance.)

A Downpour of Light: Poetry of Eternal Courage

tova above all) about the self in nature, eclipsing nature so naturally – that is, when the poet's Akhmatova! – we have written about nature in ourselves (likening it and likening ourselves); we wrote about events in nature, its distinct countenances and its hours; but however amazingly we wrote, we all wrote *about* it, no one wrote *it*,[1] itself – point-blank.

But lo! Pasternak. And again it's not certain: who is writing whom? The answer is in his penetrability. He so gives himself to be penetrated by the leaf, by the ray, that what is there is no longer himself, but a leaf, a ray. Reincarnation. A miracle. From the Lermontov avalanche to the Lebedyan' burdock[2] the whole thing is present, nothing left out, nothing missed. But more passionately than by grasses, dawns and blizzards, Pasternak was loved by the rain. (And *how* it poured down upon the poet – the whole book swims!) But far from an autumnal, drizzling, sparse little rain! Rain as a galloping Caucasian brave!

Begin:

> Сестра моя Жизнь – и сегодня в разливе
> Расшиблась весенним дождем обо всех ...

> My sister, life! Today in the flooding over
> Shattered in spring rain on us all. ...

Further: 'The Weeping Garden' (astounding from the first line to the last. I bite my fingers, having to pull it to pieces).

> Ужасный! Капнет и вслушается,
> Все он ли один на свете.
> (Мнет ветку в окне как кружевце)
> Или есть свидетель. ...

> Ни звука. И нет соглядатаев.
> В пустынности удостоверясь,
> Берется за старое – скатывается
> По кровле, за желоб, и через. ...

---

[1] 'wrote': *pisat'* means both 'to write' and 'to paint (depict)'; the thing 'painted' is the direct object of the verb, in the latter sense. I have preferred to sound un-English by using one and the same verb for 'write (about)' and 'paint (+ direct object)' rather than forfeit Tsvetayeva's slight play on this word.

[2] 'avalanche ... burdock': references to images in two poems by Pasternak.

> Appalling! it drips and listens – is it
> Alone in the world or (now it presses
> Lace-like, a twig upon the windowpane)
> Does it have witnesses?...
>
> ...No sound. No hint of espionage,
> Assured all's empty, it takes up
> Its old affairs, it sheets athwart
> The roof, brims over gutters, and across.

(Let me stress: the loneliness of the rain, not of the man being rained on!)

Next, 'The Mirror':

> ...Так после дождя проползают слизни
> Глазами статуй в саду.
> Шуршит вода по ушам....
>
> Thus after rain the slugs crawl journeying
> Like eyes of garden effigies.
> Water lisps in the ear....

And here is something wholly enchanting:

> У капель – тяжесть запонок,
> И сад слепит, как плес,
> Обрызганный, закапанный,
> Мильоном синих слез...
>
> Drops weigh as collar-studs, the garden
> Dazzles like a stretch of waters,
> All be-splotched and all be-spattered
> With a million bluish tears....

Further, in the poem 'Rain':

> Снуй шелкопрядом тутовым
> И бейся об окно.
> Окутывай, опутывай,
> Еще не всклянь темно....
>
> ...Теперь бежим сощипывать.
> Как стон со ста гитар,
> Омытый мглою липовой
> Садовый Сен-Готард.

A Downpour of Light: Poetry of Eternal Courage

>Come spin, as mulberry worm,
>Beat at the window pane,
>Come swathe, come swaddle yet,
>Thicken the murk again. . . .

>. . . And now come run, as if
>A hundred guitars made moan,
>To know the lime-washed, dim
>Saint-Gotthard, garden-adorned.

Further (my fingers will be gnawed to bits!):

>На чашечку с чашечки скатываясь,
>Скользнула по двум, и в обеих–
>Огромною каплей агатовою
>Повисла, сверкает, робеет.

>Пусть ветер, по таволге веющий,
>Ту капельку мучит и плющит,
>Цела, не дробится,–их две еще
>Целующихся и пьющих. . . .

>From calyx onto calyx sliding
>It has slipped athwart a pair of them – in both
>Like an immense drop formed of agate
>It is hung up, and dazzles there, and trembles.

>Let the wind, that breathes past meadowsweet,
>Flatten it out, that drop, and worry it,
>It's whole, and does not break apart but, **twinned**,
>The couple that it is still drink and kiss.

Next, the opening of the poem 'Spring Rain':

>Усмехнулся черемухе, всхлипнул, смочил
>Лак экипажей, деревьев трепет. . . .

>It laughed at the bird-cherry, sobbing, wetted
>Lacquer of landaus, tremor of the trees. . . .

Further ('Earth's Sicknesses'):

>Вот и ливень. Блеск водобоязни.
>Вихрь, обрывки бешеной слюны. . . .

And here's the downpour. Brilliance of hydrophobia,
Vortex, flecks of a rapid saliva....

A quatrain from the poem 'Our Storm':

> У кадок пьют еще грозу
> Из сладких шапок изобилья.
> И клевер бурен и багров
> В бордовых брызгах маляров.

Still at the waterbutts they drink the storm
From the sweet bonnets of profusion.
The clover is as tossed and crimson
As claret-coloured splotches of house painters.

A few pages later:

> Дождь пробьет крыло дробинкой....

The rain will pierce the wing with pellets....

Further (the opening of the poem 'A Sultry Night', one of the most ineffable in the book):

> Накрапывало, – но не гнулись
> И травы в грозовом мешке.
> Лишь пыль глотала дождь в пилюлях,
> Железо в тихом порошке.
>
> Селенье не ждало целенья,
> Был мрак, как обморок глубок....

A spattering came, but one that did not bend
Even the grasses in the thunder's sack.
Only the dust swallowed the rain in pellets,
Iron in powder, speck on quiet speck.

The village hoped for no alleviation,
The poppy-head was deep as fainting is...

and – let's simply list them:

> За ними в бегстве слепли следом
> Косые капли....

> Hard behind in an unseeing scurry
> Some slant drops fled. . . .

> . . . Дождик кутал
> Ниву тихой переступью. . . .

> A thin rain wrapped
> The cornfield in a quiet treading-across. . . .

> Накрапывало. Налегке
> Шли пыльным рынком тучи. . . .

> Spatter of rain. Light-footedly
> Clouds moved over a dusty market square. . . .

> Грянул ливень всем плетнем. . . .

> Rain rushed down, a solid fence. . . .

> Мареной и лимоном
> Обрызгана листва. . . .

> With madder and with lemon
> Leafage is asperged. . . .

> . . . Дождь в мозгу
> Шумел, *не отдаваясь мыслью*. . . .

> . . . rain in the brain-cells
> Roared, *not echoing back as thought* . . .

(that's why it is *rain* (life!) and not mere thoughts about it!) and on the last page of the book:

> . . . в дождь каждый лист
> Рвется в степь. . . .

> . . . in the rain each leaf
> Tears loose for the steppe. . . .

Ladies and gentlemen, now you know about Pasternak and the rain. The same thing happens with dew, leaves, dawn, earth, grass. Incidentally, I'll mention in passing the striking absence of the animal kingdom in the range of Pasternak's nature – not a tusk or horn. Only some scales slide by. Even birds are rare. As if for him the creation of the world stopped on the fourth day – and is still to be thought and understood through to the end.

But let us return to the grass, or rather let us walk after the poet:

> ... во мрак, за калитку
> В степь, в запах сонных лекарств. ...

> into the dark, past the wicker-fence,
> Into the steppe and the smell of sleepy drugs ...

(mint, camomile, sage).

Sage? Yes, ladies and gentlemen, sage. The poet, like God, like a child, or like a beggar, disdains nothing. And isn't this their horror (God's, the child's, the beggar's)?

> И через дорогу за тын перейти
> Нельзя, не топча мироздания.

> ... crossing the road and passing behind the fence
> Is not to be done but you tread the frame of the world. ...

The responsibility of every step, the trembling warning: 'Don't disturb!', and what vast – what inescapable – consciousness of power! If the poet had not said this already of God, I would say it about the poet himself: that he is one

> ... кому ничто не мелко ...
> to whom nothing is bauble. ...

Earthly indicia; his poem of genius 'The Great God of Details':

> ... Ты спросишь, кто велит,
> Чтоб август был велик,
> Кому ничто не мелко,
> Кто погружен в отделку
> Кленового листа,
> И с дней Эклезиаста
> Не покидал поста
> За теской алебастра?

> Ты спросишь, кто велит,
> Чтоб губы астр и далий
> Сентябрьские–страдали?
> Чтоб мелкий лист ракит
> С седых кариатид

A Downpour of Light: Poetry of Eternal Courage

Слетал на сырость плит
Осенних госпиталей?
Ты спросишь, кто велит?

—Всесильный Бог деталей.
Всесильный Бог любви,
Ягайлов и Ядвиг. . . .

> You ask, who stablishes
> That August be a power?
> To whom nothing is bauble,
> Who goes about to staple
> Light leaves to the maple,
> And since Ecclesiastes
> Has never left his station,
> Working the alabaster?
>
> You ask, who stablishes
> That asters taste, and peonies,
> Agonies, come September?
> That the meagre leaf of broom
> From grey of caryatids
> Come down upon dank flags of
> Infirmaries of the fall?
> You ask, who stablishes?
>
> The omnipotent God of details,
> The omnipotent God of love,
> Of Hedwigas, Yagailos. . . .[1]

In Pasternak's work there are no questions, only answers. 'Since I've given this answer, then evidently someone somewhere asked the question, perhaps it was I myself in my sleep last night, or perhaps I shall ask it in my sleep tomorrow.' The whole book is the affirmation, for everyone and everything, 'I am!' And yet how little is said directly about himself. Unmindful of himself. . . .

Pasternak and thought. Does he think? No. Is any thought there? Yes. But, beyond the gesture of his will, thought is what works in him, burrows in subterranean passages, and then suddenly – an explosion of light – it bursts outside. A revelation. An illumination. (From within.)

[1] Yagailo and Hedwiga: the Lithuanian prince and Polish queen whose marriage marked the beginning of the Polish-Lithuanian union.

> ... Но мы умрем со спертостью
> Тех розысков в груди. ...
>
> But we shall die with all the suffocation
> Of these investigations in our breast. ...

This couplet perhaps contains the chief tragedy of all those of Pasternak's kind: the impossibility of spending himself out – income tragically exceeds expenditure.

> И сады, и пруды, и ограды,
> И кипящее белыми воплями
> Мироздание – лишь страсти разряды,
> Человеческим сердцем накопленной. ...
>
> Gardens and garden-ponds and palisades,
> And, seething in white lamentations,
> The world's whole frame – are but the types of passion,
> The kinds of it man's heart accumulates.

And more helplessly and simply:

> Куда мне радость деть свою?
> В стихи? В графленную осьмину?
>
> Where shall I put this happiness of mine?
> In verses? In a rigorous eight-line stanza?

(And still they say 'the poor in spirit!')

> ... Будто в этот час пора
> Разлететься всем пружинам.
>
> Где? В каких местах? В каком
> Дико мыслящемся крае?
> Знаю только: в сушь и в гром:
> Перед грозой, в июле, – знаю.
>
> It seems this moment is the time
> For every coiled-down spring to fly apart.
>
> Where? In what places? Or in what
> Wildly envisaged region?
> The most I know is, in the drought, in thunder,
> July, a storm impending – this I know. ...

(What else but an explosion?)

> Как в неге прояснялась мысль!
> Безукоризненно. Как стон.
> Как пеной, в полночь, с трех сторон
> Внезапно озаренный мыс.

> How in bliss thought clarified itself!
> Irreproachably! As if a moan!
> As foam at midnight suddenly lights up,
> Upon three sides, a promontory.

(What else but an illumination?)
and – the last:

> Как усыпительна жизнь.
> Как откровенья бессонны!

> How drowsy living is,
> And openings-up, how sleepless!

Pasternak, when do you sleep?
I'll stop. In despair. I have said nothing. Nothing – about nothing – for before me is Life, and I haven't the words.

> ... И только ветру связать,
> Что ломится в жизнь, и ломается в призме,
> И радо играть в слезах. ...

> And only the wind can bind
> What breaks into life and breaks in the prism
> And is glad to play in tears.

What I'm writing is not a review: it's an attempt to get out, so as not to choke. This is the only one of my contemporaries for whom my lungs have not been large enough.

One doesn't write of contemporaries like this. I repent. It is solely out of professional jealousy and the wish not to surrender to the first glib pen – in some fifty years – this my heartfelt hymn of praise.

Ladies and gentlemen, this is a book for everyone. And everyone ought to know it. This book is for the soul what Mayakovsky is for the body, a release in action. It is not merely healing – like those slumbrous grasses of his – it is wonder-working.

D.L.P.

Read it trustingly, without resistance and with utter meekness: it will either sweep you away or it will save you! A simple miracle of trust: like a tree, a dog, a child, into the rain!

And there'll be no suicides, and there'll be no firing-squads. . . .

> . . . И вдруг пахнуло выпиской
> Из тысячи больниц!

> Suddenly there was a sense
> Of people being discharged from a thousand hospitals!

SOURCE: 'Svetovoi liven'', in M. Tsvetayeva, *Proza* (New York, 1953); originally published in *Epopeya*, III (Berlin, 1923).

OSIP MANDEL'SHTAM
Notes on Poetry (1923)

CONTEMPORARY Russian poetry did not drop straight from the skies, but was predicted by the whole poetic past of our country – for did not the crackling and clicking of Yazykov predict Pasternak, and is not this one example enough to show how the batteries of poetry talk to each other by long-range exchange of gunfire, not troubled in the least by the indifference of the time that divides them. In poetry there is always warfare. And only in epochs of social imbecility does there come peace or a truce. The leading roots, like battalion leaders, take up arms against each other. Roots of words wage war in the dark, snatching each other's food and earthly sap. The struggle of Russian, that is of the secular, unwritten speech, whose words have grown from domestic roots, the tongue of the lay people, against the written language of the monks, with their Church–Slavonic, hostile, Byzantine literacy – this struggle is still to be sensed.

The first intelligentsia consisted of Byzantine monks; they forced upon the language an alien spirit and an alien form. In Russia the monks, that is, the intelligentsia, have always spoken a different language from that of the lay people. The slavonicizing of Cyril and Methodius was for their age what the Volapük of the newspapers is for ours. The colloquial language loves adaptation. It fuses together inimical elements. Colloquial speech always finds the convenient middle path. In its relationship to the whole history of language it is conciliatory and is defined by a diffuse benevolence, that is, by opportunism. Poetic speech is never sufficiently 'pacified',[1] and after many centuries the old disharmonies are discovered in it: it is an amber in

---

[1] The Russian words for 'pacify' and 'secularize' have an identical-sounding root (*mir* meaning both 'peace' and 'world') so that there is a continued word-play here which cannot be reproduced in English.

which the fly still buzzes, though long since enclosed by the resin; the living foreign body continues living even within the fossil. Everything in Russian poetry that works for the advantage of an alien monastic literature, all the literature of the intelligentsia – that is, 'Byzantium' – is reactionary, that is, it is evil, it brings evil. But whatever tends to secularize the language of poetry, to drive Byzantium, the monkish intelligentsia, out of it, does good to the language, gives it longevity and helps it, as a righteous man is helped, to accomplish the feat of independent existence within the family of dialects. But just the opposite may be the case as, for instance, where a people with a native theocracy, like the Tibetans, frees itself from foreign worldly invaders, such as the Manchurians. Only the work of those who took part directly in the great laïcizing, the secularizing of the language, has been of the first importance in Russian poetry. They were Tredyakovsky, Lomonosov, Batyushkov, Yazykov, and finally Khlebnikov and Pasternak.

At a risk of seeming too elementary and of over-simplifying my subject, I would depict the negative and positive poles in the condition of the poetic language as a turbulent, morphological flowering and a hardening of the morphological lava under the crust of meaning. The speech of poetry is animated by a roaming multisignificant root.

The multiplier of the root is the consonant, which is the index of its vitality (a classical example is Khlebnikov's 'Smeyaryshnya smekho-chest' ').[1] A word multiplies by means of its consonants, not of its vowels. The consonants are the seed and the pledge of the posterity of the language.

A lessening of linguistic awareness means atrophy of the feeling for the consonant.

Russian verse is saturated with consonants; it clicks, it crackles and it hisses with them. A real secular speech. Monastic speech is a litany of vowels.

Because the struggle with the 'Byzantine' monastic intelligentsia on the battlefield of poetry subsided after Yazykov and because for a long time no new hero appeared on this glorious field, Russian poets one after the other began to grow deaf to the noise of language, became

---

[1] The poem by Khlebnikov referred to here is one consisting almost entirely of invented derivatives of the word *smekh* ('laughter').

Notes on Poetry

hard of hearing towards the beating of waves of sound, and had to use an ear-trumpet to discern their own small vocabulary amid the noise of the dictionary. An example is the deaf old man in *Woe from Wit* who is shouted at, 'Prince, prince, come back' – like Sologub, for instance.[1] A small vocabulary is not a sin, and not a vicious circle. It may even enclose the speaker in a circle of flame. But it *is* a sign that the speaker does not trust his native soil, and dare not set his foot wherever he likes. The Russian Symbolists were verily the Stylites of style: they have not more than five hundred words among them – the size of a Polynesian's vocabulary. But at least they were ascetics, anchorites. They stood upon logs. Whereas Akhmatova stands on a square of parquet – hers is a parquet stylitism. And Kuzmin sprinkles the parquet with bits of grass, to make it resemble a meadow (as in 'Otherworldly Evenings').

Pushkin has two expressions for innovators in poetry; one is: 'Only to fly away again, after stirring a wingless desire within us children of dust', and the other: 'when the great Gluck appeared and revealed new mysteries to us'.[2] Anyone who lures his native poetry with the sound and image of a foreign speech will be an innovator of the first sort, that is, a seducer. It is not true that Latin is dormant in Russian, not true that Hellas lies asleep in it. One could with as much justification conjure in the music of Russian speech Negro drums and the monosyllabic utterances of Kafirs. In Russian speech nothing at all lies dormant except itself. To say that a Russian poet's verses sound like Latin is not praise but a direct insult. And what of Gluck? Profound and fascinating mysteries? For the destiny of Russian poetry the profound and fascinating mysteries of Gluck lie not in any Sanskrit or Hellenism but in the consistent secularization of the poetic language. Give us a Vulgate, we do not want a Latin Bible.

When I read Pasternak's *My Sister Life* I experience the sheer joy of the vernacular, of the lay language freed from all extraneous influences, the common everyday language of Luther after the strained and unnecessary Latin, which was intelligible all right, everyone understood it, but it was unnecessary, and though it had once been metalogical

---

[1] By this allusion to the deaf old prince in Griboyedov's play *Gore ot Uma* (*Woe from Wit*, 1825) Mandel'shtam suggests that the poetry of Sologub (1863-1927) is the epitome of this sort of deaf-to-language poetry.

[2] Two quotations from Pushkin's *Mozart and Salieri*; they are from the speech of Salieri, envious of the genius of Mozart.

it had long ceased to be so, to the monks' great chagrin. This is the joy that the Germans felt in their tiled houses when they opened for the first time their fresh Gothic bibles, still smelling of printer's ink. And a reading of Khlebnikov can be compared to a still more sublime and instructive spectacle, the way our righteous language could and should have developed, had it been unencumbered and undesecrated by the misfortunes and the coercions of history. Khlebnikov's language is as lay, as vernacular a language as if no monks, no Byzantium, no intelligentsia's culture had ever existed. It is an absolutely worldly and secular Russian language, heard for the first time since a written Russian culture has existed. If we take this view of him, then we no longer need to regard him as some kind of sorcerer or medicine-man. He has plotted the transitional, intermediate paths in the development of the language, paths that historically it never took; they are taken solely in Khlebnikov, and made firm in his metalogy,[1] which is nothing other than those transitional forms which have not had time to acquire the crust of meaning that a rightly and justly developing language acquires.

When a ship after cruising along the coast moves out into the open sea, those who cannot bear the pitching go ashore. After Khlebnikov and Pasternak Russian poetry is again moving out into the open sea, and many of its customary passengers are having to bid farewell to the vessel. I see them already, standing, with their suitcases, beside the ladder flung across to the shore. But how welcome is a new passenger mounting the deck precisely at this moment!

When Fet appeared Russian poetry was stirred by

> the silver rocking of a sleepy stream

and when he departed Fet said:

> and with the burning salt of undying words. ...

This burning salt of certain words, this bird-whistling, crackling, rustling, flashing, splashing, this fullness of sound and fullness of life, this high tide of images and feelings sprang into being again with unprecedented force in the poetry of Pasternak. We are faced with that important patriarchal element that Fet represented in Russian poetry.

---

[1] Some of the Russian Futurist poets sought to create a new 'metalogical' (*zaumny*) language for poetry, one in which words would be 'freed' from meanings.

Pasternak's majestic everyday Russian verse is already old-fashioned. It is tasteless because it is deathless, it is styleless because it splutters from banality with the classical rapture of the trilling nightingale. Yes, Pasternak's poetry is simply birdsong (a woodgrouse in mating season, a nightingale in the spring), a direct product of the throat's anatomical structure, as much a generic sign as a bird's plumage is or its crop.

> Это — круто налившийся свист,
> Это — щелканье сдавленных льдинок,
> Это — ночь, леденящая лист,
> Это — двух соловьев поединок. . . .

> It's a steeply brimming whistle,
> It's the cracking of crushed blocks of ice,
> It is night, freezing the leaf,
> It is a duel of two nightingales. . . .

To read the poems of Pasternak is to get one's throat clear, to fortify one's breathing, to renovate one's lungs; such poems must be a cure for tuberculosis. At present we have no poetry that is healthier than this. This is *kumys* after tinned milk.

I see Pasternak's book *My Sister Life* as a collection of magnificent exercises in breathing: each time the voice is placed afresh, each time the powerful breathing apparatus is regulated in a different way.

Pasternak's syntax is that of a person talking with conviction, fervently and excitedly arguing something, and what is he trying to prove?

> Разве просит арум
> У болота милостыни?
> Ночи дышат даром
> Тропиками гнилостными.

> Can it be the arum asks
> Alms from the morass?
> Nights need not pay to inhale
> A tropical putrescence.

Thus, waving its arms and muttering, poetry takes its way, stumbling, dizzying, blessedly crazy, and yet the only thing that is sane and wide awake in the whole world.

Of course, when Herzen[1] and Ogarev stood upon Sparrow Hills as boys, they experienced physically the holy rapture of space and of the flight of birds. Pasternak's poetry has told us of these moments; it is the shining *Nikē* brought from the Acropolis to Sparrow Hills.

[1] Alexander Herzen (1812-70), Russian socialist thinker; with his friend N. P. Ogarev he had stood on Sparrow Hills in 1825 and vowed to dedicate his life to the Decembrists' (revolutionary) cause.

SOURCE: 'Zametki o poezii', in *Collected Works* of Mandel'shtam, ed. G. P. Struve and B. A. Filippov (New York, 1966); originally published in two parts, the first under the title 'Vulgata: Zametki o poezii', in *Russkoye iskusstvo*, II–III (1923), the second under the title 'Boris Pasternak', in *Rossiya*, VI (Feb. 1923); later published as one article in O. Mandel'shtam, *O poezii* (1928).

NIKOLAI ASEEV

Melody or Intonation (1923)

It is impossible to establish precisely the subdivisions of the two basic principles in the development of the Russian poetic language: the principle of melody and that of intonation. A large realm of suppositions and guesses still awaits its conscientious explorer. His task, I think, will go far beyond the frontiers of poetics, for to complete it favourably he will have to resolve the quarrel between 'the lyrical' and 'the tendentious', between that 'freedom of intuition' and that 'rational consistency' around which today's poets are distinctly grouping themselves.

To clarify my way of putting the question, let me recall that it is not only among poets of different generations and different types that these two mutually opposed slogans have arisen, but we frequently observe these apparently inimical principles in the life of a single poet, where they often destroy each other, as happened for instance with Gogol.

The formal, melodic principle which, in point of the length of time it has been in use, is the older organizing principle of speech (as in *byliny* and songs), became reduced, in literature, to a fixed number of metrical, and later also rhythmical, models, which have been canonized, studied, systematized, and consolidated by poetic theory.

It would be incautious to deny the immense organizing influence of the melodic principle on the whole of Russian poetry, starting at its very inception. It would be still more pointless to belittle its importance for the age we have just lived through. The principle of melody brought poetry out of the cul-de-sac of the hacked metre of the pre-Petrine epoch, and it gave suppleness and vitality to the fossilized imitative style that was current at the end of the nineteenth century. Finally, this same principle has determined both the vocabulary and the development of metaphor in Russian poetry. Limited by a rather narrow view of the world, and trying, as is usual in such a situation, to develop semantic depth at the expense of semantic breadth, it pushed the growth of Russian poetry towards a striving for formal perfection, giving order and refinement to craftsmanship.

The promotion of this element in poetry was moreover, assisted, in the greatest possible degree by the country's political condition. Indeed, the passive-contemplative themes invariably accompanying the melodic, 'singing', principle in poetry were themselves conditioned by that semi-oriental absolutism which received its first jolt only with the emancipation of the peasants. Under such a political régime any 'intonation' that went beyond raptures over the 'wisdom and goodness of Felitsa'[1] could hardly have been tolerated. And in fact it was not. At that time the intonation element in poetry was represented solely by the ode, that is, by the form of the classical song. Later, by tradition, but also by virtue of the above-mentioned development of rhythm and melody in the poetic language, there was created a specific kind of lyrical poem the name of which is mistakenly and quite pointlessly employed to designate a species of poem lacking in intonational power and expressiveness. 'To thrum the lyre with nonchalant hand' became the poet's honourable occupation. This is why Pisarev in his time scoffed so much at the pastime of poetry. And this is why the dissension between Fet and his contemporary critics was so acute; and why A. Grigoryev, Pavlova (in part), Tyutchev, Fofanov and a number of other first-rate poets fell into oblivion or semi-oblivion. It was the poet's own fault if the notion of a singing quality in poetry was confused with that of a lack of content, for they set up as opposites on the one hand the lyrical and on the other the civic, that is, social awareness.

At the same time there could not but exist another way of solving the question of poetic craftsmanship and of developing it: the striving for expression through intonation. By this I mean, as a counterbalance to the purely rhythmic, melodic aim, the unfolding of line and stanza on the level of oratorical or conversational speech. *Attempts* of this sort can already be clearly perceived in Pushkin and Yazykov ('The Bard in the Camp...');[2] to some extent in Tyutchev ('The Lark', etc.),

---

[1] Felitsa: a sobriquet given to the Empress Catherine II.
[2] There appears to be either a mistake or a misprint in the original. 'The Bard in the Camp of the Russian Warriors' is by Zhukovsky.

Nekrasov, Aleksei Tolstoy (the poet) and others. But these attempts were not capable of resisting the prevalent device, and they are either significant purely for their aesthetic effect or else they were diverted to 'permissible' civic themes (Tyutchev, Khomyakov, Yazykov).

Finally, in poets with a more highly formed social consciousness, they led to a certain kind of compromise, in which the two principles I have mentioned were combined and fused, so that their efficacy was weakened, and this in its turn led to a considerable lowering of the level of craftsmanship (Nekrasov, Nadson).

Hence the endless quarrels about 'the speech of slaves' and the 'language of the gods', listened to 'indifferently and haughtily' by the 'uninitiated people'.

The melodic element attained its greatest power and refinement in the poetry of Blok, who united and brought to perfection the most complex melodic and rhythmic patterns that had been heard in the lyrical work of Fet, Tyutchev and Lermontov. It was inevitable that after Blok this element should undergo a decline.

And indeed, in Igor Severyanin we see the 'laying bare of the device', and at the same time its paralysis. Severyanin was already singing his verses, unable to emphasize their melodic orientation by literary means alone.

Bely's efforts to reanimate the lifeless device – both in a series of theoretical works and in his creative prose writings – were quite hopeless and created a mist of enthusiasm for melodized prose that has not yet dissipated.

The conscious opposing of the principle of expression through intonation to the principle of melody is associated with the names of Khlebnikov, Mayakovsky, E. Guro, Pasternak. Part of the task of the present article is to examine this opposition in a book by the last-named poet – *Themes and Variations*. But let us note briefly that it was Khlebnikov who first destroyed the melodic canon in poetry by unlocking the suddenly ruptured chains of rhythm; while Mayakovsky was the first to introduce into poetry the material of colloquial speech, at first by means of quotation in the middle of a text, and then by unmotivated interruptions of the 'language of the gods' by the language of public speakers, of journalism and of the street.

To the inexperienced eye Boris Pasternak seems to stand to one side of all this. His purely 'lyrical' themes, his observance of the external, graphic forms as defined by poetics and, lastly, his rather prim and fastidious choice of words, may lead us to mistake the real nature of his skill, and give us grounds for supposing him to be closely linked with, and a successor to, the 'melodists'.

But a closer study of his work, with its independent, stubbornly pursued methods, leads us to quite a different conclusion.

In my reviews of his earlier books I have already noted the peculiar tautness of his syntactical devices. However, he had not yet at that time fully displayed the principle of expression through intonation, the amazing ability to construct a line of verse in accordance with the most ready-to-hand, most colloquial speech – a characteristic which makes some critics group him with the 'intimist' poets who write of the most complicated inner experiences, ostensibly inaccessible to the ordinary reader of today, and which makes others see him, no less mistakenly, as far too closely continuing the Futurists' methods of fashioning language.

Of course neither of these two approaches can account for the sharp freshness and heady force which emanate from every page of a book by Pasternak. Where do they come from? If he is an 'intimist', a 'personalist', the poet of his own reflections in the world, then how is it that a stanza of his is so breathtakingly vital and powerful? After all is said and done, Gumilev and Akhmatova wrote in the intimist manner of a heart-to-heart talk, a manner suitable for an audience of some twenty sensitive hearts. It will be replied that Pasternak is just as unpopular as they are. This is in fact untrue, if only because, as Bryusov rightly remarked, not one poet since the time of Pushkin has been received so attentively by all his contemporaries working with poetry.

Not twenty sensitive hearts, but at the very least two hundred poets, who have blunted their teeth on every possible poetic school, expected and still do expect new discoveries in the structure of the stanza to be made by Pasternak. And the most talented of our young poets are following, as if hypnotized, the winding of Pasternak's period.

Equally unfounded is the accusation that he is excessively close to the older generation of poets. Anyone with his eyes open can see by what centuries Pasternak's craft is divided from that of the past. Only someone who is an organizer of speech and has been through the rigorous technical school of individual culture could speak as he does. His intonational gesture is distinct and original. His poetic speech is designed for powerful vocal muscles capable of conveying these sinewy periods beyond the horizon of the age.

I will explain briefly what I mean by the terms 'expression through intonation', 'intonational gesture', and so forth, which I am using neither in a strict scientific sense nor – indeed still less – in their literal meaning. The coincidence of the movement of the rhythm with a conversational intonation of the utmost expressiveness, indeed sometimes the dependence of the rhythm upon the latter, but never the reverse (subordination of intonation to rhythm) – this I call the line's or the stanza's 'intonational gesture', for the sake of which, and in harmony with which, the line or stanza is constructed. A number of such gestures, given unity by the subject-matter and the form, make up the intonational expression of the verse.

The device used hitherto, namely that of introducing a colloquial intonation in the form of quotation, dialogue or an address to the reader, is not Pasternak's, for with him the element of intonation predominates and is the *raison d'être* of the whole poem. The continual use of this element in his work creates an impression of an immensely powerful oratory exploiting all the infinite variety of epithets and metaphors as a subsidiary means for forging a new form of speech that is organized and oriented above all on the principle of a provisional audience which has to be made to hear through to the end the ardent and vivid tale told by its contemporary. No matter that this tale is not a diary of events! No matter that it contains no biographical information about the age. Just as by looking at the bone of a prehistoric animal one can define and recognize future generations, so in the jerky, gasping, molten quality of intonational expression is to be recognized the fervent age in which man sets out upon the conscious organization of his existence and, in particular, of his speech!

One more reply, which is not even meant to object to all the so eagerly aggressive critics of Pasternak, but to stand them firmly face to the wall. Such poetry, they say, is unintelligible, therefore asocial. It is time to throw overboard all opinions of this sort! Haven't we dreamt long enough of restoring the kind of 'literary mores' where the reader does his bit of reading and the writer his bit of writing? Haven't we had enough of these

> Quiet reposes neath the linden
> With the 'Red Cornfield' in one's hand![1]

[1] 'Red Cornfield' (*Krasnaya Niva*): a popular magazine of general and literary articles which began publication in Moscow in 1922.

We need, and ought, to recognize that it is necessary and legitimate that there should exist, alongside the literature 'for reading', a literature 'for studying', which does not directly serve the practical aims of immediate general consumption. After all, do we read the theory of relativity as a propaganda pamphlet? Or the theory of electrons?

There are popular works to acquaint the ordinary reader with these things. But my whole point is that we have become accustomed to giving the same sort of interest to serious work done in the medium of language as we would give to an anecdote: if it's amusing, we remember it; if it's too complex, we forget it. And as for the equating of intelligibility with social significance we surely have here a confusion of the notions of the popular and the social. Is Karl Marx so very 'intelligible'? And Timiryazev?[2] And Romain Rolland? To whom? At what time? Under what conditions? All these question marks ought to be carved into the noses[1] of those critics who with one agonizing wail about 'unintelligibility' defend their timid entreaties for the solely correct dialectical approach to phenomena.

In *Themes and Variations*, as in his previous books, Pasternak's subjects are but faintly tinged by the contemporary scene. Whether this is his reluctance to introduce a false note into a theme that is still in process of unfolding, whether his personal manner, the manner of his life, requires that he be thoroughly well-informed before touching any plot, or whether, finally, this is a conscious turning away from facts that have not been balanced by consciousness, does not matter to us here. Let us suppose the worst: that the poet has not managed to bring his own view of the world into harmony with the objective facts of existence.

Well? Let us test the strength of his intellectual armour. For what matters to us is his active, not passive biography. Pasternak is to be valued according to the extent to which, despite and in defiance of his own subjective emotions, he represents a vast moving and organizing force. But even this last assumption falls to the ground if we look closely at the poet's vocabulary. For do we really have before us an individualist with a taste for philosophy? Is this really a bilious hypochondriac of the Khodasevich type spitting out his deathbed phlegm at every-

---

[1] 'carved into the noses': this is a literal translation of an idiomatic phrase more often rendered by something like 'Let them put it in their pipes and smoke it.'
[2] Russian natural historian, 1843–1920.

Melody or Intonation

thing around him? No. This is a slightly romantic-looking, but firm-standing, practice-hardened, well-disciplined clerk of an immense firm, who has the talents of a universal accountant and gesticulates passionately and candidly as he proves an inaccuracy in the boundless bank-balance of life. Let us recall some earlier lines of his such as these:

> Как казначей последней из планет,
> В какой я книге справлюсь, горожане,
> Во что душе обходится поэт,
> Любви, людей и весен содержанье?

> As if of the furthermost planet an accountant,
> In what book, townsfolk, shall I take account
> Of what it costs to the heart to have a poet,
> His maintenance of people, love, and springtimes?

A sturdy fellow, whose mind and muscle have been steeled in intellectual grapplings with the Kantian 'sum-total' of existence, who has gone through the Marburg school of robust slaps in the face by German idealism, who has crawled in the guise of lubricator under the wrecked 'special express' of the great European culture – he is well suited to the rôle of verbal engineer on the main railway of Russian poetry.

Pasternak's vocabulary? It is the inventory of that same vast commercial firm, where forest and flax, gardens and snow, all in heaps, in stacks, are tightly packed away and registered in the files, ready for sending off on the long journey of a new world-view. And this world inventory is checked over, with business-like lips pressed together, right at the very height of the embarkation! It has the smell that is only smelt in great colonial warehouses. It is romantic as only distant voyages are. This is a genuine business and a genuine register!

A mere superficial glance at the 'contents' of *Themes and Variations* is sufficient to convince one of that vitality in Pasternak's poetry that I have spoken of. Master of the comparison that is thrown off in passing (the very method of oratory) and that yet is always perfectly apt, he is infinitely inventive in ways of stowing this 'universal stock' of comparisons, which, though, are invariably faithful to the sole principle of their commonplace everyday, meaning.

> Поэзия! Я буду клясться
> Тобой и кончу, прохрипев:
> Ты не осанка сладкогласца,[1]
> Ты—лето с местом в третьем классе,
> Ты пригород и не припев!
>
> Poetry! I will swear by
> You, and end up croaking:
> You are not a posture of the liquid-throated,
> You are summer, seated in a third-class coach;
> A suburb, not a refrain.

This quotation alone would be enough to confirm all I have said here about Pasternak. Not to speak of the declaratory nature of its content, it is clearly founded upon colloquial speech. The first two lines are tightly bound together by the knot of the intonation: 'I will swear by you!' The remaining three lines are, one negative and the other two positive, definitions of a concept.

Is not this a verbal composition on the lines of an agitator's speech? If one were to construct a political speech on this framework – keeping the same freshness and strength in the comparisons – it would stand as a paradigm of syntactical balance and tautness of phrase.

The precision and distinctness of Pasternak's definitions, most of which, as I have said, draw on a stock of ordinary everyday things, evidently confuse those critics who are accustomed to the 'refined' comparisons of a specifically poetic vocabulary. Nothing else could explain the accusation levelled against Pasternak that his imagery is over-complicated. Certainly he is far from simple and he never employs a cliché; yet even in his most difficult similes or contrasts he always remains realistic and exact to the point of reproducing everything to scale, whether he is comparing morning to a frame-maker walking along with a baguette, or making the blizzard whirl 'like a bicycle' over his wallpaper, or noting the 'elegism of the telegraphic wave' or the 'rumbling roar of girders, like a washing-jug chucked by the bath'. Everywhere, as if from the edge of a precipice, there 'is revealed' to the reader a 'sector of the earthly globe' never before seen or observed, where the impression of this world is refreshed by a new foreshortened view and yet where, down to the smallest trifles and details (which Pasternak is so fond of), the correspondence between the indelibly real

[1] See note on p. 82.

Melody or Intonation

and the clarity of something seen for the first time is always preserved.

The central cycle of *Themes and Variations* is the cycle of nine poems under the general title 'The Break'. Their exceptional expressiveness and the power and tension of their intonational gesture lift these poems to the height of a unique, unsurpassable 'poèma' of emotion. At the same time they constitute a magnificent speech of indictment, amplified, as through a megaphone, by a grief and irony such as no poetry of the last decade has even come close to. This is not the hysterics of a nature lacerated by the pangs of love, this is sheer consciousness, its lips bitten till the blood comes, not yet able to govern but already capable of curbing an elemental emotion and of forcing it to the wall with the help of the intellect. The poem begins with an explosion of accusatory apostrophes:

> О, ангел залгавшийся, сразу бы, сразу б,
> И я б опоил тебя чистой печалью!
> Но так я не смею, но так – зуб за зуб!
> О, скорбь зараженная ложью в начале,
> О, горе, о горе в проказе!

> Angel of prevarications, on the spot, on the spot
> Had I but, even I, stifled you with a clean sadness!
> As it is, I do not dare to and as it is, it is tooth for a tooth.
> Sorrow infected with lies from the start,
> Grief, leprous grief!

The whole stanza is like the continuing of a conversation that has been going on for a long time. The periods are chopped up by purely intonational stops: 'As it is, I do not dare', 'on the spot, on the spot . . .'. Only in a passionate address brooking no digressions could their logical completion be thus omitted. And the whole poem is a predominantly intonational address of just this sort. Let us look closely at the structure of the second stanza:

> О ангел залгавшийся, – нет не смертельно
> Страданье, что сердце, что сердце в экземе!
> Но что же ты душу болезнью нательной
> Даришь на прощанье? Зачем же бесцельно
> Целуешь, как капли дождя, и как время,
> Смеясь, убиваешь за всех, перед всеми.

> Angel of prevarications – no, not fatal
> The throe by which the heart, the heart gets eczema!
> But why in the world does the soul get a skin sore as
> Your present at parting? Why unconscionably do you
> Kiss as the drops of rain do, and as time
> Laughingly kills, for the lot of us, there before us!

Here not one line is correct according to the canons. The lines are all fastened to one another by knots of intonation which carry the voice without pause for breath from one line to the next. The stops are conditioned solely by the taking of new breaths. Who will assert after this that a stanza thus constructed observes the principle of rhythm but not that of intonation? Clearly the author meant to lay out the rails of his verse over the track not of tunefulness but of intonational expressiveness, that is, what mattered to him was not the melodic but the colloquial organization of speech.

Incidentally – for the bewilderment of certain comrades who ascribe to Pasternak a tendency to idealism: it is true that he often speaks about the soul. But it will have to be agreed that a soul which is sick with a 'skin disease' is a pathological rather than an idealistic notion. Such a soul can be examined. And it should be noted that Pasternak's 'idealistic' terminology is always so material that it would seem a good deal more dubious to a mystic than to a materialist.

The whole of the next poem is remarkable both for the dynamics of its intonation and for the way it asks, point-blank, 'idealistically – materially', its question about human existence.[1]

> О, стыд, ты в тягость мне! О, совесть, в этом раннем
> Разрыве столько грез, настойчивых еще!
> Когда бы, человек – я был пустым собраньем
> Висков и губ и глаз, ладоней, плеч и щек,
>
> Тогда б по свисту строф, по крику их, по знаку,
> По крепости тоски, по юности ее,
> Я б уступил им все, я б их повел в атаку,
> Я б штурмовал тебя, сокровище мое.

---

[1] In the first published version of this article the concluding part of this sentence reads, 'its question about the *élan vital* of human existence'.

Melody or Intonation

My shamefastness, you are a weight upon me! Conscience, this so soon come
Break is imbrued with fantasies, still so many!
If but, a man – I were a void amalgam
Of temples, and lips, and eyes, cheeks, shoulders, palms of the hand,

Then had I, by the whistle of strophes, by their sign and cry,
And by yearning's hold and the youth of it, given up
Everything to them, and with them launched the assault
And taken you, my treasury, by storm.[1]

Here, with the slowing down of the expression the intonation, in the first stanza, is weakened to the point where it merely links the lines in pairs, and then increases, growing into the unbroken period of the second. And once again, this is a model of oratory, with the diapason transposed in the second part of the speech, and the speech ending in a voice that breaks off on the very highest notes (an agitator's device).

From the same point of view the fourth and fifth poems of the cycle are no less telling. The periods similarly interrupted for breathing, the same intonational concrescences, constantly modified and varied. The third and sixth poems, designed to give the voice a rest, are again only characterized by the way the lines combine in pairs in their first stanzas. However, in the seventh and eighth, just as in the fourth and fifth, there is the continuous unfolding of an intonation that has now gained in strength. Finally, the last, the ninth, as though to sum up the whole cycle, is composed of abrupt rejoinders, the most fitting imaginable for a voice that has made prolonged exertions in exceptionally powerful intonational gestures. This is the conclusion to the speech, almost a calm one, though not lacking in all the force of sarcasm that has imbued the whole cycle.

Я не держу. Иди. Благотвори.
Ступай к другим. Уже написан Вертер.
А в наши дни и воздух пахнет смертью:
Открыть окно – что жилы отворить.

I do not hold you. Go, and do good works.
Be off to some others. *Werther* is written already.
But in our days the very air smells of death:
Opening windows, it is a vein we open.

[1] Here, as elsewhere, Aseev is evidently quoting from an earlier (undiscoverable) version of the poem than the one commonly known. (Because of misprints it is difficult always to be sure of this, but it does seem to be the case with l. 3 of the poem quoted on p. 80 where I have substituted the familiar version.)

I have analysed only one cycle in one book of poems by Pasternak. Those interested in my method are recommended to turn to direct observation to test whether it is right for Pasternak's poems in general. I will just mention that in *Themes and Variations*, the clearest and most exemplary poems in this sense are: 'Shakespeare', 'The Kremlin in a Storm at the End of 1918', 'In the twilight you still seem to me a schoolgirl', 'Neskuchny', 'The air is cut by a fine drizzle', 'Poetry', the cycle 'Autumn', 'Here is its mark left, thumb nail of enigma'.

I mention the most telling ones for the benefit of those who are distinguishing between melody and intonation in poetry for the first time. But of course there are elements of intonational expression in all Pasternak's verse. It would be over-punctilious and fruitless to multiply examples. As it is, my article has spread beyond its limits, only lightly touching the question of the unequalled power of this poet, whose rôle as a remarkable organizer of speech would require, were one to account for its whole genuine importance, a long and careful specialist study.

But the modest aim of this article is to offer some guide-lines for critic and reader to approach this enormous talent without short-sightedness and inattention, for inattention will lead to distressing knocks and bruises against a phenomenon which, despite its sudden emergence into eminence, is in fact an organic whole.

SOURCE: 'Melodika ili intonatsiya?', in N. Aseev, *Dnevnik pisatelya* (Leningrad, 1929); originally published under the title 'Organizatsiya rechi', in *Pechat' i revolyutsiya*, VI (1923).

A. LEZHNEV

The Poetry of Boris Pasternak (1927)

> Я клавишей стаю кормил с руки
> Под хлопанье крыльев, шум и клекот.

> The covey of the keyboard I was feeding from my hand
> To the buffet of wing-beats, honk and hubbub.

These words could only be spoken by a great poet. Reading these amazing lines about the steppe:

> Столетняя полночь стоит у пути,
> На шлях навалилась звездами,
> И через дорогу за тын перейти
> Нельзя, не топча мирозданья…

> Right by the track stands midnight, centuries-old,
> There on the highway it has collapsed in stars,
> And crossing the road and passing behind the fence
> Is not to be done but you tread the frame of the world,

we cannot help thinking of Tyutchev. Here is the fullness and intensity of sensation peculiar to poets of Tyutchev's stamp and scale.

The extracts could be continued. More and more stanzas could be quoted to surprise and wound us, showing us a side of things that we have never seen before, whether it be a storm, 'instantaneous ever more':

> А затем прощалось лето
> С полустанком. Снявши шапку,
> Сто слепящих фотографий
> Ночью снял на память гром.

> The summer took its leave
> Of the country halt. Doffing its cap, by night
> A hundred blinding snapshots
> The thunder took, to treasure as mementoes.

Or summer rain:

> Скорей со сна, чем с крыш; скорей
> Забывчивый, чем робкий,
> Топтался дождик у дверей,
> И пахло винной пробкой.

> Rather from sleep than from the eaves, and rather
> Absent-mindedly than diffident,
> The small rain stamped its feet at the doors.
> There came up a smell of wine-corks.

Or the painful sundering of love:

> О, ангел залгавшийся, — нет, не смертельно
> Страданье, что сердце, что сердце в экземе!
> Но что же ты душу болезнью нательной
> Даришь на прощанье? Зачем же бесцельно
> Целуешь, как капли дождя, и как время,
> Смеясь, убиваешь за всех, перед всеми!

> Angel of prevarications — no, not fatal
> The throe by which the heart, the heart gets eczema!
> But why in the world does the soul get a skin sore as
> Your present at parting? Why unconscionably do you
> Kiss as the drops of rain do, and as time
> Laughingly kills, for the lot of us, there before us!

One's first impression, even before one can account for it, is that this is genuine poetry, 'an artistic product of high quality'. Whence then the disputes around the name of Pasternak? Why is it that while some regard him as the greatest master of our age, others — and they are in the great majority — find him obscure, pretentious, incomprehensible, meaningless? To understand this we must take a close look at him. We will take not just some isolated stanza, but a complete poem. Let us look at the following:

Попытка душу разлучить
С тобой, как жалоба смычка,
Еще мучительно звучит
В названьях Ржакса и Мучкап.

Я их, как будто это ты,
Как будто это ты сама,
Люблю всей силою тщеты
До помрачения ума.

Как ночь, уставшую сиять,
Как то, что в астме — кисея,
Как то, что даже антресоль
При виде плеч твоих трясло.

Чей шопот реял на брезгу?
О, мой ли? — Нет, душою — твой,
Он улетучивался с губ
Воздушней капли спиртовой.

Как в неге прояснялась мысль!
Безукоризненно! Как стон!
Как пеной, в полночь, с трех сторон
Внезапно озаренный мыс.

It sounds still, like the plaint
Of a fiddlebow, the attempts made
To estrange my soul from you
In Rzhaks, Moochkap – those place-names.

I love these names, as it might be they were
You – yes, you yourself,
With all the strength of unavailing
I love them to the blacking out of reason.

Like a night that is tired of shining,
Like what to asthma muslin is,
Like what, at the sight of your shoulder, sets
The very hallway shaking.

Whose whisper sailed upon the daybreak?
Mine, was it? No, in soul 'twas yours,
More aery than a drop of spirits, it
Evaporated from the lip.

> How in bliss thought clarified itself!
> Irreproachably! As if a moan!
> As foam at midnight suddenly lights up,
> Upon three sides, a promontory.

The 'classical' poem was usually built upon the unfolding of one definite idea, a thought idea or a feeling idea. As it unfolded, the wave of emotion mounted, reached its apogee, then fell away. If we were to represent this graphically, we would get a curve something like that of a pulse beat.[1] Pushkin's 'Prophet' could serve as a model of such construction: the wave climbs up as far as the words 'I lay in the desert like one dead', at which point there begins the catharsis, the resolution, the descending phase of the wave; or Yesenin's 'To the Memory of Shiryayevtso' (where there is an ascent as far as the stanza 'Happy in that I have kissed some women', which is the poem's apogee; the last two stanzas are its falling off.) There are other ways in which the rise and the fall of the wave of emotion can be related to each other. Thus, in Pushkin's 'I recall a miraculous moment' the apogee comes at the end of the poem, its lowest point in the middle. What is important, though, is not these differences but the fact that in every case there is a unified idea and an undulating pattern of emotion. The poems of Pasternak are constructed on quite a different principle: that of linking things together by association, and linearity.

Let me explain what I mean by these terms. Whereas for the classical poets a poem was the unfolding of a single idea, for Pasternak it consists of a series of links, connected one to the other by means of some sort of association. Goethe says that a poem is good when it retains its meaning even in a prose paraphrase. If you try to follow this advice and paraphrase Pushkin's 'Prophet' or 'I recall a miraculous moment', you will find it can be done, although the paraphrased works will have lost a considerable part of their poetic value. But attempt to paraphrase the poem which I have just quoted and you will only manage to reproduce a number of separate moments: night, tired of shining; a hallway; a whisper, evaporating more aerily than a drop of spirit; a promontory, suddenly lighted up by foam at midnight, and so on – that is, a series of notions and perceptions, connected to each other by memory or by resemblance. Evidently Goethe's advice, which amounts

---

[1] Or, rather, of the interval in the repetition, the isolated wave of the curve. *A. Lezhnev.*

to the stripping clear of the basic idea, is inapplicable here. And this is not because Pasternak is no good, but because his works are constructed on a different principle: not that of a single basic idea, one big theme – but that of a multitude of brief themes linked by association.

This is related to the other peculiarity of Pasternak, which I called 'linearity'. Let us return to the poem we were looking at. Its emotional tone is given with the very first stanza, and goes on being heard, as the poem proceeds, as an even note that grows neither stronger nor weaker. It does not rise or sink, does not change its speed or its intensity. Its graphic representation would not be an undulating curve, but a horizontal. And this is understandable: there can only be a wave-like mounting and descending where one theme – an emotion – is being developed, not where a large number of themes – of sensations – intersect. In the latter case there can be only short and random ascents.

Linearity, and connection according to associations – these are the characteristics of the vast majority of Pasternak's poems. His best and most popular pieces are constructed like this, for instance the well-known (and indeed very fine) poem which captivated Ehrenburg: 'My sister, life! today in the flooding over . . .'. Here, a whole series of brief themes – squeamish people in monocles, who sting like snakes in the oats; eyes and lawns that are lilac in the storm; a horizon smelling of moist mignonette; a train timetable which you read in May in your compartment, and which seems grander than the Holy Scriptures; the third bell,[1] floating away like a continuous apology; the steppe, crumbling from the footboard to a star – intersect with each other and add up to one general and complete impression (which is expressed the most exactly in the poem's opening lines: 'My sister, life! today in the flooding over/Shattered in the spring rain on us all'). The fact that this impression is a complete one cannot conceal, however, the basic fact that it is still an *impression* and not an *idea* (which is why it is so difficult to formulate), and that it is achieved by the intersection of various themes rather than by the development of *one*. Even in those of Pasternak's works – few enough in number – which are not built up on a concatenation of associations (for example, 'The Break') the principle of linearity remains in force. The poet here begins on a very high note ('O angel of prevarications, on the spot, on the spot . . .')

---

[1] The third bell is that which rings immediately before the train's departure.

and he finishes on the same high note. The level of intensity does not change. It is still a horizontal, only it is more elevated.

To construct a poem on the principle of linking by association already makes for difficulty in understanding it. Instead of one distinctly developing idea, you have a whole series of short, intersecting themes, leading now in one direction, now in another. Not one of them has time to take possession of you to such a degree that you could 'feel your way into' it. But the obstacles to understanding are made still greater by another peculiarity of Pasternak: the omission of one or another associative link.

> Я и непечатным
> Словом не побрезговал бы,
> Да на ком искать нам?
> Не на ком и не с кого нам.
>
> Разве просит арум
> У болота милостыни?
> Ночи дышат даром
> Тропиками гнилостными.
>
> Будешь—думал, чаял,
> Ты с того утра виднеться,
> Век в душе качаясь
> Лилиею, праведница.
>
> Луг дружил с замашкой
> Фауста, что ли, Гамлета ли,
> Обегал ромашкой,
> Стебли по ногам летали.
>
> Или еле-еле
> Как сквозь сон овеивая
> Жемчуг ожерелья
> На плече Офелиином.
>
> Ночью бредил хутор:
> Спать мешали перистые
> Тучи. Дождик кутал
> Ниву тихой перетупью
> Осторожных капель. . . .

The Poetry of Boris Pasternak

> From an unprintable
> Word, I would not have flinched.
> To whom, though, should we look?
> To none, nor can claim from any.
>
> Can it be the arum asks
> Alms from the morass?
> Nights need not pay to inhale
> A tropical putrescence.
>
> 'Twould be – I thought, I hoped –
> You from that morning forward
> For an age in the soul visible
> Swaying, lily-like, righteous woman.
>
> The field was friendly with
> Faust's manner, was it, Hamlet's,
> Swarmed like the daisy, stalks
> Flew round at ankle level.
>
> Or else, now glimpsed, now not,
> As athwart a dream, fanned out
> Pearl-cluster of the clasped
> String on Ophelia's shoulder.
>
> Come night, it raved, the farmstead:
> Sleep was broken by the feathered
> Clouds. And a thin rain wrapped
> The cornfield in a quiet treading-across
>
> Of scrupulous drops.

In this excerpt it is not hard to note at what places the omission of an association leaves a hiatus. It comes between each two stanzas: it is particularly noticeable between the third and fourth stanza, where there is a real break in the sense. A similar break in the sense also comes right in the middle of the fourth stanza. ('The field was friendly with Faust's manner, was it, Hamlet's') where incidentally we have to do not so much with an omitted as with an inadequately developed association. Not even the most diligent and attentive reading will help the reader. He will not guess why the poet goes from

the righteous woman – who is to sway in the soul for an age like a lily –
to the field, or what is meant by the field being friendly with the
manner of Faust or of Hamlet.[1] The key to these mysteries is kept by
the poet. He need only restore the association for the obscure place
to become ordinary and comprehensible. Why has he not done this?

For the reason that the constructing of a poem on associations, together with the omission of associative links, is a deliberate device with Pasternak. It would be wrong of course to suppose that Pasternak's associative method was brought about by his particular kind of thinking. It is a feature of all thinking. It would also be wrong to regard Pasternak's poems as the naïvely subjective record of the poet's sensations in the very same form in which he experienced them, to think that he noted them down without an eye to the reader, unmediated and unclothed. As a rule, the mechanism of associative combinations is scarcely to be noticed at all. Persistent self-observation and analysis are needed in order to reveal it. So the sort of recording of sensations which presents them in the form of a chain of associations will always be a *secondary* one, the result of analysis, of the breaking down of the original material of sensations and feeling. Thus Pasternak's poems, by their very construction, are not more but less immediate than are poems of the classical type. This does not mean they are forced or bookish. But it means that that peculiarity of theirs which seems to be the result of their complete denudation and creative naïveté is actually a deliberate device of construction.

A device then, but to what end? What is its meaning and purpose? What is its social foundation? This question can be fully answered only when we have examined other features of Pasternak's poetry that are closely related to this device. For the time being though, I shall confine myself to this.

There is no doubt that the omission of an associative link is the same sort of deliberate device – and adopted for the same reasons – as is the construction of a poem on the principle of combination by association. But the omission of associative links, as we have already seen, leads to

---

[1] Perhaps it is solely the external association: lily-field. But as for the 'manner' of the field, we possibly have to see in this a hint at the scene from *Faust* where Margarita pulls the petals off the daisy ('he loves me, he loves me not'), as well as a hint at the scene from *Hamlet* where Ophelia appears bedecked with flowers (this seems to be confirmed in the next stanza). However, such an association is, firstly, much too complicated, involved and indeterminate and, secondly, he ought to have spoken not of the manner of Faust or Hamlet, but of that of Margarita and Ophelia. *A. Lezhnev.*

obscurity and to difficulty in understanding the poem. Accordingly, when we say that such omission is a device, we are saying that Pasternak uses obscurity as an aesthetic factor, that his notorious incomprehensibility is a means he employs to enhance, one way or another, the aesthetic value of the work, that it is by no means spontaneous and accidental, but entirely deliberate. Pasternak writes unintelligibly because he wants to write unintelligibly. Why then does he want to write unintelligibly?

The poems of Pasternak are built not upon the development of a single theme but upon the concatenation of several short themes. What kind of themes are they?

For all their multiplicity they have something in common, something which I would call *psychophysiologism*. To explain this idea let me refer to one of Pasternak's prose works, his story *The Childhood of Luvers*. This is an interesting and in its way remarkable piece. It has no action and consists wholly of a very fine psychological web composed of elements which are not feelings in the proper sense, not emotions being unfolded before us, but sensations existing on the frontier between elementary, 'purely physiological' sensations and more complex 'mental' motions – sensations from things, rooms, trees, light and smell, sensations of the atmosphere of a house, a street, a spring corridor, and so on.[1] Sometimes they are simply expressed through the delicate description of an object; the sensation from the object enters into the description of the object. This is in its way a microscopy of feeling, a further refinement of the kind of psychological analysis which we find, for instance, in the early works of Lev Tolstoy.

[1] All these expressions ('sensation', 'the unfolding of an emotion', and so on), to be found frequently in the course of my article, I am using not as scientific terms, nor because my view-point is that of introspective psychology (as contrasted with the psychology of reflexes). I am well aware of their inexactitude and diffuseness, but use them as a convention, because there is at present no other terminology to take their place (the psychology of reflexes cannot as yet be very well applied to literature). However, with all their inexactness, these terms do express certain real correlations or distinctions; there is some sort of real substratum beneath them. The following should also be borne in mind: poetry (especially lyric poetry) has to do predominantly with the subjective aspect of those processes which the student of reflexes examines as objective ones. Moreover, what we have in poetry is not the 'sensations', and so forth, themselves, but their literary, that is, altered, rationalized, but at the same time also materialized (objectivized), expression. And the terms I am using refer not so much to 'mental' phenomena as to their literary expression. *A. Lezhnev.*

The Childhood of Luvers is in a sense the key to Pasternak's lyrical work: many of the latter's qualities are here expressed with greater clarity, definition and emphasis. This has to do also with psycho-physiologism (indeed, particularly with this). The themes of Pasternak's poems are not themes of emotion but themes of sensation:

> Был утренник. Сводило челюсти,
> И шелест листьев был, как бред....

Morning frost. Set of the jaw.
Leaf-rustle, like delirium....

> ... в грозу лиловы глаза и газоны
> И пахнет сырой резедой горизонт.

... in the thunder eyes and lawns are lilac,
And the horizon breathes moist mignonette.

> ... в высях мысли сбились в белый кипень
> Дятлов, туч и шишек, жара и хвои.

... thoughts in the heights have clotted in white spume
Of woodpeckers and fir-cones, and clouds and heat and needles.

> И песни колотой куски,
> Жар наспанной щеки, и лоб
> В стекло горячее, как лед....

And a bit of a chopped-up song,
Heat of a slept-upon cheek, and a brow
Burning against the windowpane like ice.

It is the way they are oriented toward sensation that gives Pasternak's poems their quality of unusual freshness (things seem to show us a new aspect of themselves, one that we have never seen before), and that requires them to be constructed according to associations. What is important to Pasternak is not the object but the emotional colouring which is put into the object by man, the subjective atmosphere in which objects are enveloped by him. The object, and the emotion from the object, are blended by Pasternak into a single whole: sensation. In this whole it is the emotion that predominates, deforming the object; the subjective impression overwhelms the objective datum. Pasternak does something analogous to what the Impressionists did in painting. Like them, he is a better colourist than draughtsman. He takes apart the objects of an emotion into their simplest psychophysiological components, so that, when they are created anew by the recombination of these, things appear cleansed and youthful, as if the dust and mould by which they had long been covered were now removed from them.

It is clear that the wave-like construction of a poem, which is natural and necessary to the setting forth of a single emotion-theme (for it is the result of the undulation of the feeling itself, of the very emotion which is being set forth), is inappropriate where there is but a brief sensation not wave-like in its structure. On the contrary, construction by association is here directly indicated. And indeed, what is the meaning of Pasternak's analysing the emotional material into the simple elements of sensation? It is a striving to convey something like the original quality of impressions, to convey the tangible, visible, audible world in the form in which our senses perceive it at the very moment when they do perceive it. To show consciousness, not in its final results, but in its initial and intermediate phases. Construction by associations, underlined by the whimsicality of the ways in which these are combined, strengthens that quality of a primal immediacy, not yet controlled and checked by consciousness, which the poet wants his verses to have.

If his breaking down of the world of emotions and objects into the simple components of sensations shows Pasternak to be an Impressionist, in his displacement, dislocation, of these elements he appears as a Futurist. He sets in a row elements that lie on different planes of meaning or association. At the beginning of this article we saw the most simple example of this displacement:

> *Скорей со сна, чем с крыш, скорей*
> *Забывчивый, чем робкий,*
> *Топтался дождик у дверей.*

> Rather from sleep than from the eaves, and rather
> Absent-mindedly than diffident,
> The small rain stamped its feet at the doors....

The following anecdotic construction is based on the same principle: 'Rain was falling and so were my hopes....' 'One man was in despair, the other in galoshes....'

Here is the same device, though less emphasized:

> Оно грандиозней святого писанья
> И черных от пыли и бурь канапэ.

> Так пахла пыль. Так пах бурьян.
> И, если разобраться,
> Так пахли прописи дворян
> О равенстве и братстве.

> It is grander than the Holy Scriptures,
> Than, blackened with dust and storms, is the settee.

> So smelled the dust. And such was the smell of the weeds.
> And if you look into it closely
> That was the smell of all the gentry's screeds
> About equality and brotherhood.

In similitudes of the type below, the dislocation of planes of meaning is no less apparent:

> ... как убитые спят снега.

> ... the snows sleep the sleep of the dead.

Another kind of dislocation is effected by the omission of associative links (see above).

These displacements make still more complicated the already complex structure of Pasternak's poems, with its counterpoint of brief themes. But in Pasternak complication goes hand in hand with thematic impoverishment.

The orientation toward sensation is in itself connected with the thematic impoverishment, of which, of course, it is not the cause but rather a result. The more complex feelings drop away, especially emotions of a social nature. Pasternak's poetry is limited almost exclusively to landscape-painting, still-life, interiors, and love poetry three-quarters of which, in its turn, consists of landscapes, still-lifes and interiors. Of the twenty-three poems in the collection *Selected Poems* only one, 'St Petersburg' – and perhaps also, in part the poem, 'Dearest, it's awful. When a poet loves...' – steps outside the circle of these themes and possesses, though none too intensively, a social colouring. The same proportion holds for Pasternak's other books. Social links, links with the community, are cut off almost at their root. The poet's question:

> Какое, милые, у нас
> Тысячелетие на дворе?
>
> Tell me, my dears, what
> Millennium is it out there?

can without much straining be placed as an epigraph to his books. The tremendous events of the past years – for Pasternak's poetry began and developed between 1914 and 1924 – pass by without any reflection at all in his poems, and if there were no dates at the bottom of them, you would never suppose them to have been written at a time of war and revolution. In Pasternak we can only discover 'what millennium it is outside' through the details of technology and transport that he mentions: tram-lines, a bicycle, a train timetable – ah yes, so it's our own age. We can see this, of course, in the form of his poems too: one is aware, though not very strongly, of the Futurist in Pasternak; we see it in their atomistic character, in how they are analysed into sensations, in the dislocation of levels, in the fundamental tendency to be difficult; but it cannot be seen from their content. Only very very rarely do we find him breaking through into the present like this:

> Остаток дней, остаток вьюг,
> Сужденных башням в восемнадцатом,
> Бушует, прядает вокруг,
> Видать – не доигрались насыто.
> За морем этих непогод
> Предвижу, как меня, разбитого,
> Не наступивший этот год
> Возьмется сызнова воспитывать.

> Remnant of the days, remnant of the snowstorms,
> Sentenced to the tower in the year 'eighteen,
> It flings, it ravens around;
> Clearly they have not had their fill.
> Beyond the seas of these foul seasons
> I, broken, look ahead to where
> This year not yet begun
> Will undertake afresh my education.

But these breakthroughs are not developed further. Of all the significant poets of our time Pasternak is the furthest removed from the social sphere, much further than Mayakovsky, Yesenin, Aseev, Tikhonov.

To some extent a poet can be characterized by the *things* which are to be found in his poems, the things of his environment, the material scenery of his life, which surround him, which he is used to and which get into his metaphors; his poetry's physical accompaniment. In Pasternak we find the following, rather telling series: bronze, wrists, pier-glass, drawing-room, hall, settee, piano, chandelier, muslin, gauze, blinds, tulle, mignonette, lawn, park, garden, pond, railway-carriage, compartment, ruler, *dacha*.[1] I realize that such enumerations are not always convincing. In the first place there arises the suspicion of how far any list like this is characteristic, whether it has not been selected artfully. In the second place, even if it is compiled wholly objectively, one needs to know how to read it. The same words can be pronounced with different intonations, the same things can be both a point of repulsion and a focus of attraction. One needs to know the list's emotional colouring. If such a register of objects were really standard for the poet, then nothing would be easier than to decipher his work: a brief extract would suffice. This incidentally is the way some people among us do think, replacing literary analysis with an inquiry into the writer's movable and non-movable property and confusing the job of the critic with the job of a financial assessor. The question as to the 'sociological equivalent' of a work of art is, on the whole, solved not by these inquiries but by an investigation of its content and its form. Yet along with such an investigation, there is also some use in defining the material world of the artist. We have already seen that Pasternak's poetry is distinguished by the prevalence of sensation over emotion, the paucity of themes, the breaking of social bonds, the closed world of landscape, still-life and interior. Against the background of these facts the list I have given acquires a concrete meaning and colouring. It cannot in any case be regarded as haphazard (which is indeed obvious to any reader of Pasternak: drawing-room, garden and *dacha* are the customary environment for the action of his poems), nor can it be regarded as neutral, nor yet as negatively loaded. The things in Pasternak's poems emphasize their indoors, 'chamber' quality, and also show the material foundation – a peaceful, comfortable, cultured, secure life – on which it grew up. Pasternak does not push away from his milieu, as Mayakovsky did. There is no negation or protest in him. On the contrary, the fact that his material world penetrates his meta-

---

[1] A far from complete series: it could be prolonged in the same direction several times its length. A. Lezhnev.
Dacha: cottage, house in the country.

phors, the fact that 'interior' poetry has such a prominent place in his work (he devotes several poems – 'Mirror', 'Little Girl' – to, for instance, the reflection of a garden in a standing mirror) proves that this milieu, at any rate in its material staging, is one that he feels close to and that he understands. But the poeticizing of 'things' is impossible without a certain poeticizing of the way of life. The matter is not altered by isolated negative statements made by the poet about his milieu, as for example:

> Он видит, как свадьбы справляют вокруг,
> Как спаивают, просыпаются,
> Как общелягушечью эту икру
> Зовут, обрядив ее, паюсной. . . .

> He sees his neighbours celebrating weddings,
> How they get roaring drunk and sleep it off,
> How they call common roe – that pickled frogspawn,
> Once ritually treated, caviare. . . .

These are too rare and fortuitous. They are caprices. They amount to saying that 'I, a poet, am above you, the philistines.' But we would hardly find a poet who didn't speak like this. And this is not surprising: the poet, as an ideologist, really is, for the most part, cleverer and better educated, more far-sighted and more able to take a broad view of things, than the generality of his class. Here are the seeds of a conflict. But often this conflict is unserious and superficial, not reaching to any deep social roots. So it is in Pasternak. There are only isolated scoffings, which are submerged in the mass of his 'interior' poetry. There is no discord between Pasternak and his milieu. It is no shore he has pushed off from, but the soil out of which he has grown.

The *materiality* of Pasternak's similes and metaphors is curious: 'The steppe, like a parachute', 'put your breast under kisses, as under a washing tap', 'drops heavy as collar studs', 'bits of chopped-up song'. He says of his beloved:

> Вошла со стулом,
> Как с полки жизнь мою достала
> И пыль стряхнула.

> She brought in a chair,
> Took my life as if from a shelf,
> And shook the dust off.

Such materiality has a twofold meaning: on the one hand it makes the compared object in the greatest degree material, gives it concreteness and simplifies it; on the other hand it diminishes, reduces it. This concretization (and, in part, reduction) appears particularly clearly in a related type of metaphor: 'grief with leprosy', 'the heart in eczema', 'the skin sore of the soul', 'sorrow, thundering like mercury in Torricelli's vacuum', where the first term of the simile is an emotion, while the second is borrowed by the poet from the vocabulary of pathology or physics.

The materiality of his comparisons relates Pasternak to the Futurists (and Imagists). But he is sharply distinguished from them by two peculiarities: by the way his work is loaded with culture, and by his vivid perception of nature – peculiarities which at first sight appear to contradict each other. Even on a cursory reading of Pasternak (if such a reading of him is possible) one is immediately struck by how saturated he is with culture, by his vital and intense bond with the past, the literary, musical and other echoes in his work. Byron, Edgar Allan Poe, Kipling, Bach, Beethoven, Rakosi, Shakespeare, Torricelli, Watteau, Faust, Werther, Margarita, Mephistopheles, Isolde, Tristan, Hamlet, Ophelia, Desdemona, Actaeon, Atalanta, Calydon, Troy, Helen, Sparta – in hardly any other contemporary poet shall we find in the space of a few dozen small pages such a wealth of proper names, which get there by virtue of some literary, musical or other 'cultural' association. If we add to these the amphorae, the Bacchantes, the Fata Morganas, the Aeolian harps, the arums, the boomerangs, the zurnas, the Daryals, the Ganges, the Andes, and so on and so forth, we shall get some idea of the gloss of bookishness which covers the poems of Pasternak and which contrasts so strikingly with the freshness of their emotional tone that perhaps it is this contrast which constitutes, in its unrepeatable strangeness, the most characteristic feature of Pasternak. Without a doubt, he is the most cultured of our poets. His enthusiasm for music and philosophy, for the German and French lyric poets, is distinctly to be seen in his verses. For him the culture of the past is not a matter of dead signs, but a meaning that is alive and that speaks out clearly. He clearly feels his link of continuity with it; across the centuries or decades he is in contact with Shakespeare and Goethe, Lermontov and Lenau. This feeling of cultural continuity distinguishes him from the Futurists, with whom he is generally grouped. The Futurists tried to reject the whole of the culture created by the past –

and more by force of feeling than of knowledge, for they had but a poor knowledge of it. Pasternak would not have placed, as did Mayakovsky, the author of the *Social Contract* in company with Methuselahs and archangels, would not have made Mechnikov[1] and Longfellow lackeys to Wilson, firstly because he has read them, and secondly because he understands them.

The other peculiarity that distinguishes Pasternak from the Futurists is, as I said, the development and even predominance of landscape in his work.[2] In this sphere the Futurists had nothing of importance to add. For Mayakovsky nature is merely an occasion for cracking jokes, for argument and for puns. His sense of nature is poor and feeble. In Pasternak, on the contrary, all that is best in his poems is connected with landscape. His sense of nature is sharp and original.

As the paintings of the Impressionists are made up of a number of coloured spots which, if we stand at some distance from them, merge or come up close to one another to create the impression of a whole picture, so too do Pasternak's nature depictions consist of a complex of sensations which are superimposed one upon the other so as to create a general emotional tone. Pasternak preserves the *pointilliste* technique. His landscapes can hardly even be called landscapes. They are not depictions of nature but sense-perceptions of it. The objective datum vanishes behind the subjective moment, is dissolved in it. If Pasternak's lyric work is that of landscape, so too are his landscapes lyrical. More than that, they are subjective, deformed, broken down into a series of sensation-atoms. To continue the comparison with painting, Pasternak will have to be compared not with the first Impressionists, of Monet's type, who were restrained, curbed by the bridle of realistic logic, but with the later Impressionists, the 'fiery' Impressionism in which the process of deformation had gone far and colours had an immensely exaggerated brilliance:

> Это вечер из пыли лепился и, пышучи,
> Целовал вас, задохнувшись в охре, пыльцой.
> Это тени вам щупали пульс. Это, вышедши
> За плетень, вы полям подставляли лицо
> И пылали, плывя по олифе калиток,
> Полумраком, золою и маком залитых.

---
[1] Russian biologist (1845–1916).
[2] Khlebnikov is an exception, but he is the least urbanistic of the Futurists. *A. Lezhnev.*

Это круглое лето, горев в ярлыках
По прудам, как багаж, солнцепеком заляпанных,
Сургучом опечатало грудь бурлака
И сожгло ваши платья и шляпы.

Это ваши ресницы слипались от яркости.
Это диск одичалый, рога истесав
Об ограды, бодаясь, крушил палисад.
Это запад, карбункулом вам в волоса
Залетев и гудя, угасал в полчаса,
Осыпая багрянец с малины и бархатцев.

    It was evening from the dust took shape and with a hot breath
    Kissed you, stifled in ochre, pollen-like.
    It was the shadows felt your pulse. And, going out
    Past the fence, you it was proffered your face to the fields,
    You it was flamed, afloat over glaze of hurdles
    Flooded in the dusk with ash and poppy-seed.

    Summer it was, all summer, aspark with tagged on labels
    On ponds, stuck all over like luggage with flecks of sun-glint,
    Printed with its sealing wax the bargeman's breast,
    Consumed in fire your dresses and your hats.

    Your lashes it was, glued together from the brightness.
    The disk it was run mad, that had hardened its horns
    Against stone dykes, now, butting, brought down the palings.
    Sunset it was, like a carbuncle into your hair
    Flown, that hummed, and in half an hour was extinguished,
    Crumbling from raspberry and marigold in crimson.

Just as typical of Pasternak as his sunny landscape is another series: night, rain, storm, dawn. Here he is more intimate, more sincere, more moving. Here most of all he is close to Tyutchev. But there remains a vast difference between them. For all his pathos Pasternak remains a *dacha*-dweller in his perception of nature. He sees nature in the garden, in the park, at the *dacha*, from a train-window. For Tyutchev a storm was a burst into the chaos hidden behind the external visibility of things, summer lightnings conversed with each other like deaf-and-dumb demons. In Pasternak

> Снявши шапку
> Сто слепящих фотографий
> Ночью снял на память гром.

> ... Doffing its cap, by night
> A hundred blinding snapshots
> The thunder took, to treasure as mementoes.

Chaos and kodak: a characteristic juxtaposition. In Pasternak's *dacha* image there is the keen awareness of a town-dweller trying to translate nature into his own eccentric language. It may be said, of course, that in the 'reductive' concreteness of a Pasternakian simile the materialistic view of nature triumphs: the world moves in accordance with 'immutable and iron'[1] laws, and there is no chaos behind the external visible world. Well, yes, this is true: there is in fact no chaos, just as there exist no demons, neither deaf-and-dumb, nor with normal hearing and speech. Nonetheless, in the mysterious deaf speech of Tyutchev's poems there is a peculiar kind of inner truth. His chaos is the chaos of man's inner world projected into nature. Nature is for Tyutchev not just a world that is perceived by the senses, but a world that is felt. Not a complex of sensations but some sort of totality, whose language and whose meaning he seeks to guess. Hence in his pictures of nature there is a grandeur which is lacking in the magnificent but *dacha*-like landscape of Pasternak.

I have attempted to establish some of Pasternak's characteristics and devices. Now I must answer the question which I put in the first part of my article: what then is their social meaning and interdependence?

From the features we have noted let us try to single out a central one, on which the rest depend. It is not hard to find it: it is the limitation of the thematic field, the rupture of social links, the indoors, 'chamber' quality.

The rupture of social ties in poetry corresponds to the rupturing or weakening of social relations in the actual milieu which gave rise to the poetry. The chamber lyric arises where the pulse of the class struggle is felt least of all. For the poetry of the 'interior' to flourish, certain material preconditions are necessary: prosperity, comfort, cultured conditions. It cannot be created by those who are compelled to struggle for their existence, to give up the greater part of their day to physical

---

[1] Goethe's phrase. *A. Lezhnev*.

labour, and to live in dark and dirty dwellings. But even material security is not a sufficient condition for its development. The bourgeoisie which is directly involved in the 'making of life', which goes in for commerce, speculation and gambling on the Stock Exchange, and which owns factories and plants, is a poor environment for the nourishing of this art: it is too active and too little cultured. The real substratum of chamber poetry is that section of the intelligentsia which has been able to win for itself a sufficiently eminent and honoured place in society, that summit of the intelligentsia which has overcome the bourgeois degeneration. It possesses the necessary degree of material security and it considerably surpasses the bourgeoisie in respect of culture, which is why its representatives often regard the bourgeoisie with disdain and look down on it. It is scattered, atomistic; social bonds are weak both within this group and also between it and other groups. It does not feel itself to be something complete, nor a part of a complete whole. It stands to one side of the immediate 'making of life'.

'Bohemians' also stand to one side of the 'making of life', they too are atomized. But they only achieve what this group has already achieved. They are therefore much more revolutionary: they negate, they rebel, they hate. Their rebellion against society is not too serious: it does not threaten the bourgeoisie with destruction or even simply with danger. There is more youthful envy in it than class consciousness. But still it *is* a rebellion. In Pasternak there is no rebellion. If Mayakovsky is a Bohemian poet, Pasternak is spokesman of the highly cultured summit of the intelligentsia, the 'hereditary' intelligentsia, on which the ruling class has set its indelible stamp.

When the range of themes is limited, the poet digs down deep, and primarily into the depths of himself. Psychological analysis (or more accurately, self-analysis) is pressed to the ultimate subtlety, to the unanalysable emotional atom, to sensation, in which psychological content is reduced to a minimum. Developing consistently, Pasternak's psychologism reaches the point of denial of the self.

But the transition from emotion to sensation can also be thought of as the conclusion of another causal sequence. That intimate interior subject-matter which is what remains for the poet as a result of his thematic limitation, is no longer new enough, is, if you like, 'hackneyed'. Analysis into sensations freshens this old material anew, showing it in an unexpected aspect; it works as a renovating device. Certainly, there is no contradiction in the existence of both these causal sequences at once. They can be demarcated only theoretically. For the poet – in his conscious or his subconscious mind – they are one and the same.

As we have seen, the transition to sensation requires, in its turn, the construction of a poem by associations, and emotional linearity. Thus there is an interdependence and inner logic in the development of Pasternak's devices: one conditions another; as we ascend them, we reach their single point of departure. But I must add something to what I have already said. The thematic limitation pushes the poet into a deep probing of 'personal' themes, and creates the possibility of a refined, analytical psychologism taken to its very limit, to denial of the self. But if this possibility is to become reality, if the analysis is to be carried over into sensations, one further element must be active: subjectivism. And this too is a result of the intelligentsia's social being; of its atomization, when the isolated human being begins to be regarded as a self-sufficient entity, and then as the sole reality. Such extreme subjectivism is possible, of course, only in an epoch of stagnation, of reaction[1] – and it was precisely in such an epoch that Pasternak's poetry was conceived. Not only emotion is atomized into sensations. The whole world is presented as a network, as a complex of sensations, where the frontier between the objective world and man's inner world disappears, and the very question of the existence of an objective world seems an idle one. Pasternak expresses in poetry the same thing that Mach expressed in philosophy. To explain this fact there is no need to look for any direct influence of the philosopher on the poet or even in the poet's being acquainted with Mach.

A further development of subjectivism is in Pasternak the omission of associative links and the dislocation of meaning levels. In part these are the consequence of constructing a poem on associations. But only in part. Neither the omitting of associations, nor the displacing of levels can be wholly inferred from the orientation toward sensations. These things occur more often and more readily than such an orientation requires. The cause of this, as it seems to me, lies in that same narrowness of Pasternak's range of material, which, to be refreshed, needs a number of devices to create the effect of unexpectedness. The displacing of levels and the omission of associative links leads to a rupture of meaning, to difficulty in understanding. Something which otherwise would have sounded workaday or banal acquires novelty and signifi-

[1] All reactionary epochs are subjective, said Goethe. *A. Lezhnev.*

cance when you are obliged to guess at it, when what is supposed to be shown is only partly visible, only an edge of it to be seen. Pasternak plays, as with a device, with the rupture of meaning and with the illusion of analogies.

But why did he choose to renovate his material precisely with *this* device, with the rupture of meaning ('incomprehensibility')? Why did he dwell on the dislocation of levels? The displacement of levels is a common device of the Futurist school, not a personal peculiarity of Pasternak. It is born of the subjectivism which is peculiar to the intelligentsia as a group and which was intensified in the epoch in which Futurism arose, in the pre-storm period, the period of the decline of bourgeois culture.

But how is the fascination of Pasternak to be explained? How shall we explain the fact that in a certain sense he has become the central figure in our poetry, from whom lines of power go out in all directions? The essence of this fascination seems to elude analysis. Let us nevertheless try to define it. In the first place an important rôle is played by Pasternak's craftsmanship, his rhyme, his very original syntax. Pasternak, like Khlebnikov (in Mayakovsky's phrase), is a poet for poets rather than for the wide public, for whom he is too difficult. His methods are pilfered ('popularized') by lesser but tougher poets, and reach the reading masses only through them. But the matter is not explained by the craftsmanship alone, especially as Pasternak is less than anyone else a master of technique (that is, a poet absorbed in 'craftsmanship', in technique).

Pasternak discovered if not a new world, at any rate a new element for poetry – sensation. Things, splintered into sensations and created anew by the combination of these, turned out to be different things, never seen before. A rejuvenated world emerged from Pasternak's poems. It was not a wide one, it was bounded by the walls of a room and the railings of a garden, but it was full of a special intensity. I do not share the commonly accepted view about Pasternak's dynamism: I think this is much exaggerated. In his poems it is something else that is felt: something like the tension before a storm, about to discharge itself. I just think one ought not to make a direct connection between this tension (or even dynamism) and the Revolution, drawing conclusions therefrom as to Pasternak's revolutionariness. This is a too elementary syllogism: the Revolution is movement, there is movement in Pasternak's poems, therefore Pasternak's poems are revolutionary.

It is the freshness and tension in Pasternak, I think, that chiefly makes for the fascination of his poems, of which Ehrenburg says that one could breathe them before dying, like bags filled with oxygen. With all his high craftsmanship, Pasternak is no poet of technique, but a genuine poet with strong blood and a heart capable not only of beating but also of feeling. He is a poet of the Fet and Tyutchev type and even, if we go a little further back in time, of the type of the German Romantics. An admirer of Scriabin, a pupil of Marburg University, a man screened off by his musical, philosophical and literary culture from the real struggle of mankind – is he not similar to our friends the 'Serapion Brothers',[1] these intelligent, talented, fine-feeling people, certainly not indifferent and certainly not egoists, but limiting their world to love and art, to old books, the tales of Gozzi and Mozart's symphonies?

Recently Pasternak has been trying to break out from the chamber-music quality of his poetry. He is writing a poem about the year 1905. What he is doing in this direction is at the moment far from perfect. His poems still splinter into rows of independent stanzas, descriptions of nature predominate, and, in the words of one poet, Pasternak speaks of the sea and of a mutiny in one identical tone. But nobody can pass from the chamber-music orientation to a social orientation. Least of all Pasternak, a poet who is honest to the end, who can either write one hundred per cent sincerely, or else not write at all. On the other hand, people of this stamp, once they do start on a new path, travel it to the end. Man is a plastic clay and the age moulds from him what the age needs.

[1] Hoffman's. *A. Lezhnev.*

SOURCE: 'Boris Pasternak', in A. Lezhnev, *Sovremenniki* (Moscow, 1927).

WLADIMIR WEIDLE

The Poetry and Prose of Boris Pasternak (1928)

I

IN contemporary Russian literature, if we see it not as what it has been, still is and perhaps always will be, but as what it is steadily becoming before our eyes – though we may believe that it will never become it – nothing is more interesting, or more essential to an understanding of its present transitory meaning, than the poetry and prose of Pasternak. Not because *My Sister Life, Themes and Variations, The Lofty Malady, Aerial Ways* or *The Year 1905* are in themselves anything outstanding, authoritative or deeply meaningful, but simply because all these works, while not ordinary, are yet average works; they do not outweigh their age, they merely indicate its weight; they are not important to humanity, they are significant only to literature. It is just because they are so central that they are more than mediocre; like a rudder without a helmsman, they mark the changing route of a ship that is no longer being steered. Now, to say that a literary 'product' is important to literature itself may indeed be to imply that there is skill and talent in it; the newness of its outward appearance, the unprecedented sound and flavour of its language, may give it a value that is irreplaceable and inalienable: these things are not to be ignored, and they exist in Pasternak's writing. But all this is not enough. There remains the threshold, difficult to cross, between, on the one hand, the 'mere writer'[1] who reveals, albeit with the utmost clarity, the technical possibilities of his craft in his age, and who may even have expanded or renewed them, and on the other hand the poet, who creates a new world, a new heaven and earth, in the image and likeness of the elemental force by which he is possessed. It is not important whether he

[1] The word *literator*, used a number of times by Wladimir Weidle in the course of his article, I have translated sometimes by 'littérateur' and sometimes by 'writer' or 'mere writer', according as it seemed appropriate in each context.

creates afresh the forms of his art or only recreates the existing ones – on earth, after all, there is never any creation out of nothing: in all creation there is some recollection, just as in all recollection there is something creative. What is important is that this creation should start from a certain relationship to the world and that it should need words – as meanings and as sounds – for its instrument, solely in order to embody that relationship; that it should not start from a relationship to the instrument and only thence acquire the appearance of a relationship to the world. But this is just how most of Pasternak's work does originate; he is an experimenter, a rebellious craftsman who in another age would have found room for his gift within the style already predestined by history, in the hierarchy of art and craft; but he was born into an age which knew neither style nor artistic hierarchies nor crafts and which, though it yearned for these, was doomed either to replace craftsmanship with art, or else, forfeiting art altogether, to make craftsmanship itself superfluous. It is true – and by virtue of this very predestination of style – that if Pasternak were not in *some* measure a poet he would not be significant as a writer either; but as the poetry in him remains a premiss rather than a conclusion, and is almost never fully realized, we shall approach him correctly if we treat him first of all as a writer, and concern ourselves primarily with the surface of his writings, with his way of working with words and with verse, and his transforming of poetic traditions – that is, with those things to which his admirers give most importance, as perhaps he would himself; for these aspects of his art are the most obviously important.

Incidentally, with regard to Pasternak, or indeed with regard to anything, it would be better not to speak of tradition being transformed. Traditions are renewed from within – in this their life-rhythm consists – but they cannot alter their primordial form without cancelling themselves out. A tradition becomes worn out when the source of its inner self-renewal dries up: form that is no longer spiritually alive becomes formula, which can never again be alive. It is when this happens that we become aware of a breach between spiritual value and its formulation, and we make a distinction between form and content, although this is essentially meaningless, for form without content is no longer form. In Russian poetry this discord was first observed in the age of the Symbolists, though it was being prepared for earlier and its roots are common to all Europe. The Symbolist poets – if they did not outgrow Symbolism – were constantly balanced on the narrow knife-edge that divides a poem from the experience that gave it birth; when they took a false step they either disappeared into life without poetry or else were engulfed by poetry without life, or rather by a world of poetic designs in which there was neither life nor poetry. So it was almost a matter of course that they were followed by people who declared all the traditions of Russian literature to be outworn, and who created nothing, for the simple reason that they decided they could create out of nothing. These people wanted to rid form of meaning: as a result they forfeited form itself; taking it upon themselves to turn words into mere sounds, they were deprived even of words. However, the very fact that Russian Futurism was so extreme meant that it was to some extent harmless. It could not succeed in destroying the Russian literary tradition, for it denied literature itself; nor could it for long mutilate the Russian language, because it denied the very basis of all language, all human speech. At any rate this was what Futurism was in Khlebnikov, a man visited by genius but marked by idiocy; he preached the destruction of language and at the same time – in both prose and verse – was deeply conscious of a very Russian linguistic heritage. The popularizers of Futurism are not worth talking about; it was not they and it was not the Futurists themselves who were breaking down tradition: both these groups merely offered it to the rag-and-bone merchant. The genuine breaking was done by other poets, poets who appeared to have stopped half-way along the road but in fact had stopped where the road came to an end anyway. Pasternak is the foremost of these.

The language of Russian verse, a beautiful and complex living thing, more developed than the language of prose, is the best thing that our literature has created, our highest achievement. Let us give Pasternak his due: if he has trespassed upon it this is not because he wanted to but because he was born to do so.

From the very first he shows, as do some great poets, a special kind of verbal awareness, a characteristic way of putting words together, an unusual skill in combining sound with sense. And he too would have become a great poet if he had managed to justify these gifts, that is, if he had been able to fill, to nourish with something of his own, the tissue of words which he had woven afresh. Had this happened, the tradition of our poetic language would not have been destroyed but renewed. For it is not true that a thing has to be destroyed before it can be remade; it can only be remade if it is left alive. But this did not happen; Pasternak does not imitate the Futurists when they rid the word of everything but its sound, or when they try to make poetry 'as simple as mooing'; words – in his work – nearly always retain both sound and meaning; nevertheless, for him practically the *whole* art of poetry consists in playing with these meanings and sounds of particular words. In his poems the word itself does have meaning, but the words, taken together, have no spiritual life. The hunt for associations, through alliteration and through contiguity, hinders, if not the meaning, at least the unity of meaning. The selection of the single word is harmful to the assemblage of words as a whole and the planning of a single line harms the plan of the whole poem. More important still, *what* Pasternak wishes to say, and is able to say, is too meagre for his *way* of saying it to claim not only an indubitable significance and perfection but some sort of historically important creative rôle. For it to have such a rôle would be at odds with the truth that even the apparently autonomous development of literary forms and a literary language depends on the inner importance of what is said in that language and put in those forms.

Such are the limitations which were bound to determine the whole of Pasternak's development as a poet. If we add to them a deficiency of taste – which was innate in him, though maybe it later became almost a matter of principle – we shall understand why he has had to go through a long struggle to free the language of his verse from various kinds of weeds all equally evident in it: near-meaningless un-Russian turns of speech, dubious stresses, incorrect cases and wrongly abbreviated endings. Even in *Themes and Variations* we find 'vglyadivayas' v prizraka',[1] in *My Sister Life* there is an abundance of phrases like 'lodkoyu bryatsat'';[2] 'ladonyu zaslonyas''[3] (at the very most one can only speak of screening one's *face* with one's palm), we find 'obrazchik'[4] instead of 'obrazets', 'proyasnit mnogo' instead of 'vyyasnit mnogoe';[5] also contractions such as 'tmimy' for 'tomimy',[6] 'ispoln'sya' for 'ispolnis'',[7] and stresses like 'naiskós'',[8] 'gospitálei',[9] and finally 'tétanus' for 'tétanos', with, in addition, the use of the word 'stolbnyak' as if this

[1] 'peering at apparitions'.
[2] 'to clank the boat'.
[3] 'screening oneself with one's palm'.
[4] 'sample' (*obrazchik*: colloquial for *obrazets*).
[5] Approximately ' "will brighten much" instead of "will elucidate many things" '.
[6] 'wearied' (*tmimy* – an unusual contraction).
[7] 'be fulfilled'.
[8] 'obliquely' (normally *náiskos*').
[9] 'of hospitals' (normally *góspitalei*).

designated something different. Still more characteristic of Pasternak is the word 'marina', which in his use does not even mean a seascape but is quite simply a synonym for sea. This outrageous example is characteristic because it shows not only a lack of taste but also a deficiency of thought, that is, insufficient realization of how words should be used; and this is something from which Pasternak will never quite escape, nor can any more lately acquired knowledge of the language cure him of it. Indeed, such knowledge will always remain somewhat inert, pointless, founded more on a reading of dictionaries than on a deepening of linguistic awareness. The basic source of this knowledge is Dal';[1] to Dal' a whole succession of forgotten words or dialect phrases can be traced back, and it is Dal' who, as it were, guarantees such out-of-use stresses as 'sumérnichat'',[2] 'shelókhnetsya'[3] or 'pláshmya'.[4] Dal' helps where he can help and where Pasternak chooses to conform to him; he did not manage to prevent him from using 'marina', and later he did not guard him from 'kafedral'ny mrak',[5] an expression used in *Themes and Variations* and as ignorant in its derivation as it is ludicrous in its redundancy. However, if Pasternak has failed to resist Dal' this is not just because he is far from fastidious but also because he does not want to be fastidious. Without the least compunction he employs clichés like 'Homeric laughter' or hackneyed forms like 'sploshnoĭ nekrolog',[6] rhymes 'fikus' with 'vesyolaya na vykaz'[7] and indulges our mind and ear with lines like these:

> Что это? Лавры ли Киева
> Спят купола, или Эдду
> Север взлелеял и выявил
> Перлом предвечного бреда?

> What's this? Above Kievan cloisters
> Do the cupolas sleep? The Edda,
> Did the North rear it to reveal
> A pearl of pre-eternal frenzies?

---

[1] Vladimir Ivanovich Dal' (1801–72) 'is remembered chiefly for his *Reasoned Dictionary of the Living Great-Russian Language* (4 vols, 1864–8), which still forms the basis of our knowledge of Russian as it was spoken by the people before the spread of standard schoolmastery'. (D. S. Mirsky, *A History of Russian Literature* (1949) p. 158).
[2] 'to rest in the twilight' (normally *súmernichat*').
[3] 'will stir' (normally *shelokhnétsya*).
[4] 'prone' (normally *plashmyá*).
[5] 'pulpit' or 'cathedral darkness'.
[6] 'a sheer obituary'.
[7] 'gay for show'.

where one simply doesn't know which to rejoice in first – the 'pearl', the 'pre-eternal frenzies', or the 'revealing' of them both. It may be, of course, that Pasternak does not rejoice in any of these words alone but only in their accumulation and disorder; he is prepared, too, to add to them words of quite another sort, transparent Pushkinesque words like 'zamety' (remarks): 'And the heart's sorrowful remarks'[1] (Pushkin). In *My Sister Life*: 'Of eccentricities, poverties and remarks.' He is bent on one thing: to combine in the smallest possible space and by whatever means are at hand the greatest possible number of heterogeneous, unrelated, disparate words. For him, poetry means above all a confusion of tongues, the building of a Tower of Babel.

Whatever the reasons, it is interesting to note that Pasternak's prose is quite different from this. Here, too, there are 'ficus-trees', 'boomerangs' and other such gems; here, too, word-play, often dangerous to the words, results in linguistic patterns of little meaning and in metaphors whose meaning has not been checked; nevertheless, Pasternak's meaning and aim are basically different in his prose. Even in *Il Tratto di Apelle* and *Letters from Tula*, which are unsuccessful, chaotic experiments, the special quality of his prose-style can already be sensed. And from the very first pages of *The Childhood of Luvers*, even though the same flaws are to be found there as we find in his verse, there is a change of perspective and we are led to expect something of quite a different order. These expectations are satisfied best in *Aerial Ways*, a short story printed for the first time in 1924. Here Pasternak really has succeeded, to a far greater extent than in his poems, in creating a wholly original linguistic tissue, unlike any that has ever existed before in Russian prose. There are still some incorrect usages (*Childhood of Luvers*: 'In their eyes it became a special *branch* of fatherhood to come to dinner rarely and never to supper'; *Aerial Ways*: '... installed in its place by the *dimensions of their chagrin*'), but now these are not typical. Much more striking are the truly successful and fresh juxtapositions of words and turns of phrase. Even Dal' is used in a different way here. 'Backed with mercury, like a mirror...' is somewhat deliberately said, but is not unsuccessful, and the chief thing is that it is a pleasure to hear these technical words with their very exact meanings, both as a contrast to the style of Pasternak's own poetry and, especially, in comparison with the over-decorative and vacuous style of the prose-writers around

[1] From the opening of *Yevgeny Onegin*.

him. This may even account for the fundamental fascination of his prose: it offers a strong contrast to the bad habits ingrained in the other works of the age: to their non-articulated syntax, their suffocating vocabulary, the incessant surge of emotions in them and the immoderate reproduction of every variety of dialect and accent. As a direction, an intention, this style is only to be welcomed, for it is attentive to the construction of a sentence and to the place a word occupies in it. It is at once abundant and yet rather dry; it is conscious, sober, real, in a way that is rarely met with among Russian writers – a literary, constructed style. Here is an excerpt from *Aerial Ways*:

> The soldier answered the lady that Polivanov had not returned yet. In his voice there sounded a threefold unconcern. There was the unconcern of a creature accustomed to liquid mud out of its element in dry dust. There was the unconcern of a man who on raiding and requisition parties was used to asking the questions, questions which just such ladies had to answer, confused and cowering; and now unconcerned because the normal order of such exchanges was in this case reversed and disrupted. And finally there was the assumed unconcern which treated something wholly unprecedented as if it were all in the day's work. Knowing perfectly well how shocking the things that had lately happened must appear to the lady, he pretended to be so obtuse that he could not guess at her feelings, as if he had breathed the air of a dictatorship all his life.

We may deny the profundity of this art, but not its interest; we may deny that it is perfect, but we cannot deny that it shows a consummate craftsmanship. It is possible to imitate Pasternak's style, to develop its fundamental idea; in any case, it deserves our attention. It is true that its interest is almost exclusively that of an experiment. It is a tool that the author has adapted to his needs but has not yet put to any use beyond establishing its possibilities and illustrating the effects it can achieve. His prose style differs from the style of his poetry only in that it has been made into a more perfect tool: this experiment has been more successful. And this is not so much because more talent or energy has been put into it as because the very circumstances of its creation were different. A future historian will doubtless say that the age in which Pasternak wrote was one of those in which Russian poetry was coming to a stop, while Russian prose was starting up anew. However that may be, let us be quite clear that while this prose and this verse *may* influence future literary development – for this may be influenced by a great many secondary factors which we hardly take into account at the moment – yet their inner significance and importance is too slight for such an influence to be inevitable, just as it is not sufficiently great for us to forget all about influence, tradition and history and simply see Pasternak's writing as an unrepeatable and eternal creation by a unique personality.

II

And yet there does exist in Pasternak this unique individuality of a poet. If this were not so, then not only would he not be worth writing about, but there would simply not be anything to say about him. Everything that we have been talking about, ever ythinghe has achieved or realized with any measure of success, he achieved and realized only because of the poet that is in him and only in proportion to the powers of that poet. Whatever there is in him beyond this, it is true, has no other interest than to show how his work fails to convey his inner being, and it is true that what may be called the drama of Pasternak – though in his eyes there is probably no drama at all – consists precisely in this failure; nevertheless, even if his roots are not to be mistaken for fruits, the fact remains that if there were no roots there would be no fruit anyway.

One may read through two or three of Pasternak's poems and not be struck by anything in them, but one cannot read many of them without glimpsing in their depths the dark, elemental, chaotic gift which gave birth to them. And the remarkable thing is that once we have caught sight of this talent the poems themselves begin to seem different: no longer merely cold experiments (though it cannot be denied that something of this is in them) but evidence of a poet's cruel failure. Everything they are directed towards is quite simply false and prevents the expression of what is genuine. Their linguistic inventiveness is unnecessary, indeed from the point of view not of literature but of poetry there is no invention in them at all; they are simply tongue-tied. What seems original in them as 'literature' is for poetry just so much tinsel; and even the poetry in them is not original. The rhythmic structure of a line, that is, the very thing that is nearly always the primary creative factor in a line of poetry, can more often than not be traced back to traditional and conventional patterns. There is at the base of the best of his poems a strongly coiled spring of feeling and rhythm;

the rhythm is generated, as it should be, by a lyrical experience, but once generated it proceeds along a ready-laid path heaped up with random, ill-assorted words. Here is an example:

> Разрывая кусты на себе, как силок,
> Маргаритиных стиснутых губ лиловей,
> Горячей, чем глазной Маргаритин белок,
> Бился, щелкал, царил и сиял соловей.
>
> Он как запах от трав исходил. Он как ртуть
> Оцумелых дождей меж черемух висел.
> Он кору одурял. Задыхаясь, ко рту
> Подступал. Оставался висеть на косе.
>
> И, когда изумленной рукой проводя
> По глазам, Маргарита влеклась к серебру,
> То казалось, под каской ветвей и дождя
> Повалилась без сил амазонка в бору.
>
> И затылок с рукою в руке у него,
> А другую назад заломила, где лег,
> Где застрял, где повис ее шлем теневой,
> Разрывая кусты на себе, как силок.

> Rending the raiment brush as 'twere a springe,
> Than Margarita's tight-pressed lips more purple,
> Hotter than whites of Margarita's eyes,
> Beat, clacked, held sway, shone out the nightingale.
>
> Like a smell from grass it issued; like quicksilver
> Of crazied rains amid bird-cherry, hung;
> Bemused the bark of trees; chokingly, mouthward
> Made its approach; and held there, hung on a plait.
>
> And when, eyes shielded with astounded hand,
> Margarita knew the pull of silver,
> It seemed there toppled, helmed in rain and branches,
> Sinews unstrung, an Amazon in the pinewood.
>
> And behind her head one hand in the hand of him
> The other she wide and backward cast, where stayed,
> Where was caught up, where hung, her shadowy casque,
> Rending the raiment brush as 'twere a springe.

This is one of the best poems in *Themes and Variations*, one of the few where the initial impulse is preserved and where it is therefore all the more evident that this impulse is the only thing of any importance; it alone saves the whole poem, notwithstanding the 'shadowy casque' and 'Amazon in the pinewood', and it alone is heard in the beautiful ninth line and in the captivating rhythmic movement of the second quatrain. Yet often that very same impulse, that very same inspiration, leads to effects worthy of the public stage:

> Помешай мне, попробуй. Приди, покусись потушить
> Этот приступ печали, гремящей сегодня, как ртуть
> в пустоте Торичелли.
> Воспрети, помешательство, мне, – о, приди, посягни!
> Помешай мне шуметь о тебе! Не стыдись, мы – одни.
> О, туши ж, о, туши! Горячее!

> Take and block me, see if you cannot. Come, assault me, clamp
> Down on this bout of my sorrow that thunders today like mercury in
>   Torricelli's vacuum.
> Inhibit me, you, my fixation. Oh assault, encroach upon me.
> Baffle my noise of you. And do not blush, for we are alone.
> Clamp down, clamp down – more heatedly, come, harder!

I am not even speaking, for the moment, of the comical 'Torricelli's vacuum', the vaudevillesque 'encroach' or the banality of the last lines; the point is not that they are bad but that the whole piece is a failure and that if one and the same lyrical impulse leads Pasternak to such varied – and often unsatisfactory – results, then it is because that impulse is too undifferentiated and chaotic, incapable of creating the complex metaphorical style which Pasternak strives to create, which his admirers value in him, and which his enemies deprecate.

It is not that he lacks breadth or vigour – he has so much that he stumbles with it; nor does he lack inspiration – if we decide to use this dangerous word – and he has intelligence; he only lacks the good sense that would have illumined everything, and the fullness of spirit by which it would all have been justified.

The kernel of genuine poetry hidden in all this verbiage is limited and meagre; nevertheless, it is better to concentrate on that than to go roaming through all the factitious secondary matter that invariably surrounds it. It is better for us, and it would be better for the poet himself. But does he know (and is he a poet if he doesn't?) that the best poems in *Themes and Variations* are full of a kind of asthmatic heaviness, something inescapably material?

> Пил, как птицы. Тянул до потери сознанья.
> Звезды долго горлом текут в пищевод,
> Соловьи же заводят глаза с содроганьем,
> Осушая по капле ночной небосвод.

> I drank, as birds drink; took, till the senses swooned.
> Long, long as stars flood in from throat to crop,
> Nightingales too, their eyes turn up in shudders,
> As drop by drop they wring night's arches dry.

and did he completely understand his own words when he wrote?

> Но вещи рвут с себя личину,
> Теряют власть, роняют честь,
> Когда у них есть петь причина,
> Когда для ливня повод есть.

> Ah but things tear the disguises from themselves,
> Lose their authority, and shed their honour,
> Whenever they have reason found for singing,
> Whenever there is pretext for a downpour.

At any rate it is only material things that sing in his work. Only things sing, and what they sing about is things. Even in the prose it is material things that are described best of all, and in the poetry nearly all the really convincing passages have been inspired by objects. Here are lines from *My Sister Life* about a whistle:

> Трепещущего серебра
> Пронзительная горошина.

> The shrill peas
> Of the palpitating silver.

and now these verses, extraordinarily saturated with materiality and corporeality, verses that you can taste, touch, smell:

> Чтобы, комкая корку рукой, мандарина
> Холодящие дольки глотать, торопясь
> В опоясанный люстрой, позади, за гардиной,
> Зал, испариной вальса запахший опять.
>
> So as to gulp a tangerine's
> Chill crescents, hurrying, kneading the rind in the hand,
> Into the looped-with-lustres, rearward, curtained-off
> Ballroom, with once more its whiff of perspiring waltzes.

It is only by wholly giving himself up to *things* that Pasternak is able to find, in the chaos of his vocabulary, the names which he needs to evoke and capture them. Whenever he leaves this track, the only authentic one for him, he loses everything; he can write successful love-poetry only by transforming love into a raw pre-human passion; his poetry is able to animate things, but it cannot spiritualize them. There is a passage in *The Childhood of Luvers* which throws a sudden sharp light on this:

> The gloss of inanimacy, the stupefying gloss of the observable, departed from the picture of white tents; the regiments faded and became a collection of individual people in soldier's uniform, and she grew sorry for them at the very moment when the meaning introduced into them animated them, exalted them, brought them close and took away their colour.

This passage tells how someone explained to the little Luvers girl what the soldiers' drill was that she watched each day from her window, but we would have to use almost the very same words to define what would happen to things and to people in Pasternak's work if he wished, and were able, to animate them, that is, if he decided to 'decolour' them. But no, the 'gloss of the observable' is the only thing he looks for in his art and the only thing he is able to look for. The way he describes the people searching for the lost child in *Aerial Ways* is very significant:

> Finding themselves at a great distance from one another, they shouted and waved their hands, and as these signals were each time misunderstood, they straightaway began to wave differently, more violently, more irritably and more frequently, as a sign that the signs had been misunderstood and that they were being altered, and that they should not go back but continue looking where they were looking. The harmonious turbulence of these figures gave the impression of people playing football at night, who had lost the ball and were searching for it in ditches, and when they found it they would continue the game.

The last sentence is especially good and this is because the 'gloss of the observable' is particularly strong in it; were it to lose this, we realize all too clearly, it would lose everything: Pasternak would have nothing to say, nothing to write about, nothing to point to.

In poetry as in prose the only thing he can do is point to things. Thus it is not surprising that the elements of plan, structure and unity in his work are so weak, and so forced, which is really the same thing. Certain themes are outlined in *The Childhood of Luvers* but they break off before they are properly developed. *Aerial Ways* is conceived as a work of complex construction: a father twice discovers a son he had known nothing of, is glad the first time when the child gets lost, but shattered the second time when he learns that his son is to die. But this plan, like so many of the words in Pasternak's verses, was not well enough thought out to become meaningful or deep but degenerated into a cleverly adorned anecdote. *The Lofty Malady* was meant to be an epic poem about the Revolution and the poet, but from its very inception it broke into pieces which could not be stuck together again. Pasternak's still unfinished novel in verse, *Spektorsky*, is unlikely to be held together by anything more than a plot that artificially couples unequal fragments. His most recent work, *Lieutenant Schmidt*, is squeezed with the greatest diligence into a chronological framework, but this framework is incapable of becoming anything more than a bare list of events following one after another. Everywhere the whole is buried beneath a pressing weight of far-fetched euphonies, ornaments, rhymes and what are at best very obtrusive details. Everywhere the thin skeleton of thought is overgrown and rendered scarcely discernible by the proud-flesh of words. It would be better, incidentally, if this thought did not show itself at all, puny and piteous as it is. In *Themes and Variations* it goes no further than lines like these:

> Горят, одуряя наш мозг молодой
> Лиловые топи угасших язычеств.
>
> Lilac swamps of extinguished paganisms
> Burn, maddening our young brain.

which are in particularly bad taste just because they try to think, to philosophize. The strained attempts of *The Lofty Malady*, *Spektorsky* and *The Year 1905*, are no better. The apostrophe to the Revolution with which this last book opens is comic in its helplessness:

> Как поэт, отпылав и отдумав,
> Ты рассеянья ищешь в ходьбе.
> Ты бежишь не одних толстосумов:
> Все ничтожное мерзко тебе.

> Like poets, all their pyres and ponderings done,
> You seek distraction, take yourself out walking.
> You shun not only those with bulging wallets:
> All things of no account you find offensive.

and no less flat is the apostrophe to the State ('O idol of the State') in *Lieutenant Schmidt*, a poem which is extremely strained and contrived, written to order unwillingly – whether to his own order or to another's makes no difference. The only thing to note in it is that, as always, the description is purely external, giving pictures of the growth, movement, thickness and density of things:

> И любопытство, любопытство:
> Трехверстный берег под тупой,
> Пришедшей пить или топиться,
> Тридцатитысячной толпой.
> Она покрыла крыши барок
> Кишащей кашей черепах,
> И ковш Приморского бульвара,
> И спуска каменный черпак.

> Inquisitiveness, inquisitiveness:
> Along three miles of shore, a throng
> Woodenly come to drink or drown
> Mills thirty-thousand strong.
> It roofs the roofs of river-barges, troops
> A seething tortoise-porridge
> Into the ladle of the Lungomore,
> The stone scoop of a footpath.

And yet in this very same book, among the poems that prefaced *Lieutenant Schmidt* and are united under the title *The Year 1905*, there are to be found the very best poems that Pasternak ever wrote. They are the best, probably, because there is in them for the first time something like a lyrical theme, rudimentary but capable of development – the theme of memory:

Мне четырнадцать лет.
Вхутемас
Еще — школа ваянья.
В том крыле, где рабфак,
Наверху,
Мастерская отца.
В расстояньи версты,
Где столетняя пыль на Диане
И холсты,
Наша дверь.
Пол из плит
И на плитах грязца.

Это — дебри зимы.
С декабря воцаряются лампы.
Порт-Артур уже сдан,
Но идут в океан крейсера,
Шлют войска,
Ждут эскадр,
И на старое зданье почтамта
Смотрят сумерки,
Краски,
Палитры
И профессора.

I am fourteen years old,
The *Vkhutemas*
Still a school for sculptors.
Under that roof now the *Rabfak* wing,
Upstairs
Is the studio of my father.
Some distance off
Where a century's dust is on Diana
And there are canvases,
Is our front door,
A floor of flagstones
And on the flagstones, mud.

It is the depth of winter,
And since December under the sway of gaslamps.
Port Arthur is already fallen,

> Though the cruisers go to sea,
> The troops are on their way,
> The squadrons are expected.
> And at the old post-office building,
> The twilight is looking,
> As are the pigments,
> The palettes,
> The professors.

This theme widens to become recollections of the events of 1905. But in those events everything that is not experienced as a *personal* memory and not cloaked in a lyrical, *subjective*, remoteness, is artificial and lifeless. It is only in this lyrical subjective experiencing that there appears the feeling of history which is completely lacking in *Lieutenant Schmidt*. Here is a stanza from the poem about Gapon (and the first two stanzas from the *Funeral of Bauman* are certainly on the same level):

> Восемь громких валов
> И девятый,
> Как даль, величавый.
> Шапки смыты с голов.
> Спаси, господи, люди твоя.
> Слева — мост и канава,
> Направо — погост и застава,
> Сзади — лес,
> Впереди —
> Передаточная колея.

>> Eight thundering waves
>> And the ninth
>> Like distance mighty.
>> Caps are swept from heads.
>> Lord, save thy people:
>> To the left, a bridge, a ditch,
>> To the right, a gate, a graveyard,
>> Behind, the woods,
>> In front,
>> Railway for forward traffic.

Here, and in certain other lines in *The Year 1905*, Pasternak is unrecognizable; or rather, we recognize only the poet in them, and the *littérateur* is simply not there at all. The poet has retained his own basic features; he has merely become freer and simpler, for a moment he has become the best of all the things he is able to be. He has kept, too, his gift of seeing and of describing, a gift which has become even more concentrated in the following lines, the most perfect he has ever written:

> Точно Лаокоон
> Будет дым
> На трескучем морозе,
> Оголясь,
> Как атлет,
> Обнимать и валить облака.
> Ускользающий день
> Будет плыть
> На железных полозьях
> Телеграфных сетей,
> Открывающихся с чердака.

> Like Laocoön
> The smoke,
> Over the ringing frost,
> Bare
> As an athlete is,
> Will clasp the clouds and throw them down.
> And the diminishing day
> Will glide
> Away on the iron runners
> Of the telegraph mesh
> That opens out from attics.

Here perhaps for the first time there is born before our eyes, out of words that are separate, accurate, tough and very material, the plasticity of a whole image. Pasternak's imitators will not find any nourishment in these lines; and this is the best proof that they have been imitating not him but his tongue-tied stutterings, and that in working out his literary style and his poetic language Pasternak may have been perfecting his originality but he has crippled his poetry. After the examples just quoted one may doubt whether it is incurably crippled, although it must be pointed out that certainly not all of *The Year 1905* is of equal value, for as usual there is a great deal of verbal tightrope-walking and unnecessary conjuring-tricks, which hide an inadequacy of spirit and the meagreness of the fundamental poetic power. But one thing not open to doubt is that the literature by which Pasternak is surrounded, and Pasternak the *littérateur*, himself, have always been the worst enemies of Pasternak the poet. Of course, it was the weakness of the poet rather than the strength of the *littérateur* that made this inevitable; still, both exist in Pasternak and neither can be expunged. This is why, studying them separately, we have come to conclusions that seem at first sight to contradict each other.

In fact, there is no contradiction. Pasternak's literary work, especially in prose, has a right to our attention, and in the totality of contemporary Russian literature it is definitely of interest as a direction. But on its own account the portion of poetic talent allotted to Pasternak will remain significant, whatever the age, and whatever the literary circumstances; it is not subject to history – at any rate not until, in the hunt after novelty, it tries to fawn upon history itself. If there were no poet in Pasternak there would be no writer either; but this does not mean that the writer, while maiming and doing violence to the poet, may not play an independent, and considerably harmful, rôle in literature, provoking imitations, superficial fashions, and undermining deep traditions.

But what is more characteristic than anything else of the present state of Russian literature is not the poet and not the writer in Pasternak but precisely the conflict in him between the one and the other, and the fact that in this conflict it is the writer, not the poet, who enjoys success with his contemporaries and even with himself. This, of course, indicates not a literary blossoming but a deep, perhaps ruinous rupture.

In Pasternak's last book certain stanzas seem to speak of the possibility, for him, and at times not only for him, of a liberation and a way out. But we cannot attach very much significance to his fate beyond its merely personal significance, and indeed this fate itself is still obscure.

SOURCE: 'Stikhi i proza Pasternaka', in *Sovremennye zapiski*, XXXVI (Paris, 1928).

YURI TYNYANOV

Pasternak's 'Mission' (1924)

THE rebellion of Khlebnikov and Mayakovsky shifted the literary language from its place, discovered in it the possibility of a new colouring.

At the same time this rebellion moved the word an extraordinarily long way away. In Khlebnikov it is mainly as principles that things make themselves felt. The word, in its rebellion, shifted away, tore itself away from the thing. (Thus Khlebnikov's 'self-valuable word' coincides with the 'hyperbolic word' of Mayakovsky.) The word became free, but it became too free, it ceased to latch on. Hence the pull that the former Futurist nucleus felt toward things, toward the naked objects of everyday life, and hence their 'negation of verse', as a logical conclusion. (Too logical, in fact, for the more impeccable logic is in its application to things that are not static, and literature is such a thing; the more rectilinear, the more correct it is, the more it turns out to be wrong.)

Hence too another pull – the desire to aim the word straight at the thing and somehow to give such a turn both to words and to things that the word would not be left hanging in mid air nor would the thing be left naked, but they would be reconciled, fraternally entangled. At the same time this is a normal pull away from hyperbole, the thirst of one who already stands on a new stratum of poetic culture to use the nineteenth century as material without pushing off from it as from a norm, but without being ashamed, either, of kindred with one's fathers.

Here is the mission of Pasternak.

Although he has been writing for a long time, Pasternak did not step into the front ranks straight away – only within the last two years. He was much needed. Pasternak presents us with a new kind of thing in literature.

Pasternak's 'Mission'

Hence the extraordinary obligatoriness of his themes. A theme of his does not in the least obtrude itself; somehow it is so strongly motivated that it is not spoken of.

What are the themes that bring verse and thing into collision?

First, the very wandering, the very birth of the verse amongst things.

> Отростки ливня грязнут в гроздьях
> И долго, долго до зари
> Кропают с кровель свой акростих,
> Пуская в рифму пузыри.

> Offshoots of rainstorm muddily clump together,
> And before dawn, for what a long, long time
> These scrawl from rooftops their acrostics,
> And blow their bubbles into rhyme!

Here the words became mixed with the shower ('shower' is a favourite image and setting in Pasternak); the verse interwove itself with the surrounding scene, in image entangled amongst themselves by their sounds. This is almost an instance of 'meaningless sound-speech', and yet it is inexorably logical; it is a kind of phantom imitation of syntax, and yet the syntax here is impeccable.

And as a result of this alchemical verse-operation the shower begins to be a poem, 'and the March night and the author' walk along together, shifting to the right along a square 'like a three-tiered hexameter'; as a result the thing starts to come to life:

> Косых картин, летящих ливмя
> С шоссе задувшего свечу,
> С крюков и стен срываться к рифме
> И падать в такт не отучу.

> Что в том, что на вселенной маска?
> Что в том, что нет таких широт,
> Которым на зиму замазкой
> Зажать не вызвались бы рот?

> Но вещи рвут с себя личину,
> Теряют власть, роняют честь,
> Когда у них есть петь причина,
> Когда для ливня повод есть.

> The slantwise images, flying in on a rainstorm
> From the road outside, extinguishing my candle,
> From hook and wall propelling themselves into rhyme
> And falling into measure, I cannot stop them.
>
> What of it, that the way things are is masked
> What of it, that there are no latitudes
> Such that against the winter putty would not
> Be stuffed in eagerly, to stop their mouths up?
>
> Ah but things tear the disguises from themselves,
> Lose their authority and shed their honour,
> Whenever they have reason found for singing,
> Whenever there is pretext for a downpour.

This piece has not merely ripped off its mask, but it also 'sheds its honour'.

This is how Pasternak's 'Pushkin Variations' were composed. The 'swarthy lad' who had become a mere oleographic cliché was replaced by the descendant of 'the flat-lipped hamite', roaming about among sounds:

> Но шорох гроздий перебив,
> Какой-то грохот мёр и мучил.
>
> But breaking across the shirr of clusters
> A thundering peal of some sort died, tormenting.

Pasternak's Pushkin, like all the objects in his verse, like the garret which 'will break into declamation', rips the mask off himself, begins to ferment with sóunds.

What themes are the best springboard to jump from, to fling oneself at the thing and arouse it? Illness, childhood, and in general the accidental and therefore intimately personal angles of vision which are customarily lacquered over and forgotten.

> Так начинают. Года в два
> От мамки рвутся в тьму мелодий,
> Щебечут, свищут, – а слова
> Являются о третьем годе.

> ... так открываются, паря
> Поверх плетней, где быть домам бы,
> Внезапные, как вздох, моря,
> Так будут начинаться ямбы.
>
> ... Так начинают жить стихом.

> This way they start. At two years old
> They fly their wetnurse into murk of melodies,
> They chirrup and they whistle – words appear
> In their third year.
>
> ... And so before them opens up, in flight
> High over fences where a house should be,
> Sudden, like a sigh, the sea
> This way iambs will begin to be.
>
> ... This way they begin to live in verses.

The strangest definition of poetry that has ever been made becomes comprehensible:

> Поэзия, я буду клясться
> Тобой, и кончу, прохрипев:
> Ты не осанка сладкогласца,
> Ты лето с местом в третьем классе,
> Ты–пригород, а не припев.

> Poetry, I will swear by
> You, and end up croaking:
> You are not a posture of the liquid-throated,
> You are summer, seated in a third-class coach;
> A suburb, not a refrain.

No one else could have made this definition, unless perhaps Verlaine, a poet obscurely pulled towards material things.

Childhood, not the childhood described in our anthologies, but childhood as a turning of vision, confounds thing and verse, so that things are brought onto a level with us and verses can be felt with our very hands. Childhood justifies, and makes obligatory, images which hold together the most incongruous and most disparate things:

> Галчонком глянет Рождество.
>
> Christmas will peek like a jackdaw.

The special quality of Pasternak's language is that, difficult as it is, it has a supreme exactitude – it is a private conversation, a conversation in the nursery. (Pasternak needs the nursery in his poetry, for the same reason that Lev Tolstoy needed it in his prose.) Not for nothing is his book *My Sister Life* essentially a diary, with conscientious indications of place (Balashov) and with the required notes at the ends of the sections (required in the first place by the author, but later by the reader too): 'These diversions came to an end when she went away, relinquishing her mission to a substitute', or: 'That summer we left from Paveletsky station.'

This is the reason for the prosaic quality in Pasternak, for his homely matter-of-fact language: it comes from the nursery:

> Небо в бездне поводов,
> Чтоб набедокурить.
>
> The sky in a heap of chances
> For making mischief.

His linguistic exaggerations also derive from children's language:

> Гроза, моментальная навек...
>
> Storm, instantaneous ever more...

(In his early pieces this private, prosaic quality was different and recalled Igor Severyanin:

> Любимая, безотлагательно,
> Не дав заре с путем рассесться,
> Ответь чем свет с его подателем
> О ходе твоего процесса.
>
> Darling, this brooks no delay.
> Not giving dawn the time to settle down
> After its journey, answer by return
> With the first light, as to the progress of your case.)

From here, too, derives his strange visual perspective, the kind a sick man has, with its attentiveness to things close at hand, and, immediately behind them, infinite space.

Pasternak's 'Mission'

> От окна на аршин,
> Пробирая шерстинки бурнуса,
> Клялся льдами вершин:
> Спи, подруга, лавиной вернуся.

> A yard or so from the window,
> Plucking the woollen threads of a burnous,
> He swore by the ice of steep places:
> Sleep on, my girl, but I... return as avalanche!

Illness is of the same kind, projecting 'love' through the 'eyes of medicine phials'.

The same is true of every chance angle of vision:

> В трюмо испаряется чашка какао,
> Качается тюль, и — прямой
> Дорожкою в сад, в буреломе и хаос
> К качелям бежит трюмо.

> In the pier-glass a cup of cocoa smokes
> Up, and the tulle sways, and by a straight
> Path into the garden, through windfallen wood and chaos
> The mirror runs up to the swing.

So Pasternak's stock of images is an original one, collected according to fortuitous traits. In it things are linked somehow very loosely; they are merely neighbours, close only by virtue of proximity (the second term in any image of his is always something very humdrum and abstract); yet the fortuitous proves to be a stronger link than the strongest logical connection:

> Топтался дождик у дверей
> И пахло винной пробкой.
> Так пахла пыль. Так пах бурьян.
> И если разобраться,
> Так пахли прописи дворян
> О равенстве и братстве.

> The small rain stamped its feet at the doors.
> There came up a smell of wine-corks.
> So smelled the dust. And such was the smell of the weeds.
> And if you look into it closely
> That was the smell of all the gentry's screeds
> About equality and brotherhood.

(As a term in a simile these half-abstract 'screeds' belong with a whole vocabulary of such abstractions that is to be found in Pasternak's work: 'pretext', 'right', 'discharge'. It is interesting that Pasternak here comes close to Fet, who also has 'pretext' and 'rights' and 'honour' in the most unexpected combinations with the most concrete things.)

There is an experience that we call *déjà vu*. Someone talks to you and you feel that it has all happened before, that once before you sat in this very same place, while the person with you was saying these very same things, and you know in advance what he is going to say. And the person with you really does say the things you expect. (In fact, of course, it's the other way round – he talks and it is *while* he talks that you feel he has once said it all before.)

Something like this happens with Pasternak's images. The link by which he joins things together is not one you already know, it is fortuitous, yet once he has provided it you seem to remember it, as if it had already been there somewhere – and the image becomes an obligatory one.

Indeed both image and subject are obligatory in that they do not obtrude but are a poetic consequence and not the poem's cause. The subject is not to be extracted, it is in the cavernous bodies, in the rough rugged textures of the verse. (Roughness, cavernousness – these are the properties of a youthful tissue; age is as smooth as a billiard ball.)

The subject is not left suspended in mid-air. There is a key to the words assigned to it. The key is in the 'fortuitous' vocabulary, in the 'monstrous' syntax:

> Осторожных капель.
> Юность в счастьи плавала, как
> В тихом детском храпе
> Наспанная наволока.

> Of scrupulous drops.
> Youth in gladness swam, as might
> In quiet childish snorings
> A pillowslip much slept upon.

And the 'free' word itself is not suspended in mid air, but prods at the thing. To do this it has to collide with it; and it does collide with it – on the ground of emotion. Not the bare everyday emotion of Yesenin, emotion assigned as a subject and proposed from the very start

Pasternak's 'Mission'

of the poem; no, this is an unclear emotion, seeming to sort itself out towards the end, glimmering out through all the words, through all the things, a musical emotion, akin to that of Fet.

This is why Pasternak's tradition, or rather the points of support that he indicates, are in the poets of emotion – *My Sister Life* is dedicated to Lermontov, the epigraphs in it are drawn from Lenau, Verlaine; and this is why in Pasternak's 'variations' we glimpse the themes of the Demon, Ophelia, Gretchen, Desdemona. He has even written an Apukhtin *romance*:

> Век мой безумный, когда образумлю
> Темп потемнелый былого бездонного.

> Out of its wits, my age, when shall I account for
> The obscured tempo of the bygone, never sounded?

But above all he is akin to Fet:

> Лодка колотится в сонной груди,
> Ивы нависли, целуют в ключицы,
> В локти, в уключины – о, погоди,
> Это ведь может со всяким случиться!

> The rowing-boat throbs in the drowsy breast,
> The osiers trail and kiss on bone,
> On throat and thole-pin – wait, this might
> Happen to anyone at all.

One does not want to attach historical labels to living persons. Mayakovsky has been compared with Nekrasov. (I myself sinned even worse than this, when I compared him with Derzhavin and Khlebnikov with Lomonosov.)

Mea culpa; but this bad habit is provoked by the difficulty of forecasting, yet the necessity of orienting oneself.

Let me turn to Pasternak himself (and simultaneously to Hegel):

> Однажды Гегель ненароком
> И вероятно наугад
> Назвал историка пророком,
> Предсказывающим назад.

> Once, inadvertently, no doubt
> At random, Hegel summoned
> In the historian a prophet
> Who tells the future back to front.

I restrain myself from making any prophecy about Pasternak. The present age is an age of responsibility and I do not know which way he will go. (And this is good. It is bad when a critic knows which way a poet is heading.) Pasternak ferments and his fermentation affects others – it is no accident that no poet is to be encountered so frequently in other poets' poems as he is. He not only ferments, but he is himself the ferment, the leaven.

SOURCE: Section on Pasternak in chapter entitled 'Promezhutok', in Yu. Tynyanov, *Arkhaisty i novatori* (Leningrad, 1929); first published in 1924.

# ROMAN JAKOBSON

Marginal Notes on the Prose of the Poet Pasternak (1935)

I

Textbook categories are comfortingly simple: prose is one thing, poetry another. Nevertheless, the difference between a poet's prose and that of a prose-writer, or between the poems of a prose-writer and those of a poet, is very striking. A mountaineer walking in the plains can find no foothold and stumbles over the level ground. He moves either with touching awkwardness or with over-emphatic artistry; in either case it is not his natural gait, but involves obvious effort and looks too much like the steps of a dancer. It is easy to distinguish a secondary language that has been learnt, however perfect its command, from the mother tongue acquired by the infant. Cases of complete bilingualism are, of course, undeniable. When, however, we read the prose of Pushkin or Mácha, of Lermontov or Heine, of Pasternak or Mallarmé, we cannot help being amazed at the command these writers have of the other language and at the same time we are bound to pick out a foreign note, as it were, in the accent and inner form of their speech. Their achievements in this second language are brilliant sallies from the mountains of poetry into the plains of prose.

It is not only a poet's prose that has a particular stamp; there is also the prose peculiar to an age of poetry, the prose of a literary current oriented towards poetry, as distinct from those literary epochs and schools that are prose-oriented. The vanguard achievements of Russian verbal art in the first decades of our century belong to poetry; it is poetry that is felt to be the unmarked, canonical voice of literature, its purest incarnation. Both Symbolism and the later literary fermentation often summed up under the heading of 'Futurism' are almost exclusively represented by poets, and if many of these occasionally try an excursion into prose, it is a conscious deviation, an experimental digression by a virtuoso of verse. With but a few exceptions the standard literary prose of this period is a typical imitative product, a more or less successful reproduction of classic models: the interest of this hackwork lies either in its successful copying of the old or in its grotesque brutalisation of the canon, or else its novelty consists in cunningly adapting new themes to traditional forms. In contrast to the great internal tension of the poetry of the time, this prose can claim to be distinguished only in the first place because Gogol and after him Tolstoy have lifted the qualitative norm to such a high level, and in the second place because the requirements of modern reality are themselves so exacting. In the history of artistic prose this hundredth province of Russian classic realism has little evolutionary significance, whereas the prose of Bryusov, Bely, Khlebnikov, Mayakovsky and Pasternak—that remarkable colony of modern poets—opens up hidden paths to a revival of Russian prose. In the same way the prose of Pushkin and Lermontov heralded the approach of the great festival of prose that was opened by Gogol. Pasternak's prose is the characteristic prose of a poet in a great age of poetry.

The prose of a writer and of a literary movement primarily concerned with poetry is very clearly defined both in those items where it is influenced by the dominant, that is, the poetic, element, and in those where it breaks free from that influence by an intense and deliberate effort. No less essential is the general context of literary activity, its rôle in the whole concert of the arts. The hierarchy of artistic values changes for individual artists and artistic movements: for Classicism it is the plastic arts, for Romanticism music, and for Realism literature that is the highest, the most extreme and exemplary expression of art possible. Romantic verse is required to sing and to merge into music; in the age of Realism, on the contrary, music—in musical drama and in programme music—seeks to ally itself with literature. The Romantic's slogan of art gravitating towards music was adopted to a significant degree by Symbolism. The foundations of Symbolism first begin to be undermined in painting, and in the early days of Futurist art it is painting that holds the dominant positions. But so far as the further development laid bare the semiotic essence of any art, it was poetry which became so to say a model form of artistic experimentation. A tendency to identify art with poetry is manifested by all the poets of the Futurist generation. 'Art as a whole, in other words—poetry,' says Pasternak. But the origin of this hierarchy of values differs from poet to poet; different paths lead them to poetry, and they start from different points. Pasternak, a convinced disciple of 'the art of Scriabin, Blok, Kommissarzhevskaya and

Bely,' that is, of the Symbolist school, comes to poetry from music, to which he is connected by a cult relationship characteristic of the Symbolists. Mayakovsky's springboard to poetry is painting. For all the variety of the artistic tasks that Khlebnikov sets himself, the written word is his sole and constant material. We could say that, in the development of Russian post-Symbolist poetry, Mayakovsky embodies the 'Storm and Stress', Khlebnikov provides its most characteristic and remarkable achievement, whilst Pasternak's work is, as it were, the link between Symbolism and the school that follows it. And granted that Khlebnikov reached poetic maturity earlier than Mayakovsky, and Mayakovsky earlier than Pasternak, nonetheless it can be said that when the reader whose starting-point is Symbolism comes to tackle Pasternak, he will inevitably stumble over Mayakovsky and finally, after overcoming the latter, be faced with laying a long siege to the strongholds of Khlebnikov. However, any attempt to see writers of one and the same period as individual links in a chain of uniform literary development, and to establish the sequence of these links, is always artificial and one-sided. Whilst in certain respects the individual poet continues a tradition, in many others he breaks away from it all the more decisively; the tradition is likewise never entirely negated; the elements of negation always appear only in conjunction with persisting traditional elements. Thus Pasternak, who conceives as his literary task the continuing of Symbolist tradition, is aware that out of his efforts to recreate and perpetuate the old a new art is necessarily arising. The imitations turn out to be 'more swift and fervent' than the model, and this quantitative difference evolves naturally into a qualitative one. According to the poet's own self-observation, 'the new came into being not as a rejection of the old, . . . on the contrary, it arose as an enraptured reproduction of the existing model'. By contrast, Mayakovsky is consciously out to abolish the old poetry: nevertheless Pasternak, with his acute awareness of Symbolism, senses in Mayakovsky's 'romantic manner', and the sense of life underlying it, the condensed heritage of the very school of poetry that the aggressive Futurist repudiates. What then is at issue? Pasternak's and Mayakovsky's innovations are just as partial as is their connection with the literary past. Suppose we imagine two cognate languages which differ not only in their neologisms but also in their inherited vocabulary: what the one has retained from the common source, the other has often rejected, and vice versa. These two languages are the poetic worlds of Mayakovsky and Pasternak respectively, while the common linguistic source is the poetic system of Symbolism. The theme of the remarks that follow is that unusual element in Pasternak's work which sets him apart from his predecessors, which is in part alien and in part strikingly akin to his contemporaries, and which is most clearly to be seen in the tell-tale awkwardness of his prose.

II

The textbooks confidently draw a firm line between lyric and epic poetry. If we reduce the question to a simple grammatical formula, we can say that the point of departure and the main theme are, for the lyric, invariably the first person of the present tense; for the epic, the third person of the past tense. Whatever subject-matter the lyric narrative may have, it is never more than an appendage and accessory, a mere background to the first person; and if the past is involved, then the lyric past always presupposes a reminiscing first-person subject. In the epic, on the contrary, the present refers expressly back to the past, and if the 'I' of the narrator does find expression, it is solely as one of the characters in the action. This objectified 'I' thus appears as a variant of the third person; the poet is, as it were, looking at himself from outside. Finally, the first person may be emphasized as the point of reception but that point never fuses with the main subject of the epic poem itself; in other words, the poet as 'subject of the lyric that looks at the world through the first person' is profoundly alien to the epic.

Russian Symbolism is lyrical through and through; its excursions into the epic vein are typical attempts by lyric poets to masquerade as poets of epic. In post-Symbolist poetry the two genres diverge: while the persisting lyric strain clearly predominates, reaching its most extreme expression in the work of Mayakovsky, the purely epic element finds an outlet, too, in the quite unparalleled poetry and prose of Khlebnikov. Pasternak's work is emphatically lyrical; his prose, especially, is the characteristic prose of a lyric poet, nor are his historical poems essentially different from his cycles of intimate lyric poetry.

Pasternak confesses that Khlebnikov's achievements are even now largely inaccessible to him, and justifies himself with the declaration: 'poetry as I see it proceeds in history and in cooperation with real life'. This reproach, with its implication that he had torn himself away from real life, would certainly have astonished Khlebnikov; for he has regarded his work as an affirmation of reality, unlike the negative literature of the preceding generations. Khlebnikov's world of signs is so fully realized that for him every symbol, every created word, is endowed with a complete autonomous reality, and the question of its relations to any external object, becomes entirely superfluous. For Khlebnikov, as for the little heroine in Pasternak's story, a name possesses the complete and comforting significance it has in childhood:

> She could not possibly define what was happening on the other shore, far, far away: it had no name, no distinct colour or precise outlines. . . . Zhenya began to cry. . . . Her father's explanation was brief: 'It's *Motovilikha*'. . .
> The little girl did not understand at all and, satisfied, swallowed a falling tear. For that was all that she needed: to know the name of the incomprehensible—*Motovilikha*.

When Zhenya had grown out of childhood she was struck for the first time by the suspicion that there was something which appearances concealed or else revealed only to the elect. This attitude of childhood towards appearances corresponds perfectly to Pasternak's own. An epic attitude to his environment is naturally out of the question for a poet who is convinced that, in the world of prosaic fact, the elements of everyday existence fall dully, stupidly and with crippling effect upon the soul and 'sink to the bottom, real, hardened and cold, like drowsy tin spoons', and that only the passion of the elect can transform this 'depressingly conscientious truth' into poetry. Only feeling proves to be obviously and absolutely authentic.

> Compared with this even the sunrise took on the character of urban rumour still needing to be verified.

Pasternak bases his poetics on the personal, emotional experience—indeed appropriation—of reality. 'In this form the events did not belong to me', and so on. Both his orientation of the language of poetry toward the purely expressive language of music, and the fact that this conception is based on the triumphing of passion, with its animating power, over the inevitable, show Pasternak to be continuing the romantic line of Symbolism; but as his work matures and attains individuality, so his initially romantically emotional language evolves gradually into a language about the emotions, and it is in his prose that this declarative character finds its most extreme expression.

III

Whereas, despite the obvious echoes of Khlebnikov in Pasternak's work, these two poets are clearly distinguishable from each other, it is far more difficult to draw a line between Pasternak and Mayakovsky. Both are lyric poets of the same generation, and Mayakovsky, more than any other poet, deeply affected Pasternak in his youth and constantly won his admiration. A careful comparison of the respective tissue of metaphors of the two poets at once reveals remarkable similarities. 'I was related to Mayakovsky by the age and by common influences; certain things coincided in us,' observes Pasternak. The metaphorical structure of Pasternak's poems reveals, too, direct traces of his enthusiasm for the author of 'A Cloud in Trousers'. However, in comparing the two poets' metaphors we must bear in mind that these have a quite different rôle to play in the work of each poet. In Mayakovsky's poems the metaphor, sharpening the tradition of Symbolism, is not only the most characteristic but also the most essential poetic trope which determines the structure and development of the lyric theme. In Pasternak's pertinent phrase, poetry here began 'to speak in the language of sectarian parables'. To define the problem: the poet's absolute commitment to metaphor is known; what remains to be determined is the thematic structure of his poetry. The lyrical impulse is, as we have said, provided by the poet's own self. Images of the external world in the metaphorical lyric are made to harmonize with this impulse, to shift it onto different levels, to establish a network of correspondences and masterful likenesses amidst the diverse aspects of the cosmos, to dissolve the lyric hero into the multifariousness of Being and to merge the manifold planes of Being in the lyric hero. Metaphor works through creative association by similarity and contrast. The hero is confronted by the antithetical image of what is mortally inimical to him, protean like all the ingredients of a primarily metaphorical lyric poetry. Such poetry inevitably culminates in the theme of the hero's duel to the death. Held together by a firm and taut chain of metaphors, the heroic lyric fuses the poet's mythology and his being into an inseparable whole, and he, as Pasternak has fully understood, pays for its all-embracing network of symbols with his life. In this way we have deduced from the semantic make-up of Mayakovsky's poetry both its actual libretto and the core of the poet's biography.

However rich and refined Pasternak's metaphors may be, they are not what determines and guides his lyric theme. It is the metonymical, not the metaphorical, moves that lend his work an 'expression far from common'. Pasternak's lyricism, both in poetry and in prose, is imbued with metonymicity; in other words, it is association by contiguity that predominates. By comparison with Mayakovsky's poetry the first person is thrust into the background. But it is only an apparent relegation—here, too, the eternal hero of the lyric is present. It is merely a case of his being metonymically presented; in the same way, no railway train can be seen in Chaplin's *A Woman of Paris*, but we are aware of its arrival from the patches of light and shadows on the people in the film—as if the invisible, transparent train were making its way between the screen and the audience. Similarly, in Pasternak's poetry, images of the surrounding world function as contiguous reflections, or metonymical expressions, of the poet's self. Now and then the author reveals his poetics clearly but he egocentrically applies them to art in general. He does not believe that it is possible for art to adopt a truly epic attitude to the outside world; he is convinced that genuine works of art, while relating all sorts of things, are really telling of their own birth.

> Reality arises in a kind of new category. This category seems to us to be its own condition, and not ours. . . . We try to name it. The result is art. . . .

Thus Constantinople seemed to the pilgrim from medieval Russia to be an insatiable city because he never got tired of looking at it. It is the same with Pasternak's poems and, in particular, with his prose, where the anthropomorphism of the inanimate world emerges much more clearly: instead of the hero it is, as often as not, the surrounding objects that are thrown into turmoil; the immovable outlines of roofs grow inquisitive, a door swings shut with a silent reproach, the joy of a family reconciliation is expressed by a growing warmth, zeal and devotion on the part of the lamps, and when the poet is turned away by the girl he loves he finds that 'the mountain had grown taller and thinner, the town was become lean and black'. We have deliberately given simple examples; there is a wealth of much more involved imagery of this sort in Pasternak's work. The substitution of an adjacent object is the simplest form of association by contiguity. The poet has other metonymical devices as well; he can proceed from the whole to the part and vice versa, from the cause to the effect and vice versa, from spatial relations to temporal ones and vice versa, etc., etc. But perhaps what is most characteristic of Pasternak is his using an action instead of an actor, a man's condition, or one of his utterances or attributes, rather than the man himself, and the consequent separating off and objectifying of these abstractions. The philosopher Brentano, who steadfastly fought against the logically illegitimate objectification of such fictions based in language, would have discovered in Pasternak's poetry and prose a most abundant collection of such imaginary *entia*, treated as creatures of flesh and blood. *Sestra moya—zhizn'* (My Sister Life), the actually untranslatable title and leitmotif of Pasternak's most relevant collection of poems ('life' is feminine in Russian), graphically exposes the linguistic roots of this mythology. This same being repeatedly appears in his prose too.

> Life lets very few people know what it is doing with them. It loves its job too much and while at work it speaks at most with those who wish it success and who love its workbench. *(Childhood of Luvers).*

In *Safe Conduct* it reappears in a more complex metonymical setting:

> Suddenly I imagined, outside beneath the window, his life, which now belonged entirely to the past. It moved sideways away from the window in the form of some quiet street, bordered with trees. . . . And the first to stand upon it, right beside the wall, was our State, our unprecedented, impossible State, rushing headlong into the ages and accepted among them for ever. It stood there below, and one could call to it and take it by the hand.

Pasternak's poetry is a realm of metonymies awakened to independent life. The footsteps of the tired hero, themselves longing for sleep as he is, continue to live and move behind him. On his steep path the poet's vision gently beats: 'I am the vision'. In his reminiscenses the author relates how

> I often heard the whistling of a nostalgia that had not originated with me. Catching up with me from the rear, it frightened me and made me feel pity. . . . My silence was travelling with me, I was attached to its person for the journey, and wore its uniform, a uniform familiar to everyone from his own experience.

The sound uttered by an object assumes the latter's function:

> Somewhere nearby . . . a herd . . . was making music. . . . The music was sucked in by blue-bottles. Its skin was rippling to and fro spasmodically and surely.

The Prose

Action and actor are objects in the same degree:

> Two rare diamonds were playing separately and independently in the deep nests of this half-dark bliss: The little bird and its twitter.

As an abstraction becomes objectified, it is overlaid with material accessories:

> Those were aerial ways, on which, like trains, the rectilinear thoughts of Liebknecht, Lenin and the few minds of their flight departed daily.

An abstraction is personified even at the cost of a catachresis:

> Midday quiet reigned. It communed with the quiet that was spread out below in the plain.

An abstraction becomes capable of independent actions, and these actions are objectified in their turn:

> Lacquered sounds of giggling from a disintegrating order of life winked at each other in the quiet.

Mayakovsky, who had a predilection for continually surmounting obstacles, toyed for years with the thought of writing a novel. He even had ideas for a title—first *Two Sisters,* then *A Dozen Women.* It is no accident that the project was always postponed: Mayakovsky's element is either the lyrical monologue or the dramatic dialogue; narrative presentation is profoundly foreign to him, and he substitutes second-person for third-person themes.... Everything that is not inseparably attached to the poet's self is felt by Mayakovsky to be opposed and hostile to him, and he confronts his opponent face to face—challenges him to single combat, exposes, condemns, mocks and outlaws him. It is not surprising that the only undertaking he completed in the field of literary prose was the series of splendid stageplays written in the last years of his life. There is just as firm a logic about the path that Pasternak took towards narrative prose. There exist poems which are woven through and through with metonymies, while narrative prose may be studded with metaphors (a striking example is Bely's prose), but in the main there is an undeniably closer relationship on the one hand between verse and metaphor, on the other between prose and metonymy. Verse relies upon association by similarity; the rhythmical similarity of the lines is an essential requirement for its perception, and this rhythmical parallelism is most strongly felt when it is accompanied by a similarity (or contrast) of images. An intentionally striking division into similar sections is foreign to prose. The basic impulse of narrative moves from one object to an adjacent one on paths of space and time or of causality; to move from the whole to the part and vice versa is only a particular instance of this process. The more the prose is stripped of material content, the greater the independence achieved by these associations. For metaphor the line of least resistance is verse, and for metonymy it is a prose whose subject-matter is either subdued or eliminated (Pasternak's short stories are an example of the first alternative, and his *Safe Conduct* of the second).

IV

The essence of poetic trope does not simply lie in their recording the manifold relationships between things, but also in the way they shift or dislocate familiar relationships. The more strained the role of the metaphor in a given poetic structure, that much the more decisively are traditional categories overthrown; things are arranged anew in the light of newly introduced generic signs. Accordingly, the creative (or, as the foes of such novelty will say, the forced) metonymy changes the accustomed order of things. Association by contiguity which in Pasternak's work becomes the artist's flexible tool, transforms spatial distribution and temporal succession. This emerges particularly clearly from the poet's prose ventures, outlined as it is against the background of a prose that seeks to communicate in the customary way. Pasternak grounds this dislocation in emotion, or else, if one's starting point is the expressive function of literature, he uses this dislocation to help express the emotions.

A poetic world governed by metonymy blurs the outline of things, as April, in Pasternak's story *The Childhood of Luvers*, blurs the distinction between house and yard; similarly it turns two different aspects of one and the same object into independent objects, like the children in the same story who think that a street seen first from inside the house and then from outside it is two different streets. These two characteristic features—the mutual penetration of objects (the realization of metonymy in the strict sense of the word), and their decomposition (the realization of synecdoche) bring Pasternak's work close to the endeavours of Cubist painters. The dimensions of things change:

> The gondola was, woman-like, gigantic, as everything is gigantic which is perfect in form and incommensurable with the place taken up by its body in space.

The distances between things change so that it becomes certain that a conversation about strangers has to be warmer than a conversation about kindred; and the vision of cosmic movement in the first part of *Safe Conduct* transforms inanimate objects into a remote, motionless horizon. A striking example of how settings are transformed;

> The lamps only accentuated the emptiness of the evening air. They did not give light, but swelled from within like sick fruits, from the turrid and bright dropsy that puffed up their bloated shades. . . . The lamps came much less in contact with the rooms than with the spring sky which they seemed to be pushed close up to. . . .

Pasternak himself compares, in passing, his dislocated space with the space of Gogol's eschatology: 'suddenly it became possible to see far into the distance in all cosmic directions'. Spatial relations are mingled with temporal ones, and the time sequence loses its compulsory order—objects 'are jolted again and again from the past into the future, and from the future into the past, like sand in a frequently shaken hourglass'. Any contiguity can be construed as a causal series. Pasternak is impressed by the terminology of the child who grasps the meaning of a sentence from the situation and says, 'I did not understand it from the words but from the reason'. The poet tends to identify the situation with the reason; he consciously prefers 'the vicissitudes of guesswork to the eloquence of fact'; he proclaims that 'time is permeated with the unity of a life's events', and builds bridges between them on just those prelogical 'ridiculous grounds' which he openly opposes to the syllogisms of 'adults'. Thus it is no surprise when the chatter of Cohen's companions proves to be 'uneven on account of the steplike construction of the Margurg pavements', and when the poet's numerous 'therefores' not infrequently introduce clauses whose causal nature is a pure fiction.

The wider the range of the poetic figure of speech, the more thoroughly, to use Pasternak's language, 'the accomplished' extinguishes 'the object of the accomplishment'. A connection that has been created overshadows one that is still to be made, and governs it; 'the fascination of autonomous meaning' takes on prominence, whilst objective connectedness is subdued, sometimes to a mere glimmer. In this sense the metonymical connections which Pasternak establishes, no less than Mayakovsky's metaphorical connections or the manifold ways of condensing both inner and outer verbal form in the poetry of Khlebnikov, show a persistent tendency to dispense with the object, a tendency also characteristic of the other art-forms of the period. A connection once created becomes an object in its own right. Pasternak does not tire of underlining the inessential, random nature of the thing to be connected:

> Each detail can be replaced by another.... Any one of them, chosen at random, will serve to bear witness to the transposed condition by which the whole of reality has been seized.... The parts of reality are mutually indifferent.

The poet defines art as the mutual interchangeability of images. Any images one cares to choose harbour more than similarity alone, and can consequently be mutual metaphors ('what cannot the sky be compared with?')—all images are in some way potentially contiguous. 'Who has not something of dust, or home or a calm spring evening in him?' is Pasternak's apology for the all-embracing, metonymical elective affinity. The more unrecognizable this affinity and the more unusual the community that the poet creates, the more the juxtaposed images, and whole series of images, fall to pieces and lose their spelling-book clarity. It is noteworthy that Pasternak consistently opposes 'the meaning imported into objects' to their palpability, for which he so delights in finding pejorative epithets—in Pasternak's world meaning is inevitably etiolating and palpability de-animating.

V

To define our problem: the absolute commitment of the poet to metonymy is known; what remains to be determined is the thematic structure of his poetry. The hero is as if concealed in a picture-puzzle, he is broken down into a series of constituent and subsidiary parts, he is replaced by a chain of objectivized situations and surrounding objects, both animate and inanimate. 'Every small detail lived and arose, without regard to me ... in its significance,' Pasternak records in his early cycle of poems *Over the Barriers*, in which, as he has admitted, he had already found his own poetic system. The theme of the poem is the poet's rejected proposal of marriage, but the principal characters in the action are flagstone,

[1] 'Marburg'.

paving-stone, wind, 'innate instinct', 'new sun', chicks, cricket and dragonfly, tile, midday, Marburger, sand, impending storm, sky, etc. One and a half decades later, in his book of reminiscenses *Safe Conduct,* Pasternak mentions that he is intentionally characterizing his whole life at random, that he could increase the number of significant features or replace them by others, and that, in fact, the poet's life must be looked for under alien names.

Show us your environment and I will tell you who you are. We learn what he lives on, this lyric hero outlined by metonymies, split up by synecdoches into individual attributes, reactions and situations; we learn to what he is related, by what he is conditioned and to what he is condemned. But the truly heroic element, the hero's activity, eludes our perception; action is replaced by topography. If in the case of Mayakovsky the collision of two worlds inevitably culminated in a duel, the suggestive image of Pasternak's poems—the world is a mirror to the world—says over and over again that the collision is illusory: 'The enormous garden stirs in the room, raises its fist against the mirror, runs to the swing, catches, hits with the ball, shakes—and doesn't break the glass.' If Mayakovsky unfolds his lyric theme in the form of a cycle of hero's metamorphoses, the favourite motive power of Pasternak's lyric prose is a railway journey during which his excited hero experiences changes of contiguity and distance in enforced idleness. The active voice has been erased from Pasternak's poetic grammar. In his prose ventures he employs precisely that metonymy which substitutes the action for the actor: 'a fully awake and vigorous man . . . waits for the decision to get up to come of its own accord, without his contributing anything'. The *agens* is excluded from his thematic material. The heroine did not call, did not arrange anything—'it was all announced to her'. The height of the heroine's activity, which conjures up the inevitability of the tragedy, is the mental transformation of her neighborhood; quite 'fortuitously, uselessly and senselessly' she notices someone and in imagination she introduces him into her own life. Is man perhaps active in art? No, 'in art', according to Pasternak's aesthetic, 'man's lips are sealed'; that, indeed, is the distinctive feature of art. Is art itself active, then? No, it does not even invent metaphor, but merely reproduces it. And the poet will not present his reminiscences to the memory of their object. 'On the contrary I myself received them from the latter as a gift.' If the lyric 'I' is in Pasternak's work a *patiens,* is some active third person then the real actor?

No, the genuine agent has no place in Pasternak's poetic mythology; as a rule the individual has no idea of what 'builds him up, tunes him and stitches him together', and the poet, too, is 'perfectly indifferent as to the name of the power that has given him his book'. The third person, as it appears in Pasternak's work, denotes the instrument rather than the agent. For example in *The Childhood of Luvers:*

> Everything that came from the parents to the children came at the wrong moment, from one side, provoked not by them but by certain causes that had nothing to do with them.

The auxiliary, subordinate, marginal nature of the third person is often firmly underlined in Pasternak's themes:

> *Another* human being had entered her life, the third person, just anyone, without a name or with a random name which neither provoked hatred nor inspired love.

What is essential is solely his penetration into the life of the lyric self. Whatever is unrelated to this single hero is only 'vague accumulations without names'.

This strict body of semantic laws also determines the simple pattern of Pasternak's lyric story. The hero is either delighted or appalled at being governed by an external impulse; he is now branded by it, now suddenly loses contact with it, whereupon another impulse takes its place. *Safe Conduct* is an inspired account of how the author's enamoured admiration focuses in turn upon Rilke, Scriabin, Cohen, a 'dear beautiful girl' and Mayakovsky, and how in this process he comes up against the 'limits of his understanding' (a person's nonunderstanding is one of the most acute and compelling of Pasternak's lyric themes, just as a person's being misunderstood by others is one of Mayakovsky's). Perplexed misunderstandings develop, and the inevitable passive solution follows—the hero goes off, leaving in the lurch, one after the other, music, philosophy and romantic poetry. The hero's activity is outside Pasternak's poetic competence. When his speed does deal with action, it looks like banal quotations, and in theoretical digressions he defends his right to triviality. Mayakovsky, too, uses triviality as a part of his building materials, but with him, in contrast to Pasternak, it is used exclusively to characterize the hostile 'Other'. Also, Pasternak's short stories are similarly empty of action. The most dramatic—*Aerial Ways*—is made up of the following 'Uncomplicated incidents': the former lover of the wife and friend of the husband is expected back from a sea voyage; all three are shattered by the disappearance of the child; the new arrival is shattered by the confession that the child is his son; fifteen years later he is shattered by the confirmation of this confession and then by the news of his son's death. Everything that in any way resembles action (the causes of the boy's disappearance, his rescue and the cause of his death) is left out of the picture. All that is recorded are the different stages of the emotional turmoil and their reflections.

VI

We have tried to deduce the themes of Pasternak's and Mayakovsky's work from the basic structural features of their poetics. Does that mean that the former are determined by the latter? Mechanists of formalism would answer in the affirmative, supporting their case with Pasternak's claim that in his youth he had had formal affinities with Mayakovsky which threatened to get out of hand, thus causing him radically to alter his poetic manner and, with it, the sense of life that lay at the base of it. The position of master of metaphor was filled, so the poet became master of metonymy and drew the appropriate ideological conclusions.

Others would try in their turn to prove the primacy of content. Mechanists of the psycho-analytical school would find the sources of Pasternak's thematic material in his confession that he had languished shamefully long 'in the sphere of mistakes made by the childish imagination, boyish perversions and the hungers of youth'. From these assumptions they would infer not only the repeated theme of passive exaltation and the inevitable falls, not only the poet's agitated recourse to motifs of adolescent development, but also his metonymical deviations around every fixed object. Mechanists of materialism would note the author's witness to the apolitical nature of his environment, and would assert a socio-economic basis for his apparent blindness to social problems—particularly to the social pathos of Mayakovsky's poetry—and for the mood of perplexed, inactive, elegiac distractedness which permeates both *Safe Conduct* and *Aerial Ways*.

It is legitimate to strive to find a correspondence between the different planes of reality, as it is also to try to infer facts about one of its planes from the corresponding facts about another—the method is one of projecting a multidimensional reality onto one surface. It would be a blunder, however, to confuse this projection with reality itself and to disregard both the characteristic structure and the self-movement of the diverse levels, that is, their transformation into mechanical superstructures. From among the actual possibilities of formal development, a person or a particular milieu can choose those that correspond most closely to the given social, ideological, psychological and other conditions; just as a cluster of artistic forms, come by the laws of their development to the point where they are available for use, seek out the appropriate milieu, or the creative personality, that will realize them. But this harmony of levels should not be made idyllically absolute; it must not be forgotten that dialectical tensions are possible between the different aspects of reality. Conflicts such as these are essential motor powers of cultural history. If many individual characteristics of Pasternak's poetry are in accord with the characteristic features of his personality and his social environment, so, inevitably, there are also phenomena in his work which the contemporary verbal art forces upon every one of its poets, even if they contradict his own individual and social personality. (It is a question of the integral axes of its total structure.) And if the poet rejects these demands, he is automatically derailed. The poet's artistic mission never penetrates his biography without a struggle, just as his biography is never entirely absorbed into his artistic mission. The hero of *Safe Conduct* is a constantly unlucky wretch, because the poet Pasternak cannot do anything with the numerous successes that his original model, the historical B. L. Pasternak actually achieved. (In the same way Casanova's book could not make anything of the failures that Casanova actually experienced.) The tendency which we have identified in the work of Pasternak and his contemporaries to make the sign radically independent of its object is the basic endeavour of the whole modern movement in art which has emerged as the antithesis of Naturalism. This tendency is inseparable from the militant pathos of this movement and is to be found in all artists, not withstanding the details of their biography. The attempts of observers simply to attach this specifically artistic phenomenon to a limited social sector or a particular ideology are typical mechanistic errors: to infer from the non-representational nature of a man's art the unrealistic nature of his ideology is arbitrarily to suppress a fundamental antinomy. Rather it is the tendency of philosophy towards objectivism that corresponds most closely to the non-representational tendency in art.

The Prose

To belong to a solidary, unified collective body and to hold firmly to a particular direction are both repugnant to Pasternak, who is a passionate destroyer of customary affinities. He is at pains to convince Mayakovsky of how splendid it would be if the latter would do away with Futurism for ever. He dislikes all 'banal' agreements with his contemporaries, keeps himself separate from them and advocates excursions off the common path. Nevertheless, despite the ideological discordance of the period, so variegated as to reach a point of mutual hatred and lack of comprehension, Pasternak's "coeval ties" come out very strongly in his poetry. It is revealed both in his persistent creative annulment of the object and in his transformation of the grammar of art. This latter used to consist of past and present; and the present, opposed solely to the past, was conceived as an indefinite, unmarked "nonpast". It was Futurism that wished to introduce the future into the poetic system by rubric, theory and practice, and to introduce it as a leading category. The poems and manifestoes of Khlebnikov and Mayakovsky shout this tirelessly, and Pasternak's work is imbued with the same ethos, despite his profound inclination for 'the deep horizon of recollection'. In a new way, in the context of the new antithesis, he conceives the present as an independent, marked category and understands that 'the mere apprehensibility of the present is already the future'. It is not by chance that the strained hymn to Mayakovsky which closes *Safe Conduct* ends with the words:

> From his childhood he was indulged by the future, which surrendered to him rather early and, obviously, without much difficulty.

This 'grammatical reform' fundamentally alters the very function of poetry in its relation to other social values.

SOURCE: 'Randbemerkungen zur Prosa des Dichters Pasternak', in *Slavische Rundschau*, VIII (1935).

ANNA AKHMATOVA
Boris Pasternak (1936)

Он, сам себя сравнивший с конским глазом,
Косится, смотрит, видит, узнает,
И вот уже расплавленным алмазом
Сияют лужи, изнывает лед.

В лиловой мгле покоятся задворки,
Платформы, бревна, листья, облака.
Свист паровоза, хруст арбузной корки,
В душистой лайке робкая рука.

Звенит, гремит, скрежещет, бьет прибоем
И вдруг притихнет — это значит, он
Пугливо пробирается по хвоям,
Чтоб не спугнуть пространства чуткий сон.

И это значит, он считает зерна
В пустых колосьях, это значит, он
К плите дарьяльской, проклятой и черной,
Опять пришел с каких-то похорон.

И снова жжет московская истома,
Звенит вдали смертельный бубенец —
Кто заблудился в двух шагах от дома,
Где снег по пояс и всему конец. ...

За то, что дым сравнил с Лаокооном,
Кладбищенский воспел чертополох,
За то, что мир наполнил новым звоном
В пространстве новом отраженных строф,

Он награждён каким-то вечным детством,
Той щедростью и зоркостью светил,
И вся земля была его наследством,
А он её со всеми разделил.

He, likened by himself to a horse's eye,
Peers wall-eyed, he looks, sees, registers,
And see, already, melted diamond
They shine, the puddles, and the sapped ice stirs.

In the violet dark rest settles on backyards,
On platforms, timber-baulks, on leaf and cloud,
The whee of the locomotive, crunched rind of cantaloup,
And a hand gloved hesitant in fragrant kid.

Clack, and clap, and gnash, and the surf beating
And suddenly quiet – and this means that he's
Apprehensively gliding over pine-mast
Not to set flying the thin sleep of spaces.

And this means he is keeping count of grains
In empty barley-ears, this means that he's
To a slab in the gorge of Daryal, black and accursed,
Come once more from someone's obsequies.

And anew they burn, dog-days in exhausted Moscow,
From far away dead chink of a bauble-bell –
Who goes astray two paces away from home,
Snow waist-high, the whole thing brought to an end. . . .

For likening smoke to the Laocoön,
For celebrating cemetery thistles,
For plenishing the world with a new accord
In the new spaces of respondent stanzas,

He is awarded a kind of age-long childhood,
Such a profuseness and such keenness as
The illustrious have, the earth all his, of which
He makes all men the co-inheritors.

ANDREI SINYAVSKY

Boris Pasternak (1965)[1]

PASTERNAK'S work was for a long time known only to a fairly small circle of poetry-lovers and connoisseurs. His literary aloofness and isolation were noted over the years by many critics who explained this partly by the fact that someone coming to his books for the first time would find it difficult even to understand the text. 'The reader was confronted with a poet of an unusual stamp,' wrote one critic at the end of the 1920s, '– he had to make a special effort to understand him and, in a sense, had to transform his habitual mode of perception. Pasternak's manner of perceiving, and his very vocabulary, seemed at first sight astonishing and unacceptable, and for a long time the appearance of a book by him provoked persistent questions about his "unintelligibility"; how *could* anything be like this?'[2]

The densely metaphorical quality of Pasternak's early work was often taken to be a formal affectation, beneath which some profound content was dimly to be guessed at. Moreover, his first books gave the impression of a writer almost completely estranged from contemporary life, and he acquired the reputation of a poet far removed from the large social questions, shut away in a world of his own private experiences.

But this negative and at times intolerant attitude towards him was

[1] The footnotes to this article are, all but two, Sinyavsky's own. We have supplemented them as follows. (*a*) Where Sinyavsky refers to Russian editions of prose works by Pasternak, references have been added, where possible, in square brackets, to the same passages in the University of Michigan 1961 edition of his Collected Works (*Sochineniya*, ed. Struve and Filippov) – hereunder referred to as *Works* – as well as to the corresponding passages in English translation, especially in *Safe Conduct, an autobiography, and other writings* (various translators) (New Directions 1949, reprinted 1959) – hereunder referred to as *ND*. (The English versions referred to have not, however, been used in the present translation.) (*b*) Translations have been added of the titles of works given by Sinyavsky.

[2] K. Loks, 'Boris Pasternak. Poverkh bar'erov' ('... Over the Barriers') in *Literaturnaya gazeta* (28 Oct 1929).

not the only one; at the beginning of the twenties Mayakovsky was already numbering Pasternak's works among the models of 'the new poetry, with its supreme sensitivity to what is modern'.[1]

At the same time Bryusov remarked: 'Pasternak has not written any poems specifically about the Revolution, but, perhaps even without his knowing it, his poems are steeped in the spirit of the present; his psychology is not borrowed from the books of the past; it is an expression of his own being and could have been formed only in the conditions of our life.'[2]

Because of the nature of his talent, and his conception of the function of art, Pasternak did not belong with the tribunes and orators of the Revolution. His attitude to life and to reality was determined by abstract ideals of moral perfection and did not always answer the concrete historical situation. His work in the main is about life seen from the point of view of the 'eternal' categories of goodness, love and universal justice.

Yet many of his works, written at various periods in his life, do bear the stamp of the Revolution and the new Soviet reality, which he depicts (and this is characteristic of him) as moral transformations brought into the history of the world by our age and our people. In 1957, near the end of his life, he wrote of this in a New Year message, addressing his readers abroad: '... And there is one more thing that you have us to thank for. However great the difference between us, our Revolution set the tone for you as well: it filled the present century with meaning and content. It is not only we – our young people – that are different: the very son of one of your bankers is no longer what his father and grandfather were. ... And it's us you have to thank for this new man, who is present even in your ancient society, us you must thank for the fact that he is more alive, more subtle and more gifted than his pompous and turgid forebears, for this child of the age was delivered in the maternity hospital called Russia. Should we not therefore peaceably wish each other a Happy New Year and wish that the popping of wine corks as we welcome it in shall not be interrupted by the thunders of war, that these thunders shall never sound again, either this year or in coming years. But if disaster must come, then remember by what events we have been brought up, what a severe and hardening

[1] *Teatral'naya Moskva* (1921) VIII 6.
[2] V. Bryusov, 'Vchera, sevodnya i zavtra russkoi poezii' ('The Yesterday, Today and Tomorrow of Russian Poetry'), in *Pechat' i revolyutsiya* (1922) VII 57.

school they have been for us. No one is more desperate than we are, no one readier to realize the unrealizable and the fabulous, and any call to war will transform every single one of us into heroes, as happened in the trial that recently faced us.'[1]

The largeness of subject needed by the people of today and tomorrow is to be found even in the poems Pasternak dedicates to nature, which are perhaps among the best that he wrote in his half century of literary work. His landscapes with their life-affirming pathos and their renewed perception of the world are in tune with the mind of contemporary man. Not for nothing did Pasternak connect the writing of his book *My Sister Life* in the summer of 1917 with a new awareness born of the new epoch: 'I saw upon earth a summer that seemed not to recognize itself – natural, prehistoric, as in a revelation. I left a book about it. In that book I expressed everything that can possibly be learnt of the most improbable, the most elusive things about the Revolution.'[2]

I

Boris Leonidovich Pasternak was born on 10 February (29 January) 1890, in Moscow. His father was the well-known artist Leonid Pasternak, his mother the pianist Rosa Kaufman. The poet's childhood years were spent in an atmosphere of art, music and literature. The many-sided cultural interests and connections of his family were reflected very early in his inclinations. Thus, while he was still a child or young boy, an indelible impression was made on him by the German poet Rilke, by Leo Tolstoy and by Scriabin. He has spoken of these first encounters with artistic genius as having been of definitive importance for the formation of his own cast of mind. Later, his response to the poetry of Blok, which was just as personal, and just as sharply autobiographical, and his acquaintance with Mayakovsky, had a similar importance.

Pasternak's first creative interest and enthusiasm was devoted entirely to music. At the age of thirteen, under the very strong influence of Scriabin, he gave himself up to musical composition, studying

[1] 'Druz'yam na Vostoke i Zapade. Novogodnee pozhelanie' ('To Friends in East and West. A New-Year Greeting'), in *Literaturnaya Rossiya* (1965) 19.

[2] An unpublished postscript by Pasternak to his book *Safe Conduct* (1931). (Pasternak archive.)

its theory under Yuri Engel and Reinhold Glière. After six years of serious work he abandoned music for ever. In 1909 he entered the historico-philological faculty of Moscow University and began a thorough study of philosophy. He went to Germany in 1912 in order to complete his philosophical education, and spent a semester at the University of Marburg. He also made a trip to Switzerland and Italy at that time.

Pasternak had become interested in contemporary poetry in 1908-9 and had friendly connections with those involved in it. He joined the group of poets led by Anisimov, and tried his hand at writing. But not until after Marburg did it become finally clear to him where his vocation lay. He lost his enthusiasm for philosophy and gave himself up wholly to the art of poetry, which, after 1913, became the most important and permanent fact in his life.

The same sudden breaks, impetuous transitions from one circle of ideas and occupations to another (music, philosophy, poetry), the same dissastisfaction with himself and counsels of creative perfection, the same willingness to sacrifice years of work for the sake of experiencing a 'second birth', are features of his literary biography too. As he developed, he boldly crossed out his past. The early period of his questings in poetry, a period in which the influence of Symbolism crossed with that of Futurism (he joined the moderate Futurist group Centrifuga, along with Aseev and Bobrov), he later subjected to a thorough reappraisal. A great deal of what he wrote before 1917 he omitted altogether from later editions.

With the appearance of his book *My Sister Life* in 1922 it became clear that Pasternak was one of the masters of contemporary verse. It may be said that with this book he made his début as a distinctively individual poet. Everything that preceded it – *Twin in the Clouds* (1914) and *Over the Barriers* (1917) – had the character of a first attempt, a preparation, a tuning-up, and was part of his search for a voice of his own, for his own view of life, for his own place amid the diversity of literary currents. A number of poems included in these two early collections were later re-written, to appear in unrecognizable form. Although certain important traits and persistent tendencies (the striving for free, unfettered expression, for authentic reproduction of a living picture and the tendency to abrupt, dynamic descriptiveness) were already present in *Over the Barriers*, he considered it necessary to revise the book radically when preparing a new edition of it in 1929. Clichés reminiscent of the Symbolists, that characterized his early volumes, now disappeared, as did the abstraction and deliberate obscurity and what he himself later called Futuristic 'trinkets', which gave his verse an 'extraneous cleverness' to the detriment of its meaning and content.

If we divide Pasternak's work into periods we can call the years 1912–16 the period of apprenticeship in which he accumulated experience and established his poetic method, but was not yet mature nor wholly independent. The writing of *My Sister Life* (1917) was a very important milestone in his career as a poet. He worked at it with an extraordinarily vigorous headlong impulsiveness that spoke of a soaring of inspiration, of the sudden powerful pressure of a creative energy flooding into the book. Then, after *Themes and Variations*, which was published in 1923 and was in many respects an offshoot and continuation of *My Sister Life*, there comes a phase of strenuous attempts at the epic genre (1923–30): he worked at *The Lofty Malady*, the historico-revolutionary poems *The Year 1905* and *Lieutenant Schmidt*, and the novel in verse *Spektorsky*.

In the 1920s Pasternak joined the literary association Lef (Mayakovsky, Aseev, Tretyakov, Osip Brik, N. Chuzhak, etc.). Lef's aesthetic orientation towards an emphatically tendentious, agitator's art, preaching utilitarianism and technicism, was remote from Pasternak. His temporary and very unstable connection with the Lefovtsi was sustained by his friendship with Mayakovsky and Aseev and by his sharing some of their aspirations – the quest for poetic innovation and the working out of a really modern poetic language. But he felt himself to be a stranger in the Lef milieu and frankly said so in 1928. We should note, incidentally, that all organized groupings, all adherence to schools or definite literary platforms, were always alien to Pasternak. Even in his early, revolutionary, period, when he was publicly associating himself with the Futurists, his interpretation of Futurism was different from theirs, inclining towards Impressionism; and the narrowness of the group he belonged to was burdensome to him.

At the beginning of the 1930s, after accomplishing a great deal of work in the sphere of historical narrative poetry, Pasternak turned once more to lyric verse (with his book *Second Birth*). Now there was a noticeable change of key, a new manner that moved towards greater clarity and classical simplicity. The process of change took a long time and it was accompanied by a temporary loss of energy and by lengthy interruptions in his work.

The 1930s were the most difficult and critical years for Pasternak. He produced few original works but devoted his efforts chiefly to translation, which he worked at regularly from 1934 onwards and continued to work at until the end of his life. (He translated the Georgian poets, Shakespeare, Goethe, Schiller, Kleist, Rilke, Verlaine and others.)

Not until the beginning of 1941, on the eve of war, did Pasternak overcome his crisis and enter a phase of creative inspiration. A number of first-class poems appeared, which formed the collection *On Early Trains* (1943). There are direct links between this book and the poetry he wrote at the end of the 1940s and in the 1950s, that is, the work which crowned his life. (He died on 30 May, 1960.)

In the 1920s, the 1930s and later, right up to the end of his life, Pasternak is constantly trying to re-examine and revaluate his literary past. It is well known, for example, that in 1956 he declared that he disliked his pre-1940 style. Such judgements on himself, though not always just, are a part of his nature, for he preferred not to accumulate but to abandon – for the sake of further achievements. Art, as he understood it, is a continuous giving of oneself, and a movement concerned not with totalling things up but with making discoveries.

> Цель творчества – самоотдача,
> А не шумиха, не успех.
> Позорно, ничего не знача,
> Быть притчей на устах у всех...
>
> И надо оставлять пробелы
> В судьбе, а не среди бумаг,
> Места и главы жизни целой
> Отчеркивая на полях.

> The object in composition is to give yourself entire,
> Not to be a sensation, nor a big success,
> It is ignominious and meaningless
> Being the idle talk on every lip...
>
> And you have to leave the blanks
> In your fate, not among your papers,
> The passages and chapters of an entire life
> There as a note in the margin.

The persistent, lifelong desire for a renewal of his style and viewpoint as an artist does not mean, however, that there is not a great internal unity to all his work between 1911 and 1960. In its main tendencies of thought and style his work is single and unbroken. Though he changed more than once after *My Sister Life*, in which his credo for life and art was affirmed, he did not alter the fundamentals of his poetry. He went on developing and completing that which had taken shape in this book and which rang out like an original discovery.

We have outlined the path that Pasternak took as a poet; now we shall try to enter his world, which will mean giving close attention to his philosophy of life, to the texture of his language, and to the structure of his imagery. To do this we shall depart somewhat from a chronological account of his life as a writer and shall turn to the poems themselves, which, though written at different times and to some extent in different styles, are at one in certain basic impulses and conclusions.

II

The central place in Pasternak's lyrical work belongs to his nature poems. In these poems there is much more than in the usual landscape descriptions. When Pasternak writes of springs and winters, rains and dawns, he is telling us about the nature of life itself, about the very existence of the world, he is confessing his faith in life – and this, I think, is the most important thing in his poetry generally, this is its moral foundation. Life, to him, is something unconditional, eternal, absolute; it is an all-pervasive element and the greatest miracle. Wonder at the miracle of existence – this is the attitude in which we see Pasternak throughout, forever amazed and enchanted by his discovery that 'it's spring again'.

> Где я обрывки этих речей
> Слышал уж как-то порой прошлогодней?
> Ах, это сызнова, верно, сегодня
> Вышел из рощи ночью ручей.
> Это, как в прежние времена,
> Сдвинула льдины и вздулась запруда,
> Это поистине новое чудо,
> Это, как прежде, снова весна.
> Это она, это она.

Where before did I hear this talk by snatches
Some time in the year just gone?
Ah, no doubt of it, over again
Out of the grove this night came a little river,
It is, as it has been time and again in the past,
That the weir has shifted its iceblocks and swelled over,
It is a new miracle, I warrant you.
It is, as it has been before, the spring.
She it is, she, none other.

From his nature poems comes a sense of freshness and health. As Mandel'shtam observed: 'To read the poems of Pasternak is to get one's throat clear, to fortify one's breathing, to renovate one's lungs; such poems must be a cure for tuberculosis.'[1]

Рассвет расколыхнет свечу,
Зажжет и пустит в цель стрижа.
Напоминанием влечу:
Да будет так же жизнь свежа!

Заря, как выстрел в темноту.
Бабах! – и тухнет на лету
Пожар ружейного пыжа.
Да будет так же жизнь свежа.

Dawn will make the tapers flap,
Spark and propel house-martins to their mark,
A making-mindful, in I dart:
May life be always as bran-new as this!

Dawn, like a shot into the dark,
Bang, bang! – the wadding as it flies
Out of the rifle sees its spark go out.
May life be always as bran-new as this!

Day by day, line by line, Pasternak never tires of affirming the salutary, all-triumphant vitality of nature. Trees, grasses, clouds, streams – all in his verse assume the exalted right to speak in the name of life itself, and to set us on the path of truth and goodness. ('There's

---

[1] O. Mandel'shtam, 'Boris Pasternak', in *Rossiya* (1923) VI 29. [See above, p. 71.]

D.L.P.

no sadness on earth that snow cannot cure.') The highest value and beauty may be contained in a single willow branch:

> Когда случилось петь Дездемоне,—
> А жить так мало оставалось,—
> Не по любви, своей звезде, она,—
> По иве, иве разрыдалась. . . .
>
> Когда случилось петь Офелии,—
> А горечь грез осточертела,—
> С какими канула трофеями?
> С охапкой верб и чистотела.

> When it fell to Desdemona
> To sing, so little living left,
> She made her moan not of her love, her star,
> But all of willow, willow only wept. . . .
>
> When it befell Ophelia
> To sing, harsh-tasting dreams gone sour,
> She sank among what trophies? In her arms
> The sprigs were willow, celandine the flower.

In Pasternak landscape is often not so much the object of a description as the subject of an action, the principal hero and mover of events. All the fullness of life in all its diverse manifestations enters into one scrap of nature which seems capable of acting, feeling and thinking. In Pasternak the comparison of nature with man, which is characteristic of poetry, goes to the point where landscape takes on the rôle of mentor and moral example. 'The forest drops its crimson raiment . . .' is the traditional classical formula for autumn in Russian poetry. With Pasternak we often find the opposite process of thought: 'You throw off your dress in just the same way as the grove throws off its leaves. . . .' 'Your meaning is unself-seeking as the air . . .,' the poet says to his beloved. Man is defined through nature, and it is through comparison with her that he finds his place in the world. This power which nature possesses, or rather this intercession on the part of nature, does not involve any humiliation of man, for by submitting to her and comparing himself with her he is following the voice of life. Moreover, nature is so close to man that while it pushes him aside and takes his place he nevertheless comes to life in it afresh. The world is so humanized that as we walk through these woods and fields, we have to do, essentially, not with pictures of woods and fields, but with their very characters, their psychology.

Writing of his stay in Venice Pasternak recalls: 'And so I too was touched by this happiness. I too had the joy of knowing that one can go day after day to meet a piece of built-up space, as if it were a living personality.'[1]

This is the kind of meeting that takes place in his verse between himself and nature, seen as a unique independent personality.

> И вот ты входишь в березняк.
> Вы всматриваетесь друг в дружку.
>
> And there you are, going into the birch-grove.
> The pair of you look into each other's faces.

Nature acquires all the features of a person. We are accustomed to read 'it is raining'; now we read 'Rather from sleep than from the eaves, and rather/Absent-mindedly than diffident,/The small rain stamped its feet at the doors....' Pasternak's landscapes have their own character, sympathies and favourite amusements: clouds play at catch, the thunder takes photographs, streams sing a song. They are even endowed with the features of a portrait:

> И лес шелушится, и каплями
> Роняет струящийся пот.
>
> И блестят, блестят, как губы,
> Не утертые рукою,
> Лозы ив, и листья дуба,
> И следы у водопоя.
>
> And the forest rustles, and in beads
> Lets fall its streaming sweat.
>
> And shine there, shine, like lips
> Not wiped by any hand,
> The willow's spars, the oak-tree's leaves,
> And the tracks by the standing water.

'The face of the azure', 'the face of the river', 'the face of the storm that has torn off its mask' – such is the world of nature for him, a crowd of many persons, many faces.

---

[1] Boris Pasternak, *Okhrannaya gramota* (*Safe Conduct*) (Leningrad, 1931) p. 81. [*Works* (Prose) II 259; *ND*, p. 95.]

Pasternak's poetry is metaphorical through and through. But often we do not notice that all his analogies are metaphorical, so vivid is the action taking place before our eyes. 'The garden weeps', or 'the storm runs', not metaphorically but literally, presented with all the verisimilitude of something that really and truly takes place.

> Гроза в воротах! на дворе!
> Преображаясь и дурея,
> Во тьме, в раскатах, в серебре,
> Она бежит но галерее.

> Storm at the gates! storm in the yard!
> Transformed and in tomfooleries
> In the dark, in thunder-peals, in silver,
> It runs the galleries.

In Pasternak's verse the chief rôle of metaphor is to connect one thing to another. Instantly and dynamically it draws the separate parts of reality into a single whole, and thus embodies the great unity of the world, the interaction and interpenetration of phenomena. Pasternak proceeds from the idea that two objects, set side by side, closely interact with and penetrate each other – so he connects them, not by their similarity but by their proximity, using metaphor as the link. The world is described 'whole', and the work of unifying it is done by means of the figurative meanings of words:

> Весна, я с улицы, где тополь удивлен,
> Где даль пугается, где дом упасть боится,
> Где воздух синь, как узелок с бельем
> У выписавшегося из больницы.

> Spring, I am from the street, where the poplar is astonished,
> Where the distance is alarmed, the house is afraid of falling,
> And where the air is blue like the bundle of linen
> Of one who is discharged from hospital.

The last line explains why the 'distance is afraid' and the 'house is afraid of falling down': they, too, have only just been discharged from hospital, like the man whose bundle has made the air turn blue.

Landscape, and – more generally – the whole of the world surrounding us, acquires a heightened sensitivity. It reacts sharply and instantly to changes taking place in man, and does not merely respond to his feelings, thoughts and moods (something common enough in literature) but becomes his complete likeness, an extension of him, his *alter ego*. In the prose work *A Tale* there is a passage which lays bare the mechanics of these transformations. The hero, who is in love, suddenly observes: 'Of course the whole lane, all full of dusky gloom, was utterly and entirely Anna. Serezha was not alone in this and knew it. And indeed, who had experienced it before him? However, his feeling was still vaster and more exact, and here the help of friends and predecessors stopped. He saw how painful and difficult it was for Anna to be the morning in the town.... Silently beautiful in his presence, she did not cry to him for help. And faint with longing for the real Arild... he watched her, overcast with poplars, as with icy towels, being sucked in by the clouds and slowly throwing backwards her Gothic brick towers.'[1]

Note: the feeling by which Serezha was seized was 'vaster and more exact' than similar phenomena experienced by other people, by his friends and predecessors. And Pasternak is in fact speaking of himself here, and of what makes him different from his predecessors and his contemporaries. His *correspondences* differ from the traditional ones (landscape as the accompaniment to man's inner experiences) precisely in the scope and exactness of his imagery: everything, 'utterly and entirely', is transformed into Anna Arild.

Here Pasternak is probably closest to the metaphorical sprints of Mayakovsky, who likened the world to the passions and sufferings of his hero. ('From my lament and laugh the snout of the room was distorted with horror.') But in his case the extending of emotion to objective reality is motivated by a restlessness intensified to an extreme degree ('I cannot be more calm'), and by the power and grandeur of the poet's inner experiences. Pasternak is 'calmer', 'quieter', 'more restrained' than Mayakovsky; in him such displacements are brought about not so much by the exclusiveness of passion as by the delicacy of his feeling for reflexes and resonances, and by the way each object is sensitive to the object nearest to it. For him their reactions and responses do not attain such hyperbolic dimensions, but there is not a drop of water that does not reflect a gleam of light, and all objects, even the most insignificant ones, have an influence on one another and take on

[1] Boris Pasternak, *Vozdushnye puti* (Aerial Ways) (Moscow, 1933) p. 134. [*Works*, II 196; *The Last Summer* (*A Tale*, translated under new title by George Reavey) (1959) pp. 129-30, and Penguin (1960) p. 84. Sinyavsky refers here to the collection of stories entitled *Aerial Ways*, not to the particular story of that name. The quotation is from the story *A Tale*.]

one another's lineaments. In Pasternak's poetry one cannot distinguish between man and his surroundings, or between living feeling and dead matter. By means of the shorthand of metaphor, reality is depicted in the merging of heterogeneous parts, the intersection of facets and contours, as a single indivisible whole.

Pasternak was fascinated by the task of recreating within the limits of a poem the all-embracing atmosphere of being, and of communicating his sense of 'intimacy with the universe'. In his poems the lyrical narration does not develop consistently from one thing to the next but leaps 'over the barriers', tending to a broad sketch and bold depiction of the whole. Through allegory, and the figurative meanings of words, objects shift from their long-occupied places and are set going in a stormy chaotic movement whose mission is to record reality in its native disorder.

> Мне хочется домой, в огромность
> Квартиры, наводящей грусть.
> Войду, сниму пальто, опомнюсь,
> Огнями улиц озарюсь.
>
> Перегородок тонкоребрость
> Пройду насквозь, пройду, как свет.
> Пройду, как образ входит в образ
> И как предмет сечет предмет.

> I want to be home, to be going into the vast
> Spaces of my flat that make me mournful,
> I shall go in and take my coat off and
> Come to myself, I shall be lit by the street-lamps.
>
> The slender rib-case of a partition-wall
> I shall pass through, pass through like light,
> Pass through, as image enters into image,
> As solid object shears through solid object.

In this transparent space intersected by metaphors the image of the poet, of the artist, has a peculiar place. Except in a very few works he in no way stands out nor is he shown as a distinct independent person. The lyrical voice is rarely that of the poet himself. Pasternak thus differs from Blok, Tsvetayeva, Mayakovsky and Yesenin, for whom the poet's personality is central, his work unfolding like a diary of many years, a tale told 'of the times and of oneself', a sort of saga or dramatic biography acted out before the eyes of the readers and surrounded by the halo of legend. Pasternak abandoned this conception, which he called 'romantic', and the 'notion of [the poet's] life as a spectacle'.[1] He says very little about himself, or from himself, and keeps his own 'ego' carefully hidden. Reading his poems we sometimes have the illusion that there is no author there at all, not even as a narrator, or as a witness of the things being depicted. Nature declares herself in her own name!

> ... В раскрытые окна на их рукоделье
> Садились как голуби, облака.
> Они замечали: с воды похудели
> Заборы – заметно, кресты – слегка.

> ... Through wide-open windows on their needlework
> Clouds settled, as a dove might settle, lightly.
> They took note: water made the fence stitch finer
> Conspicuously, the cross-stitch also, slightly.

It is not the poet observing, but 'the clouds observed', just as in another place, it is not the poet remembering his childhood, but, 'the snow recalls in a flash, a flash: it was called "bye-bye", in whispering sweetness the day would slowly go down behind the cradle...'. In one of his late poems, 'First Frosts', we again come across this rather unusual sort of description in which the scene and the spectator appear to have exchanged rôles: the picture itself looks at the person standing before it:

> Холодным утром солнце в дымке
> Стоит столбом огня в дыму.
> Я тоже, как на скверном снимке,
> Совсем неотличим ему.
>
> Пока оно из мглы не выйдет,
> Блеснув за прудом на лугу,
> Меня деревья плохо видят
> На отдаленном берегу.

---

[1] Boris Pasternak, *Okhrannaya Gramota (Safe Conduct)* pp. 111–13. [*Works*, II 282; *ND*, p. 129.]

> On a cold morning the sun stands up
> A smoke-haze shaft, afire but dim,
> And I too, as in a faulty snapshot,
> Am wholly indistinct to him.
>
> Until he comes up out of the dark,
> Flashing in the field beyond,
> The trees can hardly make me out
> On the far shore of the pond.

While Mayakovsky and Tsvetayeva want to speak for the whole world in their own person, Pasternak prefers that the world should speak for him and in his stead: 'not I of the spring but the spring speaks of me'; 'not I of the garden, the garden of me'.

> ... У плетня
> Меж мокрых ветох с ветром бледным
> Шёл спор. Я замер. Про меня!
>
> About a stretch of fencing
> Damp branches quarrelled with the pallid wind
> Sharply. I froze. I was the point at issue!

Nature herself is the chief lyric hero. And the poet is everywhere and nowhere. Rather than one looking on from outside at a panorama spread out before him, he is its double, becoming now the sea, now the forest. For instance, in the poem 'The Weeping Garden', the usual parallel 'I and the garden' is turned around to become the equation 'I am the garden', and Pasternak uses the very same words to speak 'about it' and to speak 'about myself':

> Ужасный! – Капнет и вслушается:
> Всё он ли один на свете
> Мнёт ветку в окне, как кружевце,
> Или есть свидетель ...
>
> К губам поднесу и прислушаюсь:
> Всё я ли один на свете,
> Готовый навзрыд при случае,
> Или есть свидетель.
>
> Appalling! it drips and listens – is it
> Alone in the world or (now it presses
> Lace-like, a twig upon the windowpane)
> Does it have witnesses? ...

> To my lips I will raise it, and intently listen,
> Am I alone in the world
> And ready endowed with weeping, if the need be,
> Or am I overheard?

This union with nature in the absence of witnesses or spies makes his verse specially intimate and genuine.

A garden is again the hero of his well-known poem 'The Mirror', but here the garden is reflected in a standing mirror where it lives, as it were, a second life, glimpsed in the mysterious mirror-depth: 'The huge garden stirs in the room in the mirror – and doesn't break the glass!' It is interesting that in an earlier publication this poem bore the declaratory title 'Myself': the poet regarded his account of the mirror absorbing the garden as an account of himself. And Pasternak does in fact think of himself as being a mirror like this, related to life and its equal. In the poem 'A Little Girl', which continues the imagery of 'The Mirror', he establishes the reverse connection – the mirror recognizes itself in a twig that has rushed in from the garden: the poet sees in nature a likeness of himself, a repetition of himself:

> Родная, громадная, с сад, а характером—
> Сестра! Второе трюмо!

> Dear one, immense as the garden, but in character
> Sister! Second mirror!

Thus Pasternak developed his artistic system – in a book whose title sounds like a poetic manifesto – *My Sister Life*. And thus he asserted his first and fundamental credo – the poet's oneness with nature.

> Казалось альфой и омегой,–
> Мы с жизнью на один покрой;
> И круглый год, в снегу, без снега,
> Она жила, как alter ego,
> И я назвал ее сестрой.

> It seemed the alpha and the omega –
> That I and life were cut to the self-same pattern,
> And the entire year, now in snow, now not,
> Life lived it through as if my alter ego,
> And sister was the name I called her by.

Pasternak was deeply convinced that poetry was a direct product and consequence of life. The artist does not think up his images, he gathers them from the street, helping nature in her work of creation, but never supplanting her by his own interference.

> Бывало, снег несет вкрутую,
> Что только в голову придет.
> Я сумраком его грунтую
> Свой дом, и холст, и обиход.
>
> Всю зиму пишет он этюды,
> И у прохожих на виду
> Я их переношу оттуда,
> Таю, копирую, краду.
>
> Time was, the snow would fiercely whirl
> Whatever slight thing I'd a mind to say.
> Now with the murk of it I prime and ground
> My house, my canvas and my day-to-day.
>
> It writes all winter long its own *études*,
> And in full sight of passers-by I pitch them
> On to my back and carry them away
> And I conceal them, copy them, and filch them.

His favourite theme is that art is conceived in the womb of nature. This is presented in various forms, but is invariable in one thing: the primary source of poetry is life itself, and the poet is at best a collaborator, or co-author, whose only task is to watch and wonder as he holds out his writing-book and collects the rhymes that drop into it ready-made. Hence the abundance of literary terms in Pasternak's nature descriptions.

> Для этой книги на эпиграф
> Пустыни сипли....
>
> For this book, by way of epigraph,
> Deserts grew hoarse....
>
> Отростки ливня грязнут в гроздьях
> И долго, долго, до зари,
> Кропают с кровель свой акростих,
> Пуская в рифму пузыри.

Offshoots of rainstorm muddily clump together,
And before dawn, for what a long, long time
These scrawl from rooftops their acrostics,
And blow their bubbles into rhyme!

Зовите это как хотите,
Но всё кругом одевший лес
Бежал, как повести развитье,
И сознавал свой интерес.

Call it what you will, the forest,
By whom all things around were dressed,
Ran on like the unwinding of a tale,
Acknowledged its own interest.

Но вот приходят дни цветенья,
И липы в поясе оград
Разбрасывают вместе с тенью
Неотразимый аромат. . . .

Он составляет в эти миги,
Когда он за сердце берет,
Предмет и содержанье книги,
А парк и клумбы – переплет.

But now, look, days of blossoming come
And limetrees belted round with fences
Squander around, along with shadow,
A not to be withstood aroma. . . .

It composes in these instants
When it clutches at the heart
The theme and substance of a book,
The park and flowerbeds the binding.

This identification of art with life, of poetry with nature, this handing over of authorial rights to the landscape, serves, in the main, one purpose: by offering us verses composed by nature herself the poet is assuring us of their authenticity, and this, the truth of the image, is for him the highest criterion for art. His views on literature and his poetic practice are filled with the concern 'to be able not to distort the voice of life that sounds in us'.

'Inability to find and to tell the truth is a fault that cannot be covered up by any amount of ability to tell untruths,'[1] Pasternak wrote. Realism, in his understanding of it (the artist's sharpened receptivity and conscientious communication of real being, which like a living human person is always entire and always unique), is present in all true art; it is seen in the work of Tolstoy and Lermontov, Chopin and Blok, Shakespeare and Verlaine; while romanticism is for Pasternak more a negative notion: it is something that tends toward fantasy and the neglect of fidelity in its depictions.

These views of his are all the more interesting in that he was for a long time connected with the group of Futurists, later called 'lefovtsi', who favoured the so-called formal method, which treated the work of art as the sum of its technical devices. 'People nowadays imagine', wrote Pasternak at the beginning of the 1920s, 'that art is like a fountain, whereas it is a sponge. They think art has to flow forth, whereas what it has to do is absorb and become saturated. They suppose that it can be divided up into means of depiction, whereas it is made up of the organs of perception. Its job is to be always a spectator and to look more purely, more receptively, more faithfully than anyone else; but in our age it has come to know pomade and the make-up room, and it displays itself from a stage....'[2]

We find the same image – poetry as a sponge – developed in one of Pasternak's early poems; he sees a heightened receptiveness to sensation as the decisive feature of his work:

> Поэзия! Греческой губкой в присосках
> Будь ты, и меж зелени клейкой
> Тебя б положил я на мокрую доску
> Зеленой садовой скамейки.
>
> Расти себе пышные брыжжи и фижмы,
> Вбирай облака и овраги,
> А ночью, поэзия, я тебя выжму
> Во здравие жадной бумаги.
>
> Poetry! suppose you an absorbent
> Aegean sponge, amongst this sticky verdure
> I'd have you placed, upon the dewy plank
> Of some green garden bench.

---

[1] Boris Pasternak, 'Neskol'ko polozhenii' ('Some Theses'), in *Sovremennik*, 1 (Moscow, 1922) 6. [*Works* (Later Poetry) III 153.]

[2] Ibid. p. 5 [*Works*, III 152.]

> Grow yourself sumptuous frills and farthingales,
> Soak up the cloud-caps and earth's furrowings,
> And come night, poetry, I shall squeeze you dry
> To the health and glory of the thirsting paper.

As we learn more of Pasternak's ideas on literature we are struck by the insistence of his warnings: don't disturb, don't frighten things away! These fears are largely directed against the habit of approaching nature with preconceived notions, and against thinking in ready-made stereotyped formulas that are not one's own, against cliché in the broad sense of this word. For Pasternak it was a necessary condition of art that the artist's perception of the world be powerful, pure and immediate, and innovation in art identical with the search for the greatest possible naturalness and truth to life. This is why, for instance, in his article on Chopin he observed that Chopin's work was 'utterly original, not because it is unlike its rivals but because it is like nature, from which he painted'.[1]

Such a view of art presupposes that the artist looks at the world anew and understands it as if for the first time. Pasternak saw the creative process as starting at the moment when we 'cease to recognize reality' and endeavour to speak of it with as little constraint and as little artificiality as would the first poet on earth; hence the emphases and aspirations characteristic of his poetry – the extraordinary and fantastic quality in everyday things, which he prefers to all fairy-tales and inventions; the morning freshness of his vision (his characteristic pose is that of a man who has just woken up – 'I wake. I'm embraced by things revealed. . . .'); and the sense of a newly created world in which everything that happens around him is new ('The whole steppe is as it was before the fall . . .').

His poetry is noticeably free from stylization. In his style and in his vision of the world there is no place for any kind of imitation except the imitation of nature. When he turns to a historical person, such as Balzac, he creates an image comparable to, say, the Balzac of Rodin, so originally does he embody him.

> Он грезит волей, как лакей,
> Как пенсией – старик бухгалтер,
> А весу в этом кулаке,
> Что в каменщиковой кувалде.

---

[1] Boris Pasternak, 'Chopin', in *Leningrad* (1945) XV–XVI 22. [*Works*, III 172.]

He is lost in dreams of freedom, like a lackey,
As an old man, a book-keeper, dreams about his pension,
And yet the weight in that clenched fist
Is what a stonemason has in his sledgehammer.

A poem dedicated to Anna Akhmatova begins by announcing:

Мне кажется, я подберу слова,
Похожие на вашу первозданность,
А ошибусь, – мне это трын-трава,
Я всё равно с ошибкой не расстанусь.

It seems to me I shall be picking words
To suit that first-hand quality you have,
And botch it, and yet make no bones about it,
Botching away in ways I shall not part with.

The poem continues, showing the essence of Akhmatova's poetry, but Pasternak remains himself. He does not write '*à la* Akhmatova'. Unable to part with his own 'mistake', he chooses his words not to resemble another's style, but to resemble the new-created quality of the world. This is why, in particular instances, Pasternak is not afraid of approaching sometimes very closely indeed to the classics, and does not fall into banality when he takes the risk of choosing as an epigraph such oft-anthologized lines as 'A little golden cloud slept on the breast of a giant rock',[1] or of opening a poem with the famous lines: 'On the shore of the empty waves/ He stood, full of mighty thoughts.'[2] Encounters like these with classical models hold no danger for him: the freshness of his vision and novelty of his manner insure him against literary echoings, and he can allow himself, as he does in *Themes and Variations*, to base a work wittingly upon traditional images, for he treats them in a wholly original way.

In his work as a poet Pasternak came into contact with a very wide range of works of art, of the past and of his own age. Though his ideas and style are very distinctly his own, his inclination is not to break with the past but to keep in constant touch with his cultural heritage and affirm a historical continuity in the development of art. This singled him out still further from the Futurists of the 1910s and 1920s, for theirs was a spirit of destruction and of breaking with artistic traditions.

In answer to a questionnaire in 1927 designed to show the attitude of

---

[1] Opening of a poem by Lermontov. *Translator*.
[2] Opening of Pushkin's 'Bronze Horseman'. *Translator*.

contemporary writers to classical literature Pasternak wrote: 'It seems to me that in our day there is less reason than ever to depart from the aesthetics of Pushkin. And by an artist's aesthetics I mean his idea of the nature of art, of the rôle of art in history and of his own responsibility to it.' In the same answer he partly explained in what specific ways Pushkin had influenced his work: 'The aesthetics of Pushkin is so broad and so elastic that one can interpret it differently at different stages in one's life. His impetuous descriptiveness even allows us to see him as an Impressionist, as I myself did see him fifteen years ago, in accordance with my own predilections as well as with the literary trends of the day. My conception of him is broader now and has come to contain a moral element.'[1]

It is also significant that in his early Futuristic phase Pasternak joined the Centrifuga group who, as distinct from the Cubo-futurists with their extremely aggressive tendencies, had a more tolerant attitude both towards the poetic tradition of the nineteenth century and towards their nearest teachers, the Symbolists.[2]

As for the 'legacy' of Russian Symbolism, Pasternak's sympathies lay with Annensky, Bely and – especially – Blok; in the work of these poets he sought above all that same 'impetuous descriptiveness', by which he meant something in the spirit of Impressionism and something that characterized his own writing of that time, for its chief quality was the 'vivid and instantaneous sketching of movement'. Many years later in his *Essay in Autobiography* (1956) Pasternak confesses that of the many and various qualities of Blok's poetry it was his 'headlong swiftness', the 'wandering intentness' of his glance, the 'fleetness' of his observations and descriptions, that were the closest to him personally and that left the greatest mark upon his style. 'Adjectives without a noun, predicates without a subject, alarm, excitement, hide-and-seek, abruptness, whisking shadows – how well this style accorded with the spirit of the time, itself secretive, hermetic, underground, only just out of the cellars and still using the language of conspiracy, the spirit of a time and of a tale in which the chief character was the town and the street was the chief event.... Of all the

---

[1] *Na literaturnom postu* (1927) v–vi 62.
[2] Recommending the poets of this group, Bryusov, for instance, noted that their Futurism 'is combined with an attempt to link their activity with the artistic work of preceding generations', and that they are 'more closely related to the legacy of the past'. (*Russkaya Mysl'* (June 1914).)

Petersburgs conceived by artists of our time, his is the most real....
And yet the features of this portrait of a town are drawn by so sensitive a hand and are so spiritualized, that the whole of it is also the absorbing image of a most remarkable inner world.'[1]

It is clear that Blok here receives, so to speak, a typical Pasternakian orchestration. This very individual and clearly expressed point of view regarding his predecessors and contemporaries is also to be found in his interpretations of Shakespeare, Verlaine, Rilke, Tolstoy, Chekhov, Mayakovsky and other writers who in one way or another are germane to him. In his aesthetic judgements and interpretations Pasternak is always biased and sometimes paradoxical. Here especially we see how profoundly original he was in combining a liking for the traditions of world art with the boldest spirit of innovation. In *Safe Conduct* he writes of his youth and of the influence of his immediate predecessors: 'What kind of art was it? It was the youthful art of Scriabin, Blok, Komissarzhevskaya, Bely – a forward-looking, exciting, original art. And it was so amazing that it not only did not provoke thoughts of its replacement, but on the contrary made you want to confirm it by repeating it all again from its very foundations, but more swiftly, fervently and wholly. You wanted to say it all again in a single breath, and this was unthinkable without passion, but passion kept leaping away to one side and in this way something new came into being. But the new came into being not as a substitute for the old, as is commonly supposed; on the contrary, it arose as an enraptured reproduction of the existing model.'[2]

In the striving to look at reality and poetry with new eyes, to refresh his aesthetic perception of the world and recreate his poetic system accordingly, Pasternak had much in common with a number of poets who on the eve of the Revolution and after it fought to free literature from antiquated forms. In this general movement embracing all spheres of art in the twentieth century, there was more than a little wastage, many empty attempts to be original, but there was also that healthy renovating force which is essential to the development of a genuinely modern art, and a real demand of life itself could be heard in it, for life does not submit to being described in the language of

---

[1] Pasternak archive. [This passage in English is taken from Boris Pasternak, *An Essay in Autobiography*, translated from the Russian by Manya Harari (1959) pp. 55–7.]

[2] Boris Pasternak, *Okhrannaya gramota* (*Safe Conduct*) pp. 91–2. [*Works*, II 267; *ND*, p. 107.]

outworn conventions and the clichés that we are all sick and tired of. Mayakovsky said, on this subject:

> И вдруг
> все вещи
> кинулись,
> раздирая голос,
> скидывать лохмотья изношенных имен.

> And at once
> all things
> propelled themselves
> rending the voice
> to throw off the rags, of threadbare names.

The same cry is heard in Pasternak's lines:

> Что в том, что на вселенной – маска?
> Что в том, что нет таких широт,
> Которым на зиму замазкой
> Зажать не вызвались бы рот?
>
> Но вещи рвут с себя личину,
> Теряют власть, роняют честь,
> Когда у них есть петь причина,
> Когда для ливня повод есть.

> What of it, that the way things are is masked?
> What of it, that there are no latitudes
> Such that against the winter putty would not
> Be stuffed in eagerly, to stop their mouths up?
>
> Ah but things tear the disguises from themselves,
> Lose their authority, and shed their honour,
> Whenever they have reason found for singing,
> Whenever there is pretext for a downpour.

As always when he speaks of a renewal of art Pasternak means that things must first be liberated from their literary impersonality, from the literary clichés that have masked them.

Seeking new words to restore individuality to the world Pasternak turned to the living colloquial language and thus took part in that decisive democratization of the poetic language which in the 1910s and 1920s affected many poets and ran most violently in the work of Mayakovsky. But Mayakovsky broadened his vocabulary by drawing on the language of the street which had begun to speak in its own full voice, mixing vulgarisms with the vocabulary of political speeches, and was led to this by the broadening of his subject matter, which came to include the town, the War, the Revolution, whereas Pasternak long continued to use the traditional themes well-worn by poets past and present. However, he spoke in a new way of the traditional springtimes and sunsets, he spoke of the beauty of nature not with the usual poetic banalities but with the words we currently use in our ordinary everyday prose. In this way he restored its lost freshness and its meaning for art, transforming a hackneyed subject into a vital event.

Pasternak did not disdain bureaucratic terms, words of common parlance or conversational idioms, but boldly brought the low language of life and of the modern city into the lofty diction of poetry. Forms worn down by daily use like coins that are passed from hand to hand now sounded fresh and unexpected. So the cliché in general use becomes a weapon in the fight against the literary cliché. Pasternak is inclined to express himself on the most exalted themes without ceremony, in homely language, and conveys the turbulent greatness of the Caucasus in the tone of simple everyday conversation: 'it was out of sorts', or 'the Caucasus was spread out as if on your hand and was all like a rumpled bed ...'. What is new in him is that he makes the world poetic with the help of prosaisms which pour the truth of life into his verses, so that they cease to be works of invention and become genuine poetry.

In the story *The Childhood of Luvers*, tracing the inner development of the heroine as she comes into collision with reality, Pasternak remarks: 'Life ceased to be a poetic trifle and began fermenting like a stern black fairy tale, in proportion as it became prose and turned into fact.'[1] In his work the prose of real fact is the source of the poetic, for it is through this that his images acquire authenticity. The following paradoxical statement by him becomes clear in connection with this: 'We pull everyday life into prose for the sake of poetry. We draw prose into poetry for the sake of music.'[2] Later, speaking of Shakespeare's *Romeo and Juliet*, he again declares that the prose in poetry

---
[1] Boris Pasternak, *Vozdushnye puti (Aerial Ways)* p. 20. [*Works*, II 100; *ND*, p. 204.]
[2] Boris Pasternak, *Okhrannaya gramota (Safe Conduct)* p. 22. [*Works*, II 216; *ND*, p. 32.]

is the bearer of life. 'This is an example of the very highest poetry of which the best models are always pervaded with the simplicity and freshness of prose.'[1]

Because of their prosaic and popular vocabulary Pasternak's images are very concrete; abstract ideas are made physical and are brought close to us. The syntactical and the rhythmical structure of his poems is subordinated to the same end; to create a poetry so supple that its tonality will evoke (but, of course, only evoke) the speech of conversation and will permit the poet to speak in verse just as freely as we speak in real life. He sets out his poetic sentence with all the complexity of subordinate phrases, interrupts himself and, just as in ordinary speech, leaves out certain connecting links, and, most important of all, seeks to create a free unfettered poetic idiom that will breathe in large breaths and will be based upon the unfolding of large unbroken intonational periods. The ability to think and speak not in separate lines but in whole stanzas, whole periods or phrases, is something that Pasternak especially valued in other poets; in particular, he spoke very highly of the verbal art of Tsvetayeva, which in this respect is like his own.

However, it was not simply a matter of making verse approximate to conversational forms. The natural and uninhibited intonation of his work is related to the larger aesthetic demand he made on himself – that a poet's perception be broad and entire, for its task was to recreate in verse some one single scene or atmosphere of life. One of his poems in which this is very tangibly felt is 'Death of the Poet', a poem dedicated to Mayakovsky: the life of the genius in the centuries, his sudden death, the talk and dumbfounded confusion of those who witness the catastrophe, the clamour of the spring street, which is presented both as a fragment of the drama that has broken out and as its wretched accompaniment – all this is gathered together and is set in motion by the irrepressible thrust of the voice that rushes after the event, encompasses it, flows around it and packs it into several periods rolling after each other with mighty cadence.

Не верили, считали-бредни,
Но узнавали от двоих,

[1] Boris Pasternak, 'Zametki k perevodam shekspirovskikh tragedii' ('Notes on the Translation of Shakespeare's Tragedies'), in *Literaturnaya Moskva* (Moscow, 1956) p. 798. [*Works*, III 198.]

Троих, от всех. Равнялись в строку
Остановившегося срока
Дома чиновниц и купчих,
Дворы, деревья, и на них
Грачи, в чаду от солнцепека
Разгоряченно на грачих
Кричавшие, чтоб дуры впредь не
Совались в грех, да будь он лих.
Лишь был на лицах влажный сдвиг,
Как в складках порванного бредня.

Был день, безвредный день, безвредней
Десятка прежних дней твоих.
Толпились, выстроясь в передней,
Как выстрел выстроил бы их.
Как, сплющив, выплеснул из стока б
Лещей и щуку минный вспых
Шутих, заложенных в осоку,
Как вздох пластов нехолостых...

They would not credit it, dismissed it as
So much wild talk – then two advised them, three,
Then all the world. There aligned themselves in the series
Of a term run out and halted
The houses of Mistress Clerk, of Mistress Huckster,
Yards of those houses, trees, and on the trees
The dulled rook, stupefied in the sun's eye, screamed
His inflamed curses after Mistress Rook
That, what the deuce, henceforward boobies should not
Obtrude their offices, bad cess to them.
Only upon the faces came a damp
Subsidence, as a tattered fishnet crumples.

A day there was, a blameless day, still more
Blameless than a dozen you have lived through.
They crowded in, they dressed their ranks in the forecourt
Like a shot, as if a shot had dressed them,
As if, though razed, there fountained out of channels
Pike and bream, as when a mine explodes,
So from the fire-squib charged and laid in the sedges
Was this exhaled as from sediments still ungelded.

Pasternak often introduces what appear to be digressions (like the rooks in the trees at the beginning of the poem) but in fact are a sign of the breadth and sweep of the intonation, for they draw into the action the whole of its environment, and leave no neutral background in the poem. Sometimes he seems to stumble and go back to what has already been said, starting again from the beginning, but then, having beaten all 'about the bush', he'll move on, putting the entire picture into the flow of speech which is very far from being arbitrary. Despite the immense amount of work put into them and the high degree of craftsmanship, Pasternak's poems do not give the impression of exquisitely fashioned *objets d'art*. On the contrary, their language is rather ungainly, in places so hampered as to be tongue-tied, with unexpected stoppages and repetitions; a speech of gulps and sobs, overloaded with words that get in one another's way. Later it was to become light, winged and transparent, but it would always keep the same quality of immediacy. It is in this naïve, artless outpour of words which seems at first sight not to be regulated by the poet but to be carrying him along with it that Pasternak achieves that naturalness of the live Russian language which he desires. In many respects we can apply to him what he wrote about Verlaine: 'He gave to the language in which he wrote that boundless freedom which was his own lyrical discovery and which is found only in the masters of prose dialogue in the novel and the drama. The Parisian phrase in all its virginal and bewitching accuracy flew in from the street and lay down entire in his lines, not in the least cramped, as the melodic material for the whole of the subsequent composition. Verlaine's principal charm lies in this directness and spontaneity. For him the idioms of the French language were indivisible. He wrote not in words but in whole phrases, neither breaking them into separate units, nor rearranging them. By comparison with the naturalness of Musset, Verlaine is natural without any anticipation, that is, he is simple not in order to be believed but so as to avoid disturbing the voice of life that bursts from him.'[1]

In Pasternak's works the organization of sounds in a line has a special significance. It is not just a question of rhyme, though his use of rhyme, too, is extremely new and varied (Bryusov had reason to consider him, even more than Mayakovsky, as the creator of a new kind of rhyme). In his poems, not only the ends of the lines rhyme but essentially any

[1] Boris Pasternak, 'Paul Marie Verlaine', in *Literatura i iskusstvo* (1 April 1944). [*Works*, III 171.]

words in the text can rhyme. Words are assimilated to each other in an original way by their sound, whether they stand side by side or are at some distance from each other.

> Париж в златых тельцах, в дельцах,
> В дождях, как мщенье, долгожданных. . . .

> Paris all golden calves and businessmen,
> All rains, like vengeance, long in coming. . . .

> Parízh v zlatýkh tel'tsákh, del'tsákh,
> V dozhdyákh, kak mshchénye, dolgozhdánnykh.

What we have here is something more than euphony and more significant than the melodious ordering of speech customary in poetry. Phonetic links are the expression of links of meaning, neighbouring images are fastened together by a similarity of sound which tells ultimately of the harmony of the different aspects of existence, interconnected and interpenetrating. The instrumentation of sound aids that transference of meaning from one object to another which is done by means of metaphor and which is provoked by the poet's aspiration to show and to stress the inner unity of the world. In Pasternak's figurative definition, rhyme is not a mere 'echoing of lines' but immensely more: in it is heard the 'roar of roots and meadows', through it the 'polyphony of worlds enters as truth into our little world'.

Such sharp attention to the 'acoustic character' of words, and their selection on a phonetic-semantic pattern, reminds one of Khlebnikov. But Khlebnikov invented a logic for phonetics, linking every sound with a definite abstract notion, a precise 'scale of energy' by which to calculate the laws for his poetic cosmogony. This linguistic rationalism, the notion that sounds possess an *a priori* necessary significance, is foreign to Pasternak, as is the emphasis Khlebnikov puts on the hidden abstract content of a word rather than on its concrete meaning. In his poems the bridges that are thrown between words that have sounds in common are not the bridges of abstract logic but bridges of metaphor and association, and they are built up upon the closeness of things to each other or simply on chance comparisons.

> Лодка колотится в сонной груди,
> Ивы нависли, целуют в ключицы,
> В локти, в уключины — о, погоди,
> Это ведь может со всяким случиться!

> The rowing-boat throbs in the drowsy breast,
> The osiers trail and kiss on bone,
> On throat and thole-pin – wait, this might
> Happen to anyone at all.

'Thole-pin' (*uklyuchini*: 'thole-pins') here appears side by side with 'throat' (*klyuchitsi*: 'collar-bones') for the same reason that willows kiss, and the boat rocks in the breast, that is, this is the Pasternakian world in which nature, human beings and things are all likened to each other, and the likeness is corroborated by phonetic resemblances.

In his poetry the frequent assonances and alliterations arise unintentionally, and as if involuntarily. They do not disrupt the basic conversational intonation. Like his metaphors, they are non-obligatory, fortuitous, for

> ... Чем случайней, тем вернее
> Слагаются стихи навзрыд.
>
> ... the more at random, so the more in fact
> Verses burst sobbing into composition.

In Pasternak's poems, Tynyanov writes, 'the fortuitous proves to be a stronger link than the strongest logical connection'. 'The link by which he joins things together is not one you already know, it is fortuitous, yet once he has provided it you seem to remember it, as if it had already been there somewhere – and the image becomes an obligatory one.'[1]

The explanation of this is to be sought in the peculiarities of Pasternak's language. We believe in the links (metaphorical, assonant, etc.) that he provides, however unexpected they are, just because they are expressed in a natural and ordinary way, with no strain, like something that is taken for granted. Here randomness merely assists naturalness. And the naturalness of intonation is a guarantee of the truthfulness of what is being said by the poem.

In the 1910s and 1920s Pasternak's poetry was often very complex and difficult. One obstacle to understanding was the way the language was over-saturated with imagery through the author's attempt to take into account and to convey in language all the manifold interconnections of life at once. Pasternak knew very well that if two objects are put side by

---

[1] Yuri Tynyanov, *Arkhaisti i novatori* (*Archaists and Innovators*) (Leningrad, 1929) pp. 566, 567. [See above, pp. 131, 132.]

side the combination of the two gives rise to a third thing. He persistently refused to divide the world into its parts and described a whole in which everything was whimsically and chaotically intermingled, where the poet did not forget for a moment 'what happens to the visible when it begins to be seen'.[1] So his complexity was a result of there being too many items. Nevertheless, by immersing nature in the flood of colloquial language, Pasternak got a great many notions up out of the sea-bed of their usual connotations and gave them new ones which, though borrowed from the familiar life of everyday, were unusual, for they had not been used before in such a combination. This most simple and natural means of expression was inaccessible to ears that had grown accustomed to the fact that the language of poetry was not the language of life.

In one of Edgar Allan Poe's stories experienced detectives searching for a stolen document find themselves utterly baffled, while all the time the thief has hidden it by putting it in the most prominent place he could find. The most obvious thing, explains the author, is often the very thing that eludes our attention. Something like this sometimes happens with Pasternak's images: they are 'unintelligible' because they are too close to us, too obvious.

For instance, in 'Death of the Poet', he says of the dead man:

> Ты спал, прижав к подушке щеку,
> Спал—со всех ног, со всех лодыг
> Врезаясь вновь и вновь с наскоку
> В разряд преданий молодых—

> You slept, you pressed the pillow with your cheek.
> You slept, and with clean heels, with raking strides,
> Now with one turn of speed, now with another, you
> Entered the constellation of young legends.

Here the immortality of Mayakovsky, the subject of the poem, is as convincing as it is, and marches into the future really, not figuratively, just because the words used for it are those of our ordinary life, of conversation, or of a matter-of-fact report. To meet these familiar terms in a poem is very rare and unexpected, and all the more so in a solemn lofty metre long inclined to verbal piety. Because a piety has

[1] Boris Pasternak, *Okhrannaya gramota (Safe Conduct)* p. 85. [*Works*, II 262; *ND*, p. 99.]

been violated, because the language is unorthodox and fresh, the reader may have the illusion of some sort of 'complexity', although the example quoted is in fact not complex in its form and one needs only to put off one's literary blinkers, the usual conventions for understanding a poetic text, to feel its direct and penetrating content.

Pasternak's linguistic innovation is to a large extent dictated by his search for the greatest possible unfettering and naturalness of expression. This he fully discovered and confirmed in his work of the thirties and, especially, the forties and fifties, which I shall dwell on later. In those years this tendency, previously cloaked under an irrepressible wealth of imagery, showed itself distinctly and was sharply intensified. But at first it was not obvious and acted, as it were, under cover, not often accessible to the reader, although the author was fully aware of it. At the beginning of the 1930s Pasternak wrote of this in his cycle of poems 'Waves':

> В родстве со всем, что есть, уверясь
> И знаясь с будущим в быту,
> Нельзя не впасть к концу, как в ересь,
> В неслыханную простоту.
>
> Но мы пощажены не будем,
> Когда ее не утаим.
> Она всего нужнее людям,
> Но сложное понятней им.

> Assuring yourself of kinship with all that is,
> And acquainted with what is to be, in your everyday,
> It is impossible not in the end to fall,
> As into a heresy, into unheard-of plainness.
>
> And yet we shall not be allowed exemption
> If we have not contrived to keep it dark.
> It is of all things most what people need,
> And yet they grasp the complicated sooner.

'Complicated' here means the hackneyed and stereotyped in poetry. Simplicity, on the other hand, is affirmed as the inner basis, the spur and the final goal of the efforts and explorations in poetry which at that stage he had not completed.

III

The depiction of nature holds the central place in Pasternak's poetry (landscape is often used to disclose the soul of man, feelings of love, and so on). Now let us turn and see how, with such an artistic system, Pasternak was able to paint pictures of contemporary history. Considerable advantages helped him here: his sensitive attention to the 'voice of life', and his freedom from pseudo-poetical canons forbidding the use of the base language of reality. It is well known that many poets in the first years of the Revolution had a lot of trouble precisely because of this sort of thing, for their language was limited to a meagre collection of conventional poeticalities. 'You can say "nightingale" but can't say "pulverizer",' Mayakovsky mocked them. The issue was that of poetry's right to use contemporary vocabulary.

Here Pasternak was quite secure: for him 'nightingale' did not exclude 'pulverizer', and his mature poetics was not poisoned by aestheticism. Something else that could be and was an obstacle was his understanding of the function and tasks of art, and the fact that he belonged to the type of poet who is concerned with the perception of life rather than with the decisive revolutionary alteration of it. His view of art as an organ of perception, his calling the artist an attentive and sensitive spectator (but not a direct participant in reforms) made him less able to embody our epoch in images that would convey its devastating stride adequately and immediately. Here he is the direct opposite of Mayakovsky who once remarked that he and Pasternak lived in the same house but in different rooms. The very notion of art as an organ of perception, the desire to drink in, to absorb, the living colours of nature, is foreign to Mayakovsky. He is wholly immersed in the events of history, affirming the active poetry of struggle, and sees nature itself primarily as material requiring to be processed ('If Mount Kazbek itself gets in your way, tear it down!'); he regards nature with a scornful condescension, while anything made by human hands he rates much higher than any 'little ants' and 'little grasses'. Defining poetry, Mayakovsky compares it to a tool, a weapon, manufacture, starting with the rioter's knuckle-duster and ending with the bayonet, the factory, and the extraction of radium. But Pasternak defines it for the most part through 'natural' images: 'It's a steeply brimming whistle, it's the cracking of crushed blocks of ice...', and so on. Mayakovsky puts the poet in the same group as the worker, the engineer, the politician, while Pasternak generally differentiates between these concepts and sometimes sees them as opposite to each other.

He formulated his idea of the different functions of poet and social activist most sharply and directly in *The Black Goblet*, an article written before the Revolution. Poet and hero, the lyrical and the historical, time and eternity are here seen as different and incompatible categories. 'Both are equally *a priori* and absolute', and the author, giving the 'soldiers of absolute history' their due, reserves for poetry the right not to be concerned with time, with the 'preparation of history for the next day'.[1]

In practice he departed from these ideas, expressed at a time when he was still immature as a writer, but echoes and variations of them in one form or another are still to be found in his later work. He is capable of handing on all the lofty titles which belong to history, to the man of action, and to the hero, nonetheless he sets aside from them the 'vacancy of the poet'.

In his relation to history, as to the whole of nature, the poet is a receptive sponge, a percipient, and not a hammer breaking up stone. The sponge absorbs the surrounding world, grows heavy with the tokens of the time, but does not become part of society and history in the same measure in which it is a part of nature. Pasternak's depiction of history seems that of someone who is outside it, which is not the case with his depiction of nature. The glance of this outsider is sometimes very acute, but it is that of an attentive observer, and not that of a person participating actively in events.

Pasternak called art the 'extreme of the age' (not something working parallel with it) and thought works of art were related to historical events as phenomena similar in kind but on different planes. Thus Tolstoy, in his view, was equal in genius to the Revolution. Thus, he saw in his own book *My Sister Life* a certain parallel to the revolutionary epoch with which it was contemporary, and even considered it a book about the Revolution, although the storms and dawns it spoke of were not the social ones but very ordinary ones, and to treat it as allegorical would be to give a very crude and forced interpretation.

Nonetheless, history did enter Pasternak's work, indeed entered it at a time when he was demonstratively refusing to have anything to do

[1] Boris Pasternak, 'Chërny bokal' ('The Black Goblet'), in *Vtoroi sbornik Tsentrifugi* (Moscow, 1916) p. 42. [*Works*, III 151.]

with it, pretending not to remember 'what millennium, my dears, is it out there'. War and revolution echoed through many of his descriptions of nature; they were marked with the clear imprint of history. In those years, 1915-17, he was already writing about 'skies on strike' and cavalry trucks on the ice: in memory of the year 1905 the spirit of 'soldiers' mutinies and summer lightnings' was borne through the air, clouds were likened to recruits and prisoners of war:

> Шли пыльным рынком тучи,
> Как рекруты, за хутор, поутру,
> Брели не час, не век,
> Как пленные австрийцы,
> Как тихий хрип,
> Как хрип:
> «Испить,
> Сестрица».

> Clouds moved over a dusty market square
> As recruits move, in the morning, past the farmstead.
> For hours, for centuries,
> Like Austrian prisoners,
> Like the hoarse whisper:
> 'Something to drink,
> Nurse.'

Nature takes on the attributes of other things, from the world of social storms and class collisions. Such a penetration of historical reality into the realm of nature came naturally to Pasternak, for he described the countryside as it is perceived by a contemporary town-dweller who takes along with him on his walks not only the facts of his daily life but also a chain of social and political associations, drawing meadows and groves into the circle of the events amongst which he lives his life.

After the Revolution these historicized landscapes are developed in a special way in Pasternak's work; sometimes they grow into a symbol of the whole of revolutionary Russia, as, for example, in his poem 'The Kremlin in a Storm at the End of 1918'. Here a snow-storm is combined with an immaterial whirlwind that rages over the open spaces of the new epoch and is borne headlong into the future. This is the elemental quality of the time, the Revolution's weather apprehended with enthusiasm and painted with the brush of a born landscape-painter.

> ... Последней ночью, несравним
> Ни с чем, какой-то странный, пенный весь,
> Он, Кремль, в оснастке стольких зим,
> На нынешней срывает ненависть.
>
> И грандиозный, весь в былом,
> Как визьонера дивинация,
> Несется, грозный, напролом,
> Сквозь неистекший в девятнадцатый.
>
> This night, last of the year, unmatchable
> With anything, all strange and all a spume,
> Itself, the Kremlin, rigged in so many winters,
> Upon the present one expends its rancour.
>
> And, all arrayed in the bygone, moves, majestic
> Like the divination of a seer,
> Terrible, not to be stayed, across the year
> Not yet elapsed, into a nineteenth year.

In a chapter intended for his autobiographical sketch, Pasternak recalls the events of 1917: 'Forty years have gone by. At such distance in time we no longer hear the voices of the crowds that met in discussion on summer squares under the open sky as in an ancient *veche*. But even at such a distance I still see these meetings, like soundless pageants, frozen *tableaux vivants*.... Simple people unburdened their hearts and talked about what was most important, about how to live and what to live for and by what means they could bring about the only thinkable and worthy kind of existence. The infectious universality of their enthusiasm erased the boundary between man and nature. In that famous summer of 1917, in the interval between two periods of revolution, it seemed that along with the people roads, trees and stars were holding meetings and making speeches. From one end to another the air was seized by a burning inspiration, a thousand versts long, and seemed a person with a name, clairvoyant and animate.[1]

Pasternak's descriptions of that turbulent era, with their cleansing showers, whirlwinds and snowstorms, did indeed have the task of conveying the 'universal meaning' of the Revolution. The theme of revolution is sensed here as a thrusting force, as the emotional tuning

[1] Archive of N. V. Bannikov.

of the images uniting the talk of the crowd with the meeting of roads and trees. It would be difficult to locate this sense, in his verse of that time, in any particular set of 'poems about the Revolution': it is ubiquitous and elusive as air, and the presence of air in his verse, as a higher spiritualizing principle, as the meeting-place of eternity and time, has always been his chief concern. Without being in the obvious sense works about the Revolution, many of his poems were written, so to speak, in its presence and thus were in tune with the loud music of that epoch.

> Мы были людьми. Мы эпохи.
> Нас сбило и мчит в караване,
> Как тундру, под тендера вздохи
> И поршней и шпал порыванье.
> Слетимся, ворвемся и тронем,
> Закружимся вихрем вороньим
> И – мимо! Вы поздно поймете.
> Так, утром ударивши в ворох
> Соломы, – с момент на намете –
> След ветра живет в разговорах
> Идущего бурно собранья
> Деревьев над кровельной дранью.

> Folk we were, but we are epochs now.
> Knocked down we were, and are whirled away in convoy
> As the tundra is, to the sound of the sighing tender,
> The pistons and the rush of the railway sleepers.
> We shall converge in flight, break through, collide,
> Spin in a whirlwind that is raven-winged.
> And – gone by, gone! It is later you will grasp it.
> Thus, of a morning, having swirled together
> Straws, from that moment over the sweepings wind
> Lives by its track amid the interchanges
> In the assembly, stormily proceeding,
> Of trees above the shingles of the roof.

When in the 1920s Pasternak turned directly to history this was connected with the unexpected awakening of epic tendencies in his art. In 1923 in *The Lofty Malady* he 'sends out a scout into the epic'; then follow the long poems *The Year 1905*, *Lieutenant Schmidt* (1925-7), and in 1930 the finishing of *Spektorsky*. Pasternak was so attracted by the epic at this time that, though but a short while before the most convinced lyrical poet, he announced: 'I regard the epic as a form inspired by the age, and therefore in my book *The Year 1905* I move from lyrical thinking to the epic, although this is very difficult.'[1] At the same time as this he expressed the opinion that 'lyric poetry has practically ceased to be heard in our age . . .'.[2]

Such an attitude to the tastes and needs of the age is extremely portentous, although of course lyric poetry had not ceased to be heard, as is shown by the work of Pasternak himself and of others. But, together with the growth of interest in the epic that had taken place everywhere in our literature at that time, we should consider the fact that it was Pasternak's peculiarity to work always with the greatest concentration and sense of purpose, and that he felt that his mission was to revive the very genre of the book of poetry as a compact unit. He used to mark out his creative path not by scattered poems but by books, which gained the significance of landmarks, turning-points in his life, and often marked a sharp change in the direction of his work. In the mid-1920s his whole preference was for the epic, which he worked at intensively, producing one long poem after another.

All these canvases are devoted to the revolutionary epoch. First, in *The Lofty Malady*, he 'gives us an epic which stands outside its subject and is like the slow rocking and gradual growing of a theme, with the realizing of it towards the end'.[3] The poet's speech, deliberately made difficult and slowed down, absorbs into itself the 'moving rebus' of events – pictures of revolution, war and destruction, not set out in the form of a consecutive narrative, but as if dissolved in the involuntary flow of the verse. The epic 'increases' as the narrator sings his rôle, 'rambles and mumbles on', using the diverse modulations of a flow of speech to convey the course of life:

> Хотя, как прежде, потолок,
> Служа опорой новой клети,
> Тащил второй этаж на третий
> И пятый на шестой волок,
> Внушая сменой подоплек,
> Что всё по-прежнему на свете,

---

[1] *Na literaturnom postu* (1927) IV 74. [2] *Molodaya gvardiya* (1928) II 199.
[3] Yuri Tynyanov, op. cit.

Однако это был подлог,
И по водопроводной сети
Взбирался кверху тот пустой,
Сосущий клекот лихолетья,
Тот, жженный на огне газеты,
Смрад лавра и китайских сой,
Что был нудней, чем рифмы эти,
И, стоя в воздухе верстой,
Как бы бурчал: «Что, бишь, постой,
Имел я нынче съесть в предмете?»

Although as in the past the roof
Has hauled, by propping up a fresh
Closet or so, the second floor
To third floor level, and has dragged
The fifth one up to reach the sixth,
Hinting, by this switch-about,
That the world is as it was before,
However this was nonetheless
A fake. For up the watersystem
Climbed that empty gurgling scream,
Hard times, and, scorched on a fire of newsprint,
A stink of laurels and chop-sueys,
Worse tedium, even, than these verses,
And stretching up in the air like a pole,
It seemed to rumble: 'Here, hold on,
Wasn't there something I was going to eat?'

The Lofty Malady is an attempt to approach the creation of an epic by strictly linguistic means. It is essentially a long-drawn-out lyrical digression which, starting from certain contemporary facts, tries to grasp the age with epic breadth and to throw light on its image by other methods than those of plot: through imagery, syntax, and the varying intensity of the voice.

Pasternak wrote this poem in 1923, and some years later he continued and concluded it with some stanzas dedicated to Lenin. These recreate the irrepressible energy of Lenin's thought and belong among the best depictions of him in Soviet literature. At the beginning the voice of the poet is confused and retarded, but by the end it has acquired a special urgency, becoming strong and full of intense will-power, which seems to be carried into the verse straight from Lenin's tribune:

> Он был – как выпад на рапире.
> Гонясь за высказанным вслед,
> Он гнул свое, пиджак топыря
> И пяля передки штиблет.
> Слова могли быть о мазуте,
> Но корпуса его изгиб
> Дышал полетом голой сути,
> Прорвавшей глупый слой лузги.

> He was like the thrust of a fencing foil.
> He drove behind the thing he'd said.
> Making his coat stand out, and staring
> With the toe-caps of his boots, he pressed
> His own point home. It could have been
> Crude oil he spoke of, his arching frame
> Was all a trajectory of pure essentials
> Which had broken through the layers of rubble.

In the long poems written after *The Lofty Malady* Pasternak uses forms of narrative more distinctively epical. But he still does not give much room to the depiction of individual destinies and characters. Even in *Lieutenant Schmidt* his attention is chiefly devoted to reproducing the very spirit of the age and to unfolding a broad historical panorama. A lightly sketched and wide-flung imagery, a wash of colour which gives everything unity, while simultaneously erasing the contours of individual characters, and which is itself full of substance and content – these are the distinctive features of Pasternak's writing, in poetry and in prose:

> Неужто жив в охвате той картины,
> Он верит в быль отдельного лица? –

> Can it be that, having lived in the scope of that picture,
> He believes in an individual's existence?

the author inquires of the reader, constantly recalling in *Spektorsky* that:

> О личностях не может быть и речи,
> На них поставим лучше тут же крест, –

> Of personalities there can be no question.
> We'd better say goodbye to them right here.

D.L.P.

that even the person whose name is the title of the poem is really of little interest to us:

> Я стал писать Спекторского в слепом
> Повиновеньи силе объектива.
>
> Я б за героя не дал ничего
> И рассуждать о нем не скоро б начал,
> Но я писал про короб лучевой,
> В котором он передо мной маячил.

> Blindly I began to write 'Spektorsky',
> Merely obeying the power of the objective.
>
> I wouldn't have given a fig for my hero,
> Nor would I soon have started to discuss him,
> But I was writing about the cage of rays
> Which he was in, hovering before my eyes.

What Pasternak cares about is the breadth of vision, the general perspective, not Spektorsky but the spectrum in which he is placed, the piece of history torn out of the past by a ray of memory. In the structure of the poem a special rôle is played by the movement of memories, according to the logic of which the separate figures, episodes and parts are linked together and the vast historical picture is gradually reconstructed.

This broad unfolding of the theme is felt in particular in the way the motif of space becomes fraught with meaning in these poems: it embraces wide horizons, temporal and spatial distances, and the attempt to look all around oneself and take in all that the eye can see. 'Space is asleep, in love with space' – such is the world revealed to the poet, the world of history set in geometrical dimensions. Space becomes the spur to creation ('the very surveyability of space demanded poems from me...'), the motive principle of the plot ('Now through the visions of impassioned space, Let us turn our tale back by one year...'), the hero of the work, and the force which creates heroes, its elect. Schmidt, whom it makes into a hero, learns 'how easily homeless space can fall in love'.

Pushing out the frames of the narrative to their very limit, Pasternak forces images from the most varied levels into the space which has formed. There are people, sketched in with a few strokes, landscapes that have taken on human passions or the features of the age, whole classes, estates and groups, plus an account of concrete historical events. History, like nature, is described whole, all at once, in the kaleidoscopic interaction of flashing parts, and the chief emphasis is given to the *general* picture of life. In the poem *The Year 1905* there pass in succession fathers and children, peasants and factory workers, sailors and students. A storm at sea merges into an uprising on the *Potemkin*, and in the days of the December fighting on the Presnya 'the sun looks through its binoculars and listens attentively to the guns'. There are strands that lead from particular incidents to the general situation, to the destinies of the State:

> С каждым кругом колес артиллерии
> Кто-нибудь падал
> Из прислуги,
> И с каждой
> Пристяжкою
> Падал престиж.

> With every spin of the artillery's wheel
> Someone or other fell
> Of the gun-crew,
> And with every
> Horse in the team of the gun
> There fell prestige.

Heterogeneous objects and concepts are brought together under a single token:

> Снег лежит на ветвях,
> В проводах,
> В разветвлениях партий
> На кокардах драгун
> И на шпалах железных дорог.

> Snow lies along the boughs,
> Along the wires,
> Along the ramifications of parties,
> And on the dragoons' cockades,
> And on the sleepers of the railway line.

Pasternak likes to write in lists, collections, enumerations, bringing together objects from various spheres of life and putting them all together in a row. In a few lines he will give a summary picture which nevertheless has specific details and seems created with a single sweep of the hand. A momentary impression of totality is achieved in a cursory sketch. He employs this manner both to give a general characterization of the age and to recount particular episodes, such as the law-court scene in *Lieutenant Schmidt*:

> Скамьи, шашки, выпушка охраны,
> Обмороки, крики, схватки спазм.
> Чтенье, чтенье, чтенье, несмотря на
> Головокруженье, несмотря
> На пары нашатыря и пряный,
> Пьяный запах слёз и валерьяны,
> Чтение без пенья тропаря,
> Рама, и жандармы-ветераны,
> Шаровары и кушак царя,
> И под люстрой зайчик восьмигранный.

> Benches, sabres, braid on the men of the guard,
> Faintings, screeches, spasm of a brawl,
> Reading, reading, reading out, despite the
> Heads whirled and swimming, and despite
> The fumes of sal ammoniac and the spicy
> Drunken fragrance of valerian and tears,
> Reading out with no responses chanted,
> The veteran policemen and the frame,
> The sash and sharovari of the tsar,
> And under the chandelier a light-ray eight ways shafted.

Pasternak's way of depicting – indeed of perceiving – history is close to that of Blok. They are alike in their ability to catch the basic rhythm of the age, not merely in the manifest course of events taking place on a single level of reality but in all the spheres of life; they are also alike in their attempt to find some common historical equivalent to everything that takes place and to show all the constituent parts of the world as making up a single unified whole, whether this be a picture of revolution, an earthquake, or love. In the preface to his *Retribution*, Blok brings together things of such different character as the Beyliss case and the hey-day of French wrestling in the St Petersburg circuses, the heat of summer and strikes in London, the development of aviation and the assassination of Stolypin. 'All these facts,' he concludes, 'though apparently so diverse, have for me a single musical sense. It is my habit to put together the facts, drawn from all spheres of life, which are within the field of my vision at a given moment, and I am convinced that together they always create a single musical force.'[1] As we know, Blok constructed his historical panoramas upon just such collisions of outwardly contradictory but inwardly harmonious facts, for example in his portrayal of the nineteenth and twentieth centuries in *Retribution*.

Pasternak sees the indicia of the age with a similar sharpness of vision: scattered everywhere, they give every object a special meaning, making it point to something. In his long poems he also seeks the common denominator shared by human acts, sunsets and city streets. If he writes, for instance, of the time of the Russo-Japanese War, which happened on the eve of the Revolution, he makes everything, including the Kiev hippodrome, speak of the agitated state of the world. History penetrates all life's pores, transforming the minutest details of every situation into a likeness of itself.

> Поля и даль распластывались эллипсом.
> Шелка зонтов дышали жаждой грома.
> Палящий день бездонным небом целился
> В трибуны скакового ипподрома.
>
> Народ потел, как хлебный хвас на леднике,
> Привороженный таяньем дистанций.
> Крутясь в смерче копыт и наголенников,
> Как масло били лошади пространство.
>
> А позади размерно бьющим веяньем
> Какого-то подземного начала
> Военный год взвивался за жокеями
> И лошадьми и спицами качалок.
>
> О чем бы ни шептались, что бы не́ пили,
> Он рос кругом и полз по переходам
> И вмешивался в разговор и пепельной
> Щепоткою примешивался к водам.

---

[1] Aleksandr Blok, *Polnoye sobranie stikhotvorenii v dvukh tomakh* (Complete works in two volumes), 1 (Leningrad, 1946) 530.

> Fields and distances sprawled elliptical.
> Silks of umbrellas breathed a thirst for thunder,
> The scorching day was aiming a depthless sky
> Into the stands around the hippodrome.
>
> The folk perspired, like yeasty kvass in the cooler,
> Mesmerized by the melt of distances.
> Turning in spurts of hooves and stockinged fetlocks,
> Horses beat like butter the open stretches.
>
> But behind it all, like the evenly treading pulse
> Of a source of some kind underneath the earth,
> The year of war climbed up behind the jockeys,
> Behind their mounts, and the staves of rocking-chairs.
>
> Whatever they whispered of, whatever they drank,
> It grew around, it crept through passages,
> It intervened in conversations; ashy,
> A pinch of it adulterated water.

By turning to historical themes and the description of objective reality Pasternak was able to clarify his complex imagery; this change is particularly noticeable in *The Year 1905*. Gorky, who had been rather critical of Pasternak's poems, wrote to him on receiving this book: 'It is an excellent book, one of those whose value is not immediately recognized but which is destined for a long life. To be frank, before this book I have always read your poems with a certain effort, for they are excessively saturated with imagery, and the images are not always clear to me; my *imagination* found it difficult to contain your images, capriciously complicated as they are and often incompletely drawn. You know yourself that their abundance often makes you speak – or paint – too sketchily. In *1905* you are simpler and more chary of words; you're more classical in this book, which is filled with a pathos that infects me, as a reader, very quickly, easily and powerfully. Yes, it is indeed an excellent book. This is the voice of a genuine poet, and of a social poet, social in the best and profoundest sense of the word.'[1]

As is clear from their correspondence, Gorky and Pasternak did not wholly understand each other. 'An admirer of classical poetry', Gorky

---

[1] 'Gor'ki i sovetskie pisateli. Neizdannaya perepiska' ('Gorky and Soviet Writers. Unpublished correspondence'), in *Literaturnoye nasledstvo*, LXX (Moscow, 1963) 300. [See above, pp. 23–4.]

preferred more traditional forms in modern poetry too. 'For me Khodasevich is immeasurably greater than Pasternak, and I am convinced that the latter's talent will ultimately lead him onto the hard path Khodasevich took, the path of Pushkin,'[1] he said in 1922 in a letter to E. K. Ferrari. And a few years later, inscribing for Pasternak a presentation copy of his novel *The Life of Klim Samgin*, Gorky confessed that Pasternak's 'chaos' was alien to him and he wished him 'more simplicity'. 'You have a wrong idea of me,' Pasternak replied, 'I have always striven for simplicity and shall never cease to do so.'[2] His subsequent development shows how this striving was fulfilled.

From his correspondence with Gorky we learn what an immense effect the first part of *The Life of Klim Samgin* had on him; he was impressed above all by the re-creation of historical atmosphere. In his judgement of this novel and other opinions he expressed at this time as to how he visualized a work whose subject was the recent past, one cannot but sense Pasternak's own interests and tastes; he was at this time working on a historico-revolutionary subject. Space, all flung 'with changing colours', dammed up with 'crowding details', 'the noting down of a thing from all angles at once'; 'history's essence—which consists in the chemical regeneration of each one of its moments' —seized and transmitted 'with the violence of inspiration'[3]—Pasternak's descriptions of the character and texture of the epic tell us of his own method of depicting history.

IV

Because his images are so saturated with the general atmosphere of reality it is impossible to draw a line between the 'more important' and the 'less important' in his poems, or to distinguish the central thread of the story from its 'background'. The 'background' itself is extremely active and often turns out to be the foreground. In the lives of his heroes chance has the character of providence and acquires paramount importance in the development of the narrative. Thus in *Spektorsky* there are unexpected meetings, random discoveries, fragments, things half said, all deliberately unmotivated, snatched 'at a run' or 'unawares', as if by the will of chance, and all these play an important part in the portrayal of the intelligentsia, which reacts in a number of different ways to the

[1] Ibid. p. 568.   [2] Ibid. pp. 308, 307.   [3] Ibid. pp. 304–5.

events of the Revolution and which is scattered over the world, down the roads and cross-roads of history. The movement of his subject is confused and interwoven; he will begin telling a story of events on a grand historical scale and then continue it, without transition, in the description of some interior scene or of a landscape, in some everyday incident or in an unexpected acquaintance with a particular person.

Here is an example of how the chain of events stretches 'across the sky', 'across the air'; the events belong to various levels of existence but they are united and made audible by the theme of revolution which is now glimpsed in a landscape, now uttered in a broad symbolical generalization, now – switching the action from Moscow to the Urals – embodied in the concrete figure of a woman revolutionary. For the sake of abbreviation we are omitting some stanzas and directing the reader's attention to the 'aerial way' of the heroine who for Pasternak personifies the moral sources and universal significance of the Russian Revolution:

> Случается: отполыхав в признаньях,
> Исходит снегом время в ноябре,
> И день скользит украдкой, как изгнанник,
> И этот день – пробел в календаре....
>
> Вдруг крик какой-то девочки в чулане.
> Дверь вдребезги, движенье, слезы, звон,
> И двор в дыму подавленных желаний,
> В босых ступнях несущихся знамен.
>
> И та, что в фартук зарывала, мучась,
> Дремучий стыд, теперь, осатанев,
> Летит в пролом открытых преимуществ
> На гребне бесконечных степеней....
>
> И вот заря теряет стыд дочерний.
> Разбиз окно ударом каблука,
> Она перелетает в руки черни
> И на ее руках за облака....
>
> Угольный дом скользил за дом угольный,
> Откуда руки в поле простирал.
> Там мучили, там сбрасывали в штольни,
> Там измывался шахтамн Урал....

Там по юрам кустились перелески,
Пристреливались, брали, жгли дотла,
И подбегали к женщине в черкеске,
Оглядывавшей эту ширь с седла.

Пред ней, за ней, обходом в тыл и с флангов,
Курясь, ползла гражданская война,
И ты б узнал в наезднице беглянку,
Что бросилась из твоего окна.

По всей земле осипшим морем грусти,
Дымясь, гремел и стлался слух о ней,
Марусе тихих русских захолустий,
Поколебавшей землю в десять дней.

It happens time, that blazed in showings forth,
Come November melts out into snow,
And day glides self-effacing as an exile,
And that day is a blank in calendars....

Of a sudden a shriek of some little girl in a boxroom,
Door broken down, much movement, tears, high voices,
The yard is a fume of long repressed desires
And a pad of bare feet, all a rush of flags.

And she that huddled in her apron, harried,
Her dense-grown shamefastness, beside herself
Now, through a gap of opportunities opened
Flies, high on a surge of limitless advancements....

And see, the dawn flings off her daughterly
Shamefastness, shattering panes with a kicking heel,
It wings across into the rabble's arms
And on those arms it wings on past the clouds....

A house on a corner slid by a house on a corner
Whence hands were stretched out towards the open field.
There once they tortured, threw into shafts of pits,
There jeered, with their mine-galleries, the Urals....

There across open spaces clustered spinneys.
They set their sights, they sacked them, burned to cinders,
And ran to the woman in the cossack coat
Surveying these broad stretches from the saddle.

> Before her and behind her, by feints to her rear out flanking,
> Smoking there crept along the Civil War,
> And in the horsewoman you would have known
> The one on the run who hurled herself out of your window.
>
> Across the entire earth, in a sea of grief
> Gone hoarse, there smoked, there rumbled rumour of her,
> From Russia's quiet fastnesses Marusya
> Who in ten days had set the earth ashake.

Who is she, this 'fugitive'? The dawn? A sudden gust of time and space? A popular uprising? A woman whose social and mental emancipation the poet treats as the most worthy achievement, as the moral imperative of the Revolution? Clearly she is all these at once: Pasternak always strives to get several levels of reality into a single unfragmented perception of the world. Fundamental to his epic compositions is the demand, which he also expresses in *Spektorsky*: 'Poetry, do not sacrifice your breadth.'

Pasternak is more likely to tell us what the weather was like at a certain moment in history than to give a consistent exposition of the order and movement of events. The content of an event is revealed through the things bordering upon it, contiguous with it, or through the atmosphere enveloping or accompanying it, or prefiguring it in the manner of a prelude. To illumine the most various things or processes he tends to write prefaces to them or to write about their side issues (which then turn out to have been after all an account of the main thing); often his gaze will 'wander' and fix itself not on the thing he is talking about but on its prehistory, or its origination, or its general environment. He likes to define a thing through the boundaries it shares with neighbouring things; in lines about a town he will describe the suburb, and a poem about the first of May will be dated 30 April.

> Как я люблю ее в первые дни,
> Когда о елке толки одни!
>
> How fond I am of it, those early days
> When the Christmas tree is as yet only talked of!

This aspect of Pasternak's artistic vision is especially prominent in the poems he wrote in the 1930s–1950s (when the epic aspirations disappeared from his verse and were developed in his prose). For instance, the cycle of poems called 'Waves', with which the book

Second Birth (1932) opens, is entirely constructed as the introduction to a theme, but the introduction unfolds and unfolds until one realizes that it is itself the real theme. In it the poet speaks of what he wishes to write: and this intention, this promise, turns into a description of our world; for our world recedes wave-like into the future, is not yet completely embodied, hides in itself certain new possibilities and intentions – and these resemble the plans inspiring the poet which are also only half-expressed and rolling onward into the future. Thus the form of the introduction turns out to be an extremely capacious one, rich in content, and in harmony with the idea of historical and poetic development which is fundamental to it.

In Pasternak's next books, *On Early Trains* (1943), *The Vast Earth* (1945), *When the Weather Clears* (1957), we again see the very original way in which his poetry adapts itself to the reality of history. There are not many direct comments on events. But – and this is the main thing to emphasize – whenever he does offer loud direct comments on contemporary issues, as in certain poems about the Second World War (for example, 'A Terrible Tale', 'The Conqueror') his writing is noticeably inferior to the poems on the same subjects where instead of the pathos of the publicist's style he uses the mode of the personal lyric or the landscape-painting which has always been peculiarly his ('The Outpost', 'Approach of Winter' and others), and the best poems, filled with an awareness of history and of the present, often sound like an introduction or foreword to the future, and most of them convey the condition of the age through inconspicuous movements in nature and in the soul of the poet, through current details of everyday experience. Thus in the poem 'Spring' (1944), where the end of the War is in the air, the poet tries to capture the voice of the time in the respiration of ordinary life, which seems extraordinarily significant and full of promise:

> Всё нынешней весной особое.
> Живее воробьев шумиха.
> Я даже выразить не пробую,
> Как на душе светло и тихо.
>
> Иначе думается, пишется,
> И громкою октавой в хоре
> Земной могучий голос слышится
> Освобожденных территорий.

> All things are special in this present spring,
> Livelier the rumpus of the sparrow.
> I am not even trying to convey
> How clear I am in the spirit, how at rest.
>
> Thinking goes otherwise, so does writing,
> And up and down a thunderous octave sounds
> The potent voice of earth, a unison
> Chorusing from liberated countries.

Just as in the poems of the revolutionary period and of the 1920s the countryside took on the features of historical being and became full of the storms of the Kremlin and the noise and the talk of trees holding meetings, now in reverse in his later poetry history itself begins to resemble nature, its processes are those of growing and ripening – processes which have impressive results and yet are hidden and imperceptible, like the way grass grows or the seasons change ('Grass and Stones', 'After the Storm'). Of course, this marks not only a development in his style but also a change in his interests as an artist and is connected with changes in the world around him, of which he now sees new aspects. Pasternak is concerned with things of a moral order, things that concentrate not on the front stage of life but in its depth, and express themselves quietly, unobtrusively, in those daily habits, those simple incidents in the life of the nation and the person, which he believes to be the very core of history.

He was always attracted by 'life without pomp and circumstance'. But from the 1930s he more and more clearly prefers subjects that lie as it were on the periphery of the social world but are filled with a latent historical significance (see, for example, his poem 'On Early Trains'). As he said in one of his speeches, he felt that 'everything noisily high-pitched and rhetorical is without foundation and useless, and sometimes even morally dubious'.[1] The poet now feels a special affinity with provincial Russian country roads, cottages, jetties and ferry boats, with unsophisticated feelings, and simple people doing humble work. Nature herself finds her correlatives among these things: a fragrant tobacco plant is compared to a stoker off duty; spring puts on a warm jacket and makes friends in the cattle yard.

---

[1] 'O skromnosti i smelosti. Rech' tov. Borisa Pasternaka' ('On Modesty and Boldness. Speech by Comrade Boris Pasternak'), in *Literaturnaya gazeta* (16 Feb 1936). [*Works*, III 219.]

The prosaic and conversational idiom, which was already a source of his poetry, now acquires an additional *raison d'être*, the ethical one that it emphasizes his democratic sympathies, his distaste for the grand bombastic phrase.

At the same time Pasternak embodies in his verse his views on fate, on the individual's vocation and his place in history. Human personality is the bearer of high moral values; it is something outwardly inconspicuous (the common and the great are closely related for him, every man being potentially a genius, while genius is simple and unobtrusive); it lives unspectacularly a profound inner life and performs the feat of voluntary self-sacrifice, self-giving, in order that life shall triumph (life in its fullest, universal sense – of history, the world's whole being). Seeing a deep connection between the 'microcosm' and the 'macrocosm' Pasternak ascribes to the individual personality an absolute meaning – yet not separately from life, nor against it, but in union and harmony with it. In a letter to Kaisyn Kuliev (25 November 1948) he explains his view on the fate of man, on the vocation of talent, like this: 'The amazing thing is that an innate talent is a child's model of the universe which has been placed in the heart in infancy, a teaching aid for understanding the world from within, in its best and most amazing aspect. Talent teaches honesty and impartiality, because it discovers what a fabulous amount honesty contributes to the whole dramatic plan of existence. The gifted person knows just how much life gains when it is illumined completely and properly and how much it loses in the half-dark. It is personal interest that makes him proud and makes him aspire to the truth. Such a situation, with its advantages and fortune, may also be a tragedy; this is of secondary importance.'

In his poetry Pasternak develops the idea that the individual human being has an exalted historical mission. From *Lieutenant Schmidt*, where the moral ideal of man is embodied in the protagonist (Schmidt sacrifices himself, performing an act of historical renewal and accepting his tragic fate as his due), through the lyric poems of the 1930s and the war period, there run strands of connection to the works written at the end of his life. Light is thrown on their philosophical content by the observations Pasternak made on Shakespeare's *Hamlet*, which he was then translating: 'Hamlet renounces himself, in order to "do the will of Him who sent him". *Hamlet* is not the drama of a man who lacks character but a drama of duty and self-renunciation. When it becomes plain that the real and the apparent are not one but that a gulf divides them, then it is not important that a reminder of the world's falseness comes in supernatural form and that the ghost demands vengeance from Hamlet. What is far more important is that Hamlet is chosen by the will of chance to be a judge of his time and a servant of that which is more remote. *Hamlet* is a drama of high destiny, of a great deed entrusted from above, a heroic predestination.'[1]

Pasternak's later poetry discloses his attitudes to the world and his age in a rather different perspective from his earlier work. The idea of moral service becomes the prevalent one, although he continues to affirm the perceptive power of poetry and its ability to seize a living picture of reality (for him the essential thing in the artist's world-picture always was the moral element). While his central idea of art was formerly that expressed in the image of 'poetry as a sponge', now, without cancelling out the old one, a new motif reigns: 'the object in composition is to give yourself entire.' At the same time the consciousness of having fulfilled his own historical destiny sounds clearly and with full force. Hence the exceptionally bright tonality of his late poetry, notwithstanding tragic notes in certain poems, and hence the dominant feeling of confidence in the future.

There are a number of points in Pasternak's moral conception of history as well as in his view of the tasks proper to art which, although they show him to be close to his age, yet call in question some of its assumptions and demands. 'You are a suburb, not a refrain,' he said to poetry. Poetry embraces reality and borders it closely, as a suburb a town, but it does not reiterate word for word generally recognized truths. Such an analogy, which corresponds to the very structure of Pasternak's images, conveys, to some extent, the nature of his connections with his age and his divergences from it.

Pasternak's peculiar view of art is so organic to his vision as a whole that similar ideas and practices are to be found even in his translations, which from the 1930s onward occupied a very important place in his work. As a translator Pasternak tries to recreate above all the spirit of the original, to the neglect of details and literal accuracy. Like reality, the work of a genius does not require literal translation but seeks its equivalent in genius which – ideally – inspired by the original which

---

[1] Boris Pasternak, 'Zametki k perevodam shekspirovskikh tragedii' ('Notes on the Translation of Shakespeare's Tragedies'), in *Literaturnaya Moskva* (Moscow, 1956) p. 797.

it starts from, is harmonious with it and has 'its own unrepeatability'. According to Pasternak the translator must not take a mould of the object he is copying but must transmit its vital and poetic force, thus transforming a copy into an original creation that can live on a level with the original in another linguistic system.

It is clear that his thoughts on the art of translation are very like his thoughts on art as such. He is striving 'more than anything for that conscious freedom without which one can never come close to great works'.[1] Comparing his own work with that of other translators, Pasternak said: 'we don't compete with anyone in individual lines but argue with whole passages; in constructing them, at the same time as preserving fidelity to the great original, we enter into an ever greater subordination to our own system of speech ...'.[2] 'The relation between an original and a translation ought to be that of a premiss and a conclusion derived from it, or of a parent tree and its sapling. The translation must come from an author who has experienced the influence of the original for a long time before he sets to work translating it. It must be the fruit of the original and its historical consequence.'[3]

Pasternak's best translations ripened in him for years, while he prepared himself for them by the very process of his inner development. In a certain sense they are even autobiographical. For instance his translations of Georgian poetry were corroborated by his visits to Georgia in 1931 and 1936, by a friendship of many years with several Georgian poets, and finally by the grateful love for the Georgian land, people and culture with which many of his own poems are imbued. They could be called an 'offshoot' of Georgia in his life and work.

Pasternak's translation of *Hamlet* appeared in a separate edition in 1941, marking the beginning of a series of translations of Shakespeare's tragedies. But in a poem written in 1923 we already find an idea which he was to develop in his activity as a translator. 'O, all of Shakespeare is, perhaps, in this, that Hamlet converses freely with a ghost.' 'To converse freely', that is, to talk about the loftiest matters without inhibition

---

[1] Boris Pasternak, 'Ot perevodchika (Predislovie k perevodu "Gamleta" Shekspira)' ('From the Translator (Foreword to the translation of Shakespeare's *Hamlet*)'), in *Molodaya gvardiya* (1940) v–vi 16. [*Works*, III 191.]

[2] Boris Pasternak, 'Novy perevod "Otello" Shekspira' ('A New Translation of Shakespeare's *Othello*'), in *Literaturnaya gazeta* (9 Dec 1944).

[3] Boris Pasternak, 'Zametki perevodchika' ('Notes of a Translator'), in *Znamya* (1944) I–II 166. [*Works*, III 183.]

and in everyday language, is, as we have seen, the rule with Pasternak. Other of his qualities make him akin to Shakespeare's realism, freedom, and pictorial vividness. 'The influence of the original' (not of course always a direct one but often complicated, refracted in the various phenomena of world culture) in this case began long before his actual work on Shakespeare's tragedies and to some extent coincided with his own interests and plans. This is why Shakespeare took root so deeply in Pasternak, and why his translating work, which was influenced by his predilections and manner as a poet, had in its turn an influence on his original work. In this close and at the same time extremely free commerce with Shakespeare, whose greatness and power he sought to convey 'in its own unrepeatability', he realized in practice his theoretical conviction that 'translations are not a method of getting acquainted with particular works, but a medium of the age-old intercourse of cultures and peoples'.[1]

V

The meaning of existence, the purpose of man, the essential nature of the world – these are the questions that agitated Pasternak over many years, especially toward the end of his life when it could be said that he devoted the whole of his poetry to the search for fundamentals, the divining of ultimate ends and primal causes.

> Во всём мне хочется дойти
> До самой сути:
> В работе, в поисках пути,
> В сердечной смуте.
>
> До сущности протекших дней,
> До их причины,
> До оснований, до корней,
> До сердцевины.

> In everything I need to get
> Through to the kernel:
> In work, in the seeking of the road forward,
> In the mob-rule of the heart;

[1] Ibid.

> Through to the quality of times gone,
> Through to their cause
> And ground. Down to the root,
> The marrow.

Pasternak's whole work is characterized by the inclination to make sense of life philosophically; poet and thinker, he is drawn to an art of broad generalizations and large spiritual content. From very early in his life he had felt an affinity to 'that depthless spirituality without which there can be no originality, that infinity which opens up at any point in life, in any direction, without which poetry is just a misunderstanding, temporarily unexplained'.[1] In many of his works, at widely different periods, one senses the insistent desire to 'dig down to the very essence' and to show us, not just what the things he is talking about are like in themselves, but what their primordial nature is.

> Мой друг, ты спросишь, кто велит,
> Чтоб жглась юродивого речь?
> В природе лип, в природе плит,
> В природе лета было жечь.

> My friend, you ask who stablishes
> That the speech of holy simpletons should burn?
> It was in the nature of limetrees, and of roof-tiles,
> And in the nature of summer that it burn.

He does not say 'the summer was hot', but 'it lay in the nature of summer to burn' – this is a typical poetic process in Pasternak.

This concern for essences and for the nature of things puts the poet in a very interesting and ambiguous relationship with Impressionism, traces of which can be seen in his work (especially his early work): critics often called him an Impressionist. He is related to the Impressionists by the purity and immediacy of his perceptions, and by the pathos of receptivity to impressions and sensations. Some of his images make one think of paintings by Monet and Renoir, Pissarro and Vuillard. He often tries, like these painters, to set down his momentary impressions of objects and, laying aside his previous knowledge of the world, to depict it just as he sees it at a given moment. Here is an example of a sketch done in an impressionistic spirit:

---

[1] Boris Pasternak, *Okhrannaya gramota (Safe Conduct)* p. 100. [*Works*, II 273; *ND*, p. 116.]

Гремели блюда у буфетчика.
Лакей зевал, сочтя судки.
В реке, на высоте подсвечника,
Кишмя кишели светляки.

Они свисали ниткой искристой
С прибрежных улиц. Било три.
Лакей салфетной тщился выскрести
На бронзу всплывший стеарин.

A clash of crocks from the man at the serving counter,
The waiter had counted cruets, and he yawned.
Down in the river, as high as a candlestick,
A swarm of the fireflies swarmed.

Like glistening filaments they hung
From the streets of the waterfront. It was 3 o'clock.
The waiter was attempting with a napkin
To scrape the streaks of tallow from the bronze.

The lights on the shore, their reflection in the water, the steward on board ship, all are seized by a single glance that is concerned solely to take in the picture suddenly revealed and to fix it in this position, glimpsed once, 'at the height of a candlestick'.

As a rule, however, Impressionism has to do with the surface of a thing, accessible to the senses, and not with its essence. Immersed in an ocean of hues and scents it eschews all preconceived, all *a priori* knowledge, any notion or thought that might disturb the purity of perception. Impressionism is in principle not interested in external values or absolutes, but is wholly drowned in the stream of fresh impressions proceeding from *this* and only *this* nature. So it has enriched realistic art chiefly through its depiction of concrete sensuous things, and its transmission of a nature that is visible but not yet intelligible.

It is also interesting that the young Pasternak, explicitly going beyond Impressionist notions of art, invents for himself such a formula for art as 'the impressionism of the eternal'.[1] This phrase combines his predilection for the immediate apprehension of life, the sheer brushstrokes of colour, the *plein air*, with his interest in the philosophical search for absolute categories. In his poetic imagery, too, he seeks to

---

[1] Boris Pasternak, 'Chërny bokal' ('The Black Goblet'), in *Vtoroi sbornik Tsentrifugi* (Moscow, 1916) p. 41.

unite sensation and essence, the moment and eternity; describing a 'storm, instantaneous for ever', he gives the momentarily grasped picture an immutable and unconditional meaning. The 'moment', beloved by the Impressionists, is for him filled with a content of such great significance that it speaks no longer of the fleeting and unique but of the permanent and universal.

> Мгновенье длился этот миг,
> Но он и вечность бы затмил.

> This moment lasted but an instant,
> But it would have eclipsed eternity.

While the Impressionist deliberately confines himself to asking 'how is this thing perceived at this moment?', Pasternak goes further and seeks to know *what* it is. He looks deeply into it, penetrates into its heart, and often constructs an image as a definition of its attributes and essence, conveying the very idea of the object, not merely a first impression of it. Indeed some of his poems have the title 'Definition' ('Definition of Poetry', 'Definition of the Soul', etc.), and many others outwardly repeat the same pattern which one can almost trace back to the set texts of a school-book or to an explanatory dictionary:

> Поэзия, я буду клясться
> Тобой, и кончу, прохрипев:
> Ты не осанка сладкогласца,
> Ты—лето с местом в третьем классе,
> Ты—пригород, а не припев.

> Poetry, I will swear by
> You, and end up croaking:
> You are not a posture of the liquid-throated,
> You are summer, seated in a third-class coach;
> A suburb, not a refrain.

Pasternak is not afraid of drawing such apparently dry conclusions. He readily deduces the formulas of the object depicted, makes calculations about it, analyses its qualities and structure:

> Мы были в Грузии. Помножим
> Нужду на нежность, ад на рай,
> Теплицу льдам возьмём подножьем,
> И мы получим этот край.

> И мы поймём, в сколь тонких дозах
> С землей и небом входят в смесь
> Успех и труд, и долг, и воздух,
> Чтоб вышел человек, как злесь.

> We were in Georgia. We must multiply
> Bare need by tenderness, and by heaven hell,
> We should rear glaciers on a hothouse plinth,
> If we're to get this land as the result.

> And we shall grasp how scrupulous the dosage
> Has to be, of dutifulness and air,
> Of toils and triumphs, mixed with earth and sky,
> Before the sum works out to man as he is here.

But however much he seeks the essence of things, however deeply he delves at times into the most abstract realms, Pasternak always gives a picture – that is, is always entire and concrete. His 'definitions' all resemble logical constructions only externally, in reality their reasoning is provided by the picture of life upon which the whole composition rests.

In the above-quoted poem 'In everything I need to get...', which has the character of an artistic programme, Pasternak expresses a wish to write lines 'about the properties of passion', to deduce its 'law' and 'principle'. How does he envisage this cherished work that would study the essence of the object?

> Я б разбивал стихи, как сад.
> Всей дрожью жилок
> Цвели бы липы в них подряд –
> Гуськом, в затылок.
>
> В стихи б я внес дыханье роз,
> Дыханье мяты,
> Луга, осоку, сенокос,
> Грозы раскаты.
>
> Так некогда Шопен вложил
> Живое чудо
> Фольварков, парков, рощ, могил
> В свои этюды.

> I'd have laid out my verses like a garden.
> A tremble in every fibre
> They would have flowered, lime trees, each in its turn
> Steady, keeping the ranks.
>
> Over the verses I'd have let in airs of roses,
> Airs of mint,
> Meadow-airs, airs of sedge, of haycocks,
> Reverberations of thunder.
>
> Thus Chopin once induced
> The alive marvel
> Of the home-farm and the park, the coppice and the graveyard,
> Into his *études*.

Pasternak's poetry is that of the close at hand and the concrete. He depicts only what he sees himself. But what he sees has usually a widening significance, and certain of its details are constantly being carried onto a more general plane. The ordinary objects around us become the embodiment of goodness, love, beauty and other eternal categories. Uniting the concrete and the abstract, the individual and the universal, the temporal and the eternal, the poet creates as it were an ideal portrait of the real fact or person. Thus, in the poem dedicated to the memory of Larissa Reissner, her image expands until it has the generality of an abstract idea and her personality becomes the personification of life's beauty, somewhat recalling the personified virtues and the goddesses of Renaissance art:

> Лишь ты, на славу сбитая боями,
> Вся сжатым залпом прелести рвалась.
> Не ведай жизнь, что значит обаянье,
> Ты ей прямой ответ не в бровь, а в глаз.
>
> Ты точно бурей грации дымилась.
> Чуть побывав в ее живом огне,
> Посредственность впадала вмиг в немилость,
> Несовершенство навлекало гнев.
>
> Only you, gloriously moulded by battles,
> Blazed out in one clenched volley of beauty.
> If life didn't know the meaning of enthralment,
> You'd be a straight-from-the-shoulder proof of it.

> You swirled up like a tempest all of graces;
> Whatever hardly knew its living fires,
> All that was middling was that moment spurned
> And what was less than consummate called for anger.

When in the war years Pasternak began to speak in an elevated style, and 'animated frescoes' appeared in his verse, in which the heroes looked 'the centuries in the eye', fought to the death with 'the naked force of evil', were carried away 'to the abode of Thunderers and eagles', this was all unexpected, although here too the Pasternakian 'prose' showed through (a sinking corvette 'smoulders like a fag-end') and the familiar intonations of popular speech were to be heard:

> Валили наземь басурмане,
> Зеленоглазые и карие.
> Поволокли, как на аркане,
> За палисадник в канцелярию.

> The miscreants threw us down,
> Their eyes gleamed green and brown.
> They lugged us across front gardens
> To an office, as if lassoed.

Next to the front garden the archaic 'miscreants' appear too abstract, despite their living faces that are seen from below, from the position of a man who has been knocked down onto his back.

The war period naturally left its mark on Pasternak's poetry and facilitated, in particular, the appearance in it of the archaic abstractions which at that time became part of the general literary currency. But in principle this sort of combining of the elevated and abstract with the prosaic and concrete was not so new to Pasternak as it might at first seem. It did not involve any radical change in the system of his style, but rather intensified and concentrated, for a time, something that was already there. The ideal within the real was always more or less clearly visible in his images. To see this, one need only turn, for example, to his love poems of the beginning of the 1930s.

> Красавица моя, вся стать,
> Вся суть твоя мне по сердцу ...

> My beautiful, all your bearing,
> All your being is after mine own heart ...

the poet says to his beloved, and through her 'bearing' he discovers her 'being', the laws of beauty:

> Тебе молился Поликлет.
> Твои законы изданы.
> Твои законы в далях лет.
> Ты мне знакома издавна.

> You Polycleitus prayed to.
> Your laws, vouchsafed, we know.
> Your laws are from stretches of years.
> I knew you long ago.

He compares her to the future ('Measuring the silence with your footsteps, you enter, like futurity'), and sees in her an incarnation of the 'foundations' of life:

> Любить иных тяжелый крест,
> А ты прекрасна без извилин,
> И прелести твоей секрет
> Разгадке жизни равносилен.

> Loving some people is a heavy cross,
> But you are lovely without involution;
> The secret of your charm is of such power
> As having, to life's riddle, a solution.

Life, as is characteristic of Pasternak's world-view, brings the 'taste of great principles' into each of its manifestations. In its presence even the most insignificant objects become more ideal, illumined by this light that pulsates from within. A simple rest in a pinewood is the pretext for the generalization:

> И вот, бессмертные на время,
> Мы к лику сосен причтены
> И от болезней, эпидемий
> И смерти освобождены.

> And lo, we are for the time immortal,
> We are admitted to the communion
> Of pinetrees, and we are from maladies
> And epidemics freed, and freed from death.

Immortal is what gods were once called. But here ordinary people in contact with eternal nature become eternal, for immortality, Pasternak believes, is diffused everywhere ('our daily immortality') and is merely a synonym, another name for life.

This intensity of thought in his poetry is to be observed especially from the 1930s onward, and as time passes it becomes more conspicuous. In his earlier works this intensity was more difficult to discover, and the pithiness of his imagery was often taken for formal affectation. With the years Pasternak became more comprehensible and so it was natural that this aspect of his poetry came more into evidence. But his growing intelligibility was itself largely due to the acceleration of his thought which became more finely ordered and increasingly conscious of its organizing, dominant rôle in the verse.

In his early writing the philosophical idea does not show itself outwardly but is wholly concealed within the picture through which it is conveyed. We will hardly find here any explicit thinking or reasoning from the author himself, but thought is transmitted by nature in its consciousness of itself. Moreover, the author's idea is obscured by the abundance of impressions, and by associations seeming to arise fortuitously, and is complicated by the poet's insistent wish to take into account all the interacting factors of life and to combine them in a fine mesh of metaphor. The early Pasternak sticks to his perceptions much too consistently for clarity, and although, as we have seen, his language is basically natural and unforced, it is the naturalness of chaos that bursts forth, come what may, and requires disentanglement if it is to be wholly understood.

But the profound matter of Pasternak's poetry and the naturalness of his language could not remain for ever behind the locked door of 'unintelligibility'. He had always longed to be accessible, and to fuse so completely the 'depthless spirituality' of images with the 'unheard-of simplicity' of the language they are expressed in that they would be appropriated by the reader without any effort, of themselves, like a truth requiring no elucidation. This longing could already be sensed in certain of his poems of the 1920s and especially in his book *Second Birth*; starting with this book, and continuing in his verse of the thirties and forties, Pasternak moves toward simplicity and clarity.

In one of his poems the protagonist, who has been fighting in the Second World War, dreams of a play he will write when he leaves hospital:

> Там он жизни небывалой
> Невообразимый ход

> Языком провинциала
> В строй и ясность приведет.
>
> There an unprecedented life's
> Never imagined ways
> He will bring to order and clarity
> In a provincial's language.

'A provincial's language' means the living everyday language, free from all literary phrase-making, that was Pasternak's old ideal. But now the concern for 'order and clarity' is a new element in his conception of the tasks of art, and it did not get there all at once.

Pasternak achieves harmonious order and clarity largely because he ceases to play a subordinate rôle in relation to his own perceptions and departs from the extreme degree of metaphorical concentration peculiar to his poetry in the past. He makes a stricter selection among his impressions and, curbing the wilfulness of nature, frequently presents 'pure' feelings and thoughts – not translated into the language of metaphor. In his earlier work the process of making sense of life went on – so to speak – continuously, and his first look at the world was not separable from his final conclusions about it; but now we clearly distinguish the process of cognition which, as it grasps things, does not completely dissolve into them but preserves its independence and puts order into the movement of images.

For an artist who had already formed his own extremely individual view of the world and way of writing it was not easy to attain 'universal intelligibility' and accessibility. Sometimes the demand for simplicity brought with it the risk of an impoverishment of imagery, or of a too direct and declaratory solution of a problem. Sometimes, in this process of reconstructing his art, Pasternak wrote poems that were wittingly inferior to what he could write. Thus, in the mid-1930s when he was trying particularly strenuously to remake his style, there appeared a number of poems of which he said at the time (not without self-disparagement of course) that until he got used to it he was obliged to 'write badly', 'like a cobbler'. In this case a complicating factor was that his subject, which he approached somewhat generally, in the manner of the publicist, was a new one to him, and abstract. As he then said, he had to 'fly from one point to another across a space where the air had been thinned by journalism and abstractions, with little imagery in it or concreteness'.[1]

---

[1] 'O skromnosti i smelosti. Rech' tov. Borisa Pasternaka' ('On Modesty and Boldness. Speech by Comrade Boris Pasternak'), in *Literaturnaya gazeta* (16 Feb 1936). [*Works*, III 219.]

So it is understandable that for the late Pasternak the decisive condition of success for a creative work was that the picture given by its imagery should be at once spiritual and very concrete. The poem is filled with a picture that pulses with thought and is not clogged with excessive metaphor, yet its depictive power is not less than that of the earlier poems and it surpasses them in frank dazzling wealth of content. It is in his philosophical verse that Pasternak is now most successful of all, while he has not much success either with the declaratory publicistic sort of writing or with pictures of everyday life or of landscape that lack the support of a philosophical idea. For him artistic perfection is measured by the observable, the manifest importance of what is said.

While attaining the simplicity he desired, Pasternak did not forfeit that most valuable of his former gains – his way of perceiving and depicting the world as a whole. But whereas previously the barriers between things – between man and nature, the temporal and the eternal – had been overcome mainly with the help of metaphor that shifted objects and attributes from one place to another and simultaneously introduced confusion, a Babel of images, now, though still important as a means of connecting things, metaphor is not the sole mediator between things. Things now are unified through that very breadth and clarity of the poet's view of the world, that winged inspiration of thought and feeling, before which all barriers fall and life appears as one great whole where 'nothing can be lost', where man lives and dies in the arms of the Universal, and the wind

> Раскачивает лес и дачу,
> Не каждую сосну отдельно,
> А полностью все дерева
> Со всею далью беспредельной....

Agitates forest and country lodge,
Not the pine trees one by one
But a consensus of all trees
And the boundless distances, on and on....

In Pasternak's later work not only are the links between things and the poet's union with the world realized in simpler, directer forms than hitherto, but the very 'universe is simpler than some clever fellows suppose', and it is founded upon the supremacy of a few simple elemental truths available to everyone: earth, love, bread, sky. Sometimes a poem rests wholly upon the affirmation of one such cornerstone of human existence. Meanwhile a still larger place is held in his verse by everyday life, and again, not with the complicating allegoricalness which was obligatory in his earlier poems, but with the meanings that everyone knows, the straightforward meanings of everyday objects, habits and occupations. The poetry of life's prose, by which he had always been inspired, is now particularly developed.

Pasternak's work underwent a good deal of change and reconstruction through the half-century during which he wrote. But there was a series of ideas, principles and predilections to which he remained faithful to the end and by which he was guided at the different periods of his life. One of these deep convictions was that true art is always larger than itself, for it bears witness to the meaningfulness of being, the greatness of life, the immeasurable value of human existence. It is able to bear witness to these things without any declarations, profound symbols or exalted allegories: the presence of greatness shows itself in the unfeigned vitality of the narrative, in the sharpened sensibility and poetic inspiration of the artist who is possessed and amazed by the miracle of actual reality and keeps speaking of one thing alone: of its portentous presence, of life as such – even when he appears to be talking only of the falling of snow or the rustling of a forest.

This view and judgement of works of art is of course primarily applicable to Pasternak's own poetry. For him ordinary phenomena are marked by the fabulous presence in them of life as such and they are therefore significant in no less degree than, for instance, Tyutchev's ancient pre-eternal chaos or the universal music of Blok.

As always in Pasternak, the most exalted turns out to be ultimately the most simple – life, all-pervasive, all-exhaustive. 'Poetry', he said, 'will always remain that celebrated summit, loftier than all the Alps, which lies in the grass under our very feet, so that we only need to bend down, to see it and pick it up from the ground....'[1]

[1] Boris Pasternak, Address at the International Congress of Writers in the Defence of Culture in Paris (June 1935), in *Mezhdunarodny kongress pisatelei v zashchitu kul'turi v Parizhe (Stenogramma vystuplenii) (International Congress of Writers in the Defence of Culture in Paris. (Stenographic Report of Speeches)*) (Moscow, 1936) p. 375. [See *Sbornik statei, posvyashchennykh tvorchestvu Borisa Pasternaka* (Collection of articles on Pasternak), (Munich, 1962) p. 9.]

SOURCE: 'Poeziya Pasternaka', introductory article to: Boris Pasternak, *Stikhotvoreniya i poemy* (Poems and Narrative Verse), published by 'Biblioteka poeta' (Moscow and Leningrad, 1965).

MICHEL AUCOUTURIER

The Legend of the Poet and the Image of the Actor in the Short Stories of Pasternak (1966)

> You played that role so well!
> I forgot that I was the prompter....
> (*My Sister Life*, 1917)
>
> Oh, had I known that's how it happens
> when I made my stage debut....
> (*Second Birth*, 1932)
>
> All grows still. I go onstage....
> ('Hamlet', poem from *Dr Zhivago*, 1946-53)

WRITTEN and published between 1915 and 1929, Pasternak's short stories have remained the least known and least studied part of his work.[1] At the time of their publication they suffered from the proximity of a highly esteemed poetic output which eclipsed them in the eyes of

---

[1] Of the three stories studied in this article the first two have been translated into English by Robert Payne and published in the following collections: *Boris Pasternak: The Collected Prose Works*, arranged with an Introduction by Stefan Schimanski (1945); *Boris Pasternak: Prose and Poems*, ed. Stefan Schimanski, with an Introduction by J. M. Cohen (revised edition supplemented by a selection of poems translated by J. M. Cohen). The American edition, *Pasternak: Selected Writings* (New York, 1949 and 1958), does not include *Il Tratto di Apelle*.

The last of these three stories, to which we have here restored its original title, *The Narrative*, has been translated by George Reavey under the title of *The Last Summer* (London and New York, 1959).

The translations given in this article have been compared with the Russian text and, in some instances where the author has felt it necessary, they have been slightly emended.

The principal studies devoted to the three stories are R. Jakobson, 'Randbemerkungen zur Prosa des Dichters Pasternak', in *Slavische Rundschau* (1935) p. 6 [translated and reprinted in the present volume A. L.], and V. A. Aleksandrova, 'Rannjaja proza Pasternaka', in *Sbornik Statej, posvjaščennych tvorčestvu B. L. Pasternaka* (Munich, 1962). The first of these articles is a formal study of Pasternak's stories; the second is only a paraphrase of their contents. Two works on Pasternak as a whole set forth a detailed interpretation which differs from our own. They are Robert Payne, *The Three Worlds of Boris Pasternak* (New York, 1961), and Jacqueline de Proyart, *Pasternak* (Paris, 1964).

the Russian public and critics; whereas, on the other hand, the non-Russian reader, by his ignorance of the poetry, has long been deprived of the source of light illuminating their unity. Very different in aim, form, and content, these five stories do not, in fact, appear as a homogeneous and independent whole, but as so many isolated incursions of a poet into the domain of prose. It is mainly from this formal angle that they have been considered till now, the fiction being treated most often as merely an accessory and secondary element, as compared with an original language showing the indisputable freshness of vision of a great poet. It is therefore understandable that critical attention should have been focussed chiefly on *The Childhood of Luvers* which, in fact, is an unfinished novel, where the development of the subject, arbitrarily broken off, counts less than the originality of the means of investigation and description Pasternak employs to follow the paths a child's consciousness takes.

Doctor Zhivago, however, has modified this point of view by showing that these prose experiments are also, and above all, works of imagination whose subjects, situations, and characters already reveal Pasternak's fundamental and permanent novelistic motifs. Alongside *Doctor Zhivago*, *The Childhood of Luvers* thus appears as a sketch for that 'novel of feminine destiny' later incarnated in the person of Lara Antipova. Similarly, in *Aerial Ways*, written in 1924, one already sees a first sketch for the character who, under the name of Pavel Antipov, will soon portray the drama of the revolutionist. But these two themes, however important, are subordinated to the life story of Yuri Zhivago, the legendary transposition of the poet's biography, and the symbolic portrayal of his destiny. It is this 'legend of the poet', constantly associated with the image of the actor, that we wish to follow through the three stories in which it takes shape, trying to show that it is not one theme among others, but the initial ferment of all the prose work of Pasternak, that which dictates and justifies his recourse to fiction and brings out its profound necessity.

With Pasternak's first story, written in 1915, we enter at once the domain of legend. He presents *Il Tratto di Apelle*, in fact, as a kind of apocryphal anecdote: the hero is named Heinrich Heine, but the reader quickly understands that he has to do with an imaginary character, a modern namesake, or rather, legendary double of the historical Heine. The adventure takes place in Italy, but the descriptions of Pisa or of Ferrara – Pasternak had recently visited Italy – are drawn in order to take the imagination out of its familiar element rather than to situate the action; the plot itself rests upon rather implausible psychological data; and the narrative, conducted now along the lines of a fairy tale, now along those of a play in dialogue, never seeks to create the illusion of reality. Here anecdote – and the allegory it contains – alone matters: Heine, passing through Pisa, learns that a stranger has come to his hotel and left him as a calling card a simple white card bearing the imprint of a bloody thumb. By his signature he recognizes the Italian poet Emilio Relinquimini, author of a love poem entitled 'Il Sangue'. The latter has previously given him notice of his visit, summoning him to reply by a message expressing in equally laconic fashion the essence of love, a message which must be at the same time his signature as a poet (whence the title of the narrative, an allusion to the famous exchange of signatures between the painters Zeuxis and Apelles). Taking up the challenge, Heine goes to Ferrara, where he hopes to find the feminine inspirer of Relinquimini. He traces her by a ruse (inserting an advertisement in the local paper, giving out that he is in possession of a bundle of the Italian poet's manuscripts); no sooner is he in her presence than he seduces her and lets himself be seduced, a brilliant improvisation on the theme furnished him by chance. Such is the signature of Heine, his 'mark of Apelles'.

A critique of poetry? But Heine, too, is a poet; and the favors of Camilla Ardenze are those of the Muse: their love affair thus illustrates the triumph of true poetry over an attitude in which true poetry refuses to be found. It must be recalled here that *Il Tratto di Apelle* belongs to the period when Pasternak, with his second collection of poems, *Over the Barriers*, was breaking with the 'romantic manner' that still betrayed, in *A Twin in the Clouds*, the influence of symbolism.[1] The name *Relinquimini*, precisely, makes one think of a cast-off skin, whereas the namesake 'Heine' evokes that ironic splitting in two, with its sting of cynicism, by which the poet catches himself red-handed and confronts himself with the spectacle of his own naïveté in order to exorcise it. The romantic naïveté that Heine's reply denounces, is that of wanting to *tell* love, to reach its essence by a symbol, a double illusion, about love and poetry at the same time. For the essence of love is its immediate, lived-through reality, in other words, that by which it escapes speech, rejects symbol. 'Love', Pasternak was to write much later,

[1] *Safe Conduct*, trans. Beatrice Scott, in *Prose and Poems*, p. 110.

... is as simple and absolute as consciousness and death, nitrogen and uranium. It is not a state of the soul, but the first foundation of the universe. The fundamental and primordial principle, love is thus the equivalent of creation. It is not inferior to it, and its testimony has no use for the manipulations of art. Art can conceive nothing higher than to lend its ear to the voice of love itself, that voice forever new and unprecedented.[1]

To be equal to love, poetry must be something other and more than a word about love: it must be, like love, a 'second birth', an immediate experience of life in its creative principle. In love, poetry thus discovers that 'alter ego' which, as in a mirror, reveals to it its own stuff: that which Pasternak was to christen, in 1917, *My Sister Life*.

Love, in this sense, is the touchstone of symbolist metaphysics: for if it testifies to a reality superior to art, that reality is not something beyond, but on this side of speech; it does not belong to the domain of essences, but to that of existence; it is not an 'idea' one can know or merely approach through language, but a force that can be lived only, in an experience identical with that of love. This is the meaning of Heine's reply, which already contains, we see, the central poetic and philosophical intuition of Pasternak's work.

But is it really a case here of love, of poetry? Heine's victory over Relinquimini ostensibly is that of the seducer over the man in love, of the Don Juan over the poet, of the rake over the simple-hearted. Nothing seems more cynical than the substitution of a casual love affair for the poetic exploit awaited by Relinquimini; nothing more immoral than the maneuver by which Heine lures Camilla Ardenze, a maneuver that the newspaper editor, after being informed, terms blackmail; nothing more false than the game he plays to seduce her, and in which she rightly denounces an actor's pose. And yet, there comes a moment when the casual affair stops being a casual affair, when the blackmail is no longer blackmail, when the pose is no longer a pose: it is the central moment of the story, marked only by the breaking off of a chapter on an unfinished sentence that is to be continued in the following chapter at the moment when the scene of seduction, apparently uninterrupted, suddenly undergoes a change of lighting and becomes a love scene. A miracle has occurred during the scarcely perceptible interval of the suspension points separating the two chapters. Heine has foreseen this

[1] 'Translating Shakespeare', trans. Manya Harari, in B. Pasternak, *I Remember: Sketch for an Autobiography* (New York, 1959). Paperback edition, Cleveland and New York, 1960. [This is the same work as that known as *An Essay in Autobiography*. A.L.]

miracle; before leaving for Ferrara he has sent Relinquimini the following poetic fragment: 'But Rondolfina and Enrico have discarded their old names and changed them for names hitherto unprecedented, he crying wildly "Rondolfina" and she exclaiming "Enrico!"' But even foreseen, prepared for, staged, the miracle remains a miracle, its essence being precisely to escape the chain of cause and effect, not to let itself be reduced to the conditions that prepared for it. Enrico-Heinrich Heine is no longer the seducer, nor Rondolfina-Camilla Ardenze the fickle mistress too easily throwing over the man who loves her for a younger and more brilliant rival. They discover each other in love, this 'second birth', this invisible and yet total metamorphosis that, beneath unchanged appearances, strips them, along with their 'former names', of all the deadweight of their past.

Love is thus not a result justifying the artifices of the seducer, the Don Juan, the rake, but a metamorphosis that annihilates these figures. It is the expectant waiting for this metamorphosis that for Heine is a kind of justification, for it reveals the lover behind the mask of the seducer, the child behind the mask of the rake, the poet behind the mask of the adventurer. Camilla Ardenze has sensed this even before the miracle has come to pass: 'For all that, you are – will you excuse my familiarity? – you are, how shall I put it, an extraordinary child. No, that's not the right word – you are a poet! Of course, how is it I didn't find the word before: it was enough to look at you.' Rake and innocent at the same time, the poet is an actor who believes in a miracle and who is capable of welcoming it in himself. He knows that the actor's technique is only a way of making himself available for grace, for inspiration, which alone will make of his acting a 'mark of Apelles', the infallible sign of his genius, that is to say, of that supreme spontaneity, that supreme naturalness which reveals the true artist. That naturalness is not given, and if it can no more be acquired, it is won at every moment from the inert weight of hollow words, of empty gestures, of which habit makes each of us a prisoner. Such is the paradox of the actor as Heine describes it to Camilla when she reproaches him with behaving as if he were on a stage: 'We spend our whole lives on the stage,' he replies, 'and it is only with the greatest difficulty that some of us are capable of the naturalness which, like a role, is assigned to us at the moment of birth.' True naturalness is genius, in the etymological sense of the word; but as Goethe wrote, genius is a long patience.

One can see that this paradox of the actor is nothing else but the paradox of art, the synthesis of two apparently contradictory components: that of craft and that of inspiration, of technique and of creation, of artifice and spontaneity, of labor and gift, works and grace. In this, *Il Tratto di Apelle* reflects an old concern of Pasternak's, the very one that, if we are to believe *Sketch for an Autobiography*, made him give up his first calling as a musician ten years before, through having lacked the wish to acquire the indispensable technical skills:

> This discrepancy between a new musical thought, which nothing could satisfy, and its missing technical support, transformed the gift of nature which might have been a source of joy into a cause of continual suffering, which at last I could not bear. How was such a discrepancy possible? Basically, there was something that should not have existed, and should have been set right: an inadmissible adolescent arrogance, a nihilistic scorn of a half-baked scholar for all that seemed possible to him to acquire or attain. I scorned all that was not creation, all that was craft, having the cheek to think that in this matter I was a fine connoisseur. In real life, I thought, everything should be miracle and predestination, nothing premeditated or intentional, nothing arbitrary.[1]

This mystique of inspiration, which Pasternak attributes to the influence of Scriabin, is linked in a more general way to the symbolist climate in which his conceptions of art developed. The anti-symbolist generation of 1910, on the contrary, emphasized the rôle of craftsmanship in art, to the point of defining it sometimes as a mastery (to speak with the acmeists) or as a group of technical procedures (in the language of the futurists and of the formalist criticism which grew up in their wake). It is in this sense that we are tempted to interpret the famous aphorism by which the young Pasternak, switching from music to poetry, rallied to the esthetic of the new generation: 'Art, in its fashion, is nothing but a simple homework assignment, whose only requirement is to be done brilliantly.'[2] If Heine's experience does not expressly contradict this formula, it nonetheless shows that the accomplishment Pasternak expects of art is not a simple technical success justifying the artifice, but a veritable metamorphosis effacing and annihilating it; that in his eyes the opposition between artisan and creator, craftsmanship and inspiration, is vain; or at least resolves itself into the paradox of the actor, which expresses the essence and the secret of genius.

[1] *I Remember: Sketch for an Autobiography.*
[2] B. Pasternak, 'Chërny bokal', in *Vtoroi sbornik Tsentrifugi* (Moscow, 1916) and in B. Pasternak, *Sochineniya* (Univ. of Michigan, Ann Arbor, 1961) T. III.

This theme of the actor, like the word *genius*, which Pasternak was later to use in the same sense, retains, however, a certain ambiguity: extended from the domain of art to that of life, it makes the artist the possessor of a superior and autonomous morality which raises him above the crowd and puts him out of reach of its laws. This ambiguity is the one Pasternak later denounced in what he called 'the romantic conception of life'. 'This,' he wrote in *Safe Conduct*,

> ... was the conception of life as the life of the poet. It had come down to us from the Symbolists and had been adopted by them from the Romantics, principally the Germans. ... In the poet who imagines himself the measure of life and pays for this with his life, the Romantic conception manifests itself brilliantly and irrefutably in his symbolism, that is, in everything which touches upon Orphism and Christianity imaginatively. ... But outside the legend, the Romantic scheme is false. The poet who is its foundation is inconceivable without the non-poets who must bring him into relief, because this poet is not a living personality absorbed in the study of moral knowledge, but a visual-biographic 'emblem', demanding a background to make his contours visible.[1]

It is the sentiment of this ambiguity which inspired Pasternak's development of the actor-theme in *Letters from Tula* and *The Narrative*.

With *Letters from Tula*, written in 1918, the image of the actor finds itself challenged, precisely, by the reality of 'a living personality absorbed by the study of moral knowledge'. The ironic fantasy of *Il Tratto di Apelle* was that of a game of wits; the pathetic sincerity of *Letters from Tula* is that of a confession, translated into the language of fiction, but whose passionate tone suffices to betray its roots in a real experience. The form, too, is no longer that of a fairy tale, but of a realistic short story testifying to a concern for psychological verisimilitude totally absent in *Il Tratto di Apelle*. The central event, surrounded by penumbras suggesting its connections with the whole fabric of a life, is a chance meeting that illumines, like a revelation, the conscience of a young poet, and turns him utterly against what he has been until then. The hero is at the station of Tula, where he has just parted from the woman he loves; it is to her that he relates his experience in his letters. This is the psychological context of the revelation, its realistic cause: the separation here being, as is often the case with Pasternak, the moment of discomposure, of unbalance, when love is no longer just a 'state of the soul', but an impulse, a force, an unlimited power of renewal.

[1] *Safe Conduct*, in *Prose and Poems*, p. 111.

The Legend of the Poet in the Short Stories

Like the image of love, the image of the actor is shifted here from the ground of legend to that of reality: it is materialized in the confrontation of the poet with two sorts of actors. The first are film actors, 'the worst species of bohemian', who happen to be his table companions at the station buffet in Tula. 'They play at being geniuses, bandying phrases with each other, theatrically flinging down their serviettes on the table, immediately after wiping their clean-shaven lips.' The horror which this spectacle inspires in the poet stems from the fact that he recognizes himself in them:

> I am sick to my stomach over it. It is an exhibition of the ideals of the age. The vaporings they give off are my vaporings, all our vaporings. They are the stifling vaporings of ignorance and of the worst kind of insolence. It is I myself.... Here is their vocabulary: genius, poet, *ennui*, verses, untalented, *bourgeois*, tragedy, woman, she, I.... How frightful to recognize one's traits in others.

And, speaking of himself in the third person: 'The poet, who shall henceforth place this word in inverted commas, until it has been purified by fire, the "poet" observes himself in actors on a spree, in a spectacle indicting his comrades and his generation.' For, in his tablemates the poet recognizes an attitude that is not his alone:

> A style has come into being in life, such that there is no longer a place on earth where man can warm his soul by the fire of shame; shame has taken on water everywhere and no longer burns. Falsehood and confused debauchery. That is how all those who are out of the ordinary have for thirty years lived and watered shame, the young and the old; and already this has overflowed onto the crowd, onto the unknown. For the first time since the far-off years of childhood I burn....

The movement by which the poet rises against this image of himself and his time reflected back to him by the actors is a movement of shame: his revolt is a revolt of conscience. He perceives this, and formulates it, at the moment when he is aware that he is at Tula, on the very ground where Tolstoy lived: the incarnation of a literary tradition dominated by ethical preoccupations. 'The adventure lies in the nature of the place. It occurs on the *territory of conscience*, in its gravitational center, in its ore-bearing regions.' The revelation of Tula is that of an ethical domain where the character of the actor has no place.

The ham-actor doubtless is only a caricature of the actor. But the caricature is telling only if it hits what is effectively vulnerable. The ham-actor, who sets up the character of the actor as a universal standard, unveils his weak point, which is, precisely, that he cannot be set up as a standard. There is no morality of genius that is not fatally the caricature of one.

Denounced by the ham-actor, the character of the actor is rehabilitated, however, in the second part of the narrative, by an old trouper, long since retired from the stage, who, like the poet, was present at the arrival of the film players. This spectacle, incomprehensible to him at first, soon upsets him deeply; it makes him understand that his day is done, that he is old, that all that is left for him is to die. To escape the invasion, he shuts himself up in his room; and, to deliver himself from the inner tumult it has caused, he begins to recite mechanically an old part, finds inspiration again, and once more becomes the actor he used to be. And there he is, saved, delivered from the nightmare, in proportion as he becomes himself again by letting himself be taken over by the part he plays.

The poet has only a presentiment of the road to salvation: 'He told himself everything would begin when he ceased listening to himself and when an absolute physical silence would fill his soul.' The old actor is there to suggest the way to silence this invading, autonomous ego 'which makes itself the measure of life' and reduces the actor to the level of a ham. 'He, too,' writes Pasternak, 'sought physical silence. He alone of the two heroes in the narrative had found it, by making someone else speak through his own lips.' The true actor does not find his ultimate standard in himself, but in the role he incarnates. A morality of genius does really exist. It dwells in its fidelity to a density of which it is not author and master, but the one who is chosen.

This, henceforth, will be the fundamental theme of the poet-legend in Pasternak. Its richest and densest expression is to be found in the poem 'Hamlet', a parable of the destiny of Yuri Zhivago, which unites in one image the actor playing out his role to the end, the character of Shakespeare (who embodies for Pasternak the drama 'of the great destiny, the heroic mission, the destiny entrusted into the hands of man'[1]) and the figure of Christ, faithful to his divine mission to the point of sacrifice.

Pasternak links the idea of sacrifice to that of risk, which is already implied in the image of the actor as presented in *Il Tratto di Apelle*: 'You would not understand half of my words,' says Heine to Camilla

[1] 'Translating Shakespeare', in *I Remember; Sketch for an Autobiography*.

Ardenze, 'if we had not met each other in such a dangerous place. I must believe it is dangerous, although I do not know it for certain myself....' The dangerous place where Heine has met Camilla is the stage of this supreme bit of acting that in his eyes represents real life. But to have knowledge of risk is to admit a limit to the acting, to recognize that it is not genuine life: one understands, consequently, that Heine resists the knowledge. Everything changes from the moment that the actor, assuming a role, admits the existence of a norm outside of his acting. For a role is not only self-subjection; it is also an engagement, thus a responsibility and the acceptance of a risk. This is the new significance *The Narrative* gives to the image of the actor.

The originality of *The Narrative*, written in 1929, is to insert the legend of the poet into a realistic context that traces it back to its birth and illuminates its essence. At first sight, *The Narrative* appears as a rather loose series of scenes evoking the life of a young poet, Sergei, whom Pasternak had already made the hero of the verse-novel *Spektorski*. However, apart from some marginal episodes put in to suggest a vaster novelistic scheme, all the scenes converge in a central episode that gives them unity. This episode takes us back to the summer of 1913, when Sergei, having finished his university studies, takes a post as tutor in the wealthy bourgeois Fresteln family. There he meets a young Danish girl, Anna Arild Tornskjold, a widow without means engaged as a lady-companion. She confides to him the humiliations she has had to suffer from coarse employers. He falls in love with her and asks for her hand. But at the same time he has met a prostitute, Sasha, whose distress upsets him deeply.

> All of human naturalness, howling and swearing, was there, raised up as on a strappado, at the height of a catastrophe visible from all sides. In the surroundings described from this elevation, one made it a duty to spiritualize oneself, on the spot and at that very moment; and, in the sound of one's own emotion, one could hear the deserted stretches of the universe, by a common impulse, and in urgent haste, become covered with rescue posts.

The humiliation of Arild, the distress of Sasha, assume for Sergei the significance of an ineluctable appeal. He responds instantaneously, and without reflecting a single moment on the hopeless inadequacy of his enterprise, by making a sketch of his first narrative, the synopsis of a play which he intends submitting to a director of theatrical reviews, if only to obtain thereby a minimal fraction of the sums he knows are needed to deliver the women from their bondage. He imagines a young artist, whom he names Y³, as though to stress still more the abstract, non-realistic character of the story. Y³ decides one day to sell himself at auction. He appears in the sale room, transformed for the occasion into a theatrical hall, into which throng the elegant public of the capital. There he displays his talents as a musician and poet, and conquers the audience by the almost miraculous richness of his gifts. Then the sale begins; a rich patron of the arts carries him off, and Y³, having disposed of his acquired millions by distributing them in poor neighborhoods, gives himself up to the good pleasure of his buyer.

Sergei imagines also, more vaguely, a sequel to his narrative: the bounties of Y³, far from curing the evils, provoke violence and riots that increase them; the patron, burdened by his acquisition, offers freedom to his slave, who refuses it. . . . But those, Pasternak makes one feel, are only secondary details, like all accessory developments to fill out the theme, enrich the image. The essential has been said, and can be summed up in two points. It is, first, this vision of a stage which, once again, reveals the poet beneath the features of an actor. But art, here, is no more than a sum staked: it stands for everything the actor can put into the balance; it represents at the same time his grandeur and his limitations, his power over men and his powerlessness before misery, evil, and death. The true acting by which he triumphs and fulfils himself is that complete giving of himself, that acceptance of an unlimited risk symbolized by the image of an auction at which the stage of the actor becomes identified with the sacrificial stake.

Secondly, the essential consists in the birth of legend, the pure gushing of the fiction seized at its source, at the moment when it is not yet a work of art, but merely an urgent and spontaneous response of the imagination to the position in which life has placed the poet. For, seen from this angle, the legend of the poet is not a gratuitous revery, a compensatory illusion, an arbitrary invention: it is the immediate and insistent command of an imagination directly connected to reality; it has the imperative character of inspiration. By this very fact it imposes on the poet a role that has nothing arbitrary about it, and that he is not free to choose or reject. The poet is not the author of his legend, but the servant of the destiny it traces for him: the slave of a higher and more significant work than his own person.

SOURCE: *Studies in Short Fiction* (New College, S.C.) Winter 1966. Translated from the French by Paul Kirschner.

NICOLA CHIAROMONTE
Pasternak's Message (1958)

HERE is Russia, once again speaking out freely. That is the feeling one gets from the very first pages of *Dr Zhivago*, a feeling which is confirmed as one continues to read, becoming so strong that at the end one shuts the book with an emotion not far from reverence.

In the second introductory lesson to his great course in Russian history, Klyuchevsky used to deny that cultural and artistic manifestations could in themselves assume the character of historical events. 'Insofar as it is just an idea,' he would say,

> it remains personal élan, poetic ideal, scientific discovery. An idea becomes an historic factor only when it possesses itself of some practical force or power, either in the form of a popular mass or of capital, which then transforms it into laws, institutions, industrial or other enterprises, and custom, that is, proposes it to the general admiration by making it a work of art available to all: as when, for example, the pious image of Heaven is moulded into the shape of the dome of the cathedral of Saint Sophia.

So, first of all, Boris Pasternak's novel 'proposes to the general admiration' this event: a Russian writer has resumed his freedom of speech in order to make 'available to all' what he thinks of the history lived through and suffered by his people during the last forty years. His is obviously an act which has ripened for a long time in silence and solitude and which would have been impossible if Pasternak was not sure of testifying as much for the others as for himself, and, even more, of having reached just the right moment when one could no longer do without such testimony. His novel, which we now have because it was, in effect, smuggled out of Russia, tells us, quite simply, this news: after so much turmoil, so much pain and terror, so much inhuman violence – the sense of truth, the love of life, even the feeling of hope, and, finally, as firm and unshaken as in Pushkin's day, the faith in literary communication, have remained intact in the spirit of a Russian writer. This is indeed an historic event.

Pasternak attaches a great importance to this novel. To the editor of a Uruguayan magazine who expressed admiration for his poetry, he recently replied in these words:

> They are only trifles. I have the feeling that an epoch with absolutely new tasks, both of the heart and human dignity – a silent epoch which will never be proclaimed or promulgated in a loud voice – has come to birth and grows day by day without our being aware of it. Fragmentary, personal poems are hardly suited to meditating on such obscure, new and solemn events. Only prose and philosophy can attempt to deal with them. For this reason, the most important thing which I have until now succeeded in doing in my life is the novel *Dr Zhivago*. . . . I am disturbed by the very sad circumstance which gives me an exaggerated fame on the basis of my first writings, whereas nobody knows my recent work (above all, my novel), work which has an entirely different significance.

To move out of the 'fragmentary' and the 'personal', to dominate his lyrical impulse in order to render the sense of human experience, this is evidently what Pasternak has tried to do in his novel. It is, in substance, a meditation on history, that is, on the infinite distance which separates the human conscience from the violence of history and permits a man to remain a man, to rediscover the track of truth that the whirlwind of events continually cancels and confuses. One might say that all of *Dr Zhivago* is dedicated to a description of this distance, and to the insistent representation of the truth manifested in it.

The novel tells the story and meditates on the odyssey of one man (a doctor who is also a poet, but, above all, a man irremovably thoughtful and sensitive) through forty years of Russian history, from 1903, when the protagonist is barely a boy in Czarist Russia, to 1929, when, having lost his family, the woman he loves and his friends, he is killed by a heart attack on the street in the midst of a crowd in Stalin's Moscow. But in the Epilogue and the Conclusion, the novel arrives at the last war and 1945, when the memory of Zhivago, handed down to them in a small notebook of his prose and poetry, is revived in the minds of his two old friends and his experience flows into theirs, illuminated by the light of hope.

Anyone looking for adventures, the interweaving of plots, the imprint of historical events will find all these in this novel. There are the peaceful years before 1905, the Socialist and libertarian fervor, the

Pasternak's Message

revolution of 1905, the war of 1914, the February days of 1917, the October *coup d'état*, the civil war from the Ukraine to Siberia, famine, plague, massacres, the terroristic fury of the Cheka, the consolidation of Bolshevik power, the spreading of silence and fear; there are the intellectuals, the peasants, the workers, soldiers, Red and White Commissars; there are the steppes, the forests, the rivers of Russia; family life, friendship, adolescence, youth, maturity; and there is a love story, told with a truly Russian purity and seriousness. Since *War and Peace*, there has not been a novel which has embraced so vast and dense a period of history. Indeed, though described in a very different manner, the characters and events in Pasternak are even more numerous than in Tolstoy.

But the tumult, the wealth and grandiosity of events are certainly not the essential matter in *Dr Zhivago*. And even less the depiction of solid, well-rounded characters, the joy of describing life and making it palpitate which fills Tolstoy with such exuberance. In Pasternak, there are on one side the events and the vicissitudes of the individual characters, on the other – as a constant counterpoint – a certain ecstasy of the spirit outside of the immediate reality, an ecstasy found in the vision of universal life and in the effort to understand in human terms that which is happening. There is, more than a religious, a mystical feeling for nature, a powerful and proud 'yes' said to life, despite everything. But there is not a single smile, nor a single moment of joy, save for the joy of freedom during the first days of the revolution, and this is an impersonal rapture more than a true joy. The events are narrated in every detail, with bare simplicity; but they seem far-off and muffled, plunged in a kind of twilight; terrible as they are, they occur and pass away in a sort of strange silence and tranquillity, almost as though even their terror cannot disturb that which exists at the bottom of things and of the human spirit. As a result, they give us the feeling of memories which rise to the surface of consciousness, sharp yet insubstantial: shadows which ask to be placated by understanding. And they are shadows which also are characters: almost pure names, with nothing physical about them. What one is told about them is solely the part they play in each other's lives, the way in which they are twisted and beaten by the storm, a few of the essential expressions of their spirit, a few of their thoughts and judgements. Their existences are so disordered and torn to pieces that nothing is left to them (and, in particular, to the protagonist) but the pure distance of the spirit from circumstances, the meditative solitude in which they endure the raging of destiny. At the end, we know that all that has been told was told so as to describe this distance and this solitude: Doctor Zhivago's conscience and how it managed, by resisting death, to remain human.

From another viewpoint, however, Pasternak's book is an historical novel in the full, even Tolstoyan sense of the word: a re-evocation of the tragedy of Russia which has been written not only to rescue it from the 'non-truth' of the official truth ('the diabolical power of the dead letter,' says Pasternak), but also from the dull opacity of resentment and hate. At every point the novel draws its life from the will to oppose the true story of individuals to History as it is made, by force and chance, on the world's stage. In fact the great Russian novelists have never separated the story of the individual from that of his society, from that immense *persona* which Russia is for them. And it is in this way that Pasternak has certainly wished to 'continue' Tolstoy – the Tolstoy whom he venerates – by telling the truth about Russian history and proclaiming that, no matter who is entrusted with the material power, the power over consciences belongs to him who knows how to make himself its instrument and voice.

'I am here so as to try to understand the terrible beauty of the world and to know the names of things, and if my forces do not suffice, to generate children who will do it in my place.' Thus thinks the young woman Lara at the beginning of the novel, when she feels she has finally freed herself from the weakness which has made her the slave of a seducer. And her resoluteness has its correspondence in Yuri Zhivago's virile pride:

> Now he feared nothing, neither life nor death; instead everything, all the things of the world, were part of his vocabulary. He felt himself on a footing of equality with the universe and he listened to the funeral ceremony for Anna Ivanovna in a completely different way from that in which, when she had died, he had listened to his mother's. At that time he had felt that he was dying of the pain, he had been afraid and had prayed. Now he listened to the ceremony as to a communication which addressed him directly and intimately concerned him. He listened to the words and demanded a clear meaning from them, such as one demands from anything, and there was nothing in common with devoutness in the emotion he felt of dependence on the supreme forces of earth and heaven, to which he bowed as to his true progenitors.

Armed with such inner certainties – with such 'revelations', one might say – these individuals go to meet their fates; in fact the novel amounts to nothing else but the story of how pride of this sort resists disorder and violence, of how man cannot be humiliated by anybody but himself.

The revolution, justice on earth, man liberated from the superfluous which 'besmears' him and thus rendered equal to man – all this is what people such as Lara and Zhivago look forward to. When it arrives, this is how they welcome it: 'There is truly something morbid in the life of the rich. An infinity of useless things. Useless furniture and rooms in their houses, useless delicacies of feeling, useless expressions.' And, again: 'No sooner had the mass of the humble revolted and the advantages of the élite been abolished, how quickly then did everyone become stale and faded, how soon they laid aside without regret their original ideas, which they obviously had never had!' When, in the Moscow of 1917, Yuri Zhivago brings home a duck and his family enjoys this unheard-of luxury, they are filled by a feeling of guilt.

> The evening seemed to them a betrayal.... Outside the window spread Moscow, dark, mute and hungry.... They understood then that only a life similar to the life of the people who surrounded them, a life which immerses itself in life without leaving a trace, is a true life, that solitary happiness is not happiness.

It is because his spirit is so open and so disposed to accept not only what is just but all that takes place, and to evaluate it for what it means, that Zhivago, hearing about Lenin's *coup d'état*, can exclaim: 'In the manner in which this act has been carried out to the end, without the slightest hesitation, there is something of our national tradition, something ancestral and familiar. Something of Pushkin's absolute light, of Tolstoy's direct faithfulness to the concrete.'

But it is just this generous impartiality that gives Yuri Zhivago the right to judge and, confronted by the newly established power, to say:

> Everything has its measure, Larisa Fedorovna. In this in-between period it was necessary to achieve something. Instead, it seems clear that, for the inspirers of the revolution, the marasmus of upheavals and transformations is their natural element. They do not live on bread, they require something which at least equals the whole terrestial globe. The construction of new worlds, the period of transition is their goal, a goal in itself. They haven't learned anything else, they don't know how to do anything else. And do you know where the restlessness of this continual changing of theirs comes from? From the lack of definite abilities, talent. Man is born to live, not to prepare himself for life.

On the other hand, such judgements would not carry the weight of conviction they do if they did not well up from so vast and joyous a feeling for nature and the communion of all living beings, to which Pasternak continually brings back his characters: on the earth is the chaos caused by men, one endures it as inevitable and perhaps even just, but, lo! a cloud forms in the sky, a cow moos, the ice melts in the spring, and everything that happens on earth is transfigured, its burden of pain infinitely lightened, the great certainty which lies at the bottom of the human heart infinitely confirmed.

Such scenes, such spectacles (those of the hallucinatory march of Partisans across the Siberian steppes) gave the impression of something transcendental, of another world. They appeared to be fragments of an unknown existence, of other planets, transported by error on to the earth. Only nature remained faithful to history and revealed itself to the eye as the artists of the modern age had depicted it.

If there is a mysticism of nature in Pasternak (and it is in the light of this mysticism that his Christianity should be interpreted), there is also, as a direct emanation of it, a mysticism of artistic creation.

After two or three stanzas composed in a rush and a few similes which almost surprised him, the work took possession of him and he felt the approach of that which he called inspiration. In such cases the ensemble of forces that preside over creation seems to gain the upper hand. The chief role no longer is the author's nor the state of his spirit, which he is trying to render, but rather is taken over by the very language with which he wants to express it. The language ... begins to think by itself, to speak and become totally music, not in the sense of pure phonetic resonance, but as the consequentiality and rhythm of one's inner flow.... At such moments Yuri Andreevich felt that it was not he who did the essential work but something greater than himself: the situation of thought and poetry in the world.... He was only an occasion and a point of support....

It is while he is composing poetry that Zhivago happens to reflect on history:

He realized once again that he did not know how to conceive of history ... that it presented itself to his thought like the unfolding of life in the vegetable world. In the winter, beneath the snow, the stripped branches of a deciduous wood are thin and miserable as the hairs in an old man's wen. In the spring, the wood is transformed in a few days.... During this

Pasternak's Message

transformation the wood moves with a speed that surpasses that of the animals, for animals do not grow as quickly as plants. And yet this is the sort of movement nobody can observe. The wood does not move, we can't catch it in the act, or hide in such a way as to surprise it. We always find it immobile. And in this very immobility we rediscover the life of society, history, which also eternally moves, eternally changes. . . . Tolstoy . . . thought of it in just this way, but he has not expressed it with sufficient clarity. Nobody makes history, one cannot see history, just as one cannot see the growing of the grass. . . .

The capacity to give himself to life, to generously obey its rhythm – this is the true measure of a man. It is not enough that a person carries out his function perfectly, like the revolutionist Strelnikov, the perfect image of the resolute, intelligent man.

> His thoughts had an extreme clarity and equilibrium. He possessed to a rare degree the sense of justice and honesty, nobility and elevation of spirit. . . . But his intelligence lacked the gift of the fortuitous, that power which, by unforeseen discoveries, violates the sterile harmony of the foreseeable. By this same token, if he were really to do good, the consistency of his principles lacked the inconsistency of the heart. . . .

Pasternak certainly does not hesitate to make his hero say what he thinks of Bolshevik power and its 'non-truth'. But perhaps his essential judgement on what happened to Russian society under the new regime is summed up in these few words: 'They had changed their habits, having by now accepted the revolution, and they said "That's the way it is," instead of saying "Yes" or "It's right."'

Naturally, so serene and solemn a thought as that expressed in this novel implies that a man has reached that state of inner conviction for which there is no other adjective but 'religious'. The final point of Pasternak's vision is the message of Christ, and what Christ means to him is absolute faith in man's innerness and freedom:

> You do not understand that one can be an atheist, not even know if God exists or for what, and yet at the same time know that man does not live in nature but in history and that . . . history has been established by Christ and the Gospels are its foundation. But what is history? It is to begin the century-long work so as to succeed little by little in solving the mystery of death and in the future to overcome it. . . . For discoveries of this kind one needs spiritual equipment, and in this sense all the data have already been given to us by the Gospels. . . . First of all, love for one's neighbor, that

supreme form of living energy.... And then, the essential reasons of the man of today, without which he would be unthinkable, namely, the ideals of free individuality and of life regarded as sacrifice....

And, further on:

> If the beast which sleeps in man could be held down by the threat of punishment, it doesn't matter what punishment, or with a reward after death, the highest emblem of humanity would be the lion tamer in the circus with his whip, not the prophet who has sacrificed himself. But this is the point: for centuries not the cudgel but simply an inner music has placed man above the beast... the irresistible power of disarmed truth, the attractive power of the example.

And, in a singularly symbolic discourse, put in the mouth of an inspired, prophetic woman: 'The Gospels, which counterpose the Sabbath to the ordinary days of the week, intend, despite all kinds of coercion, to edify life.'

To read these passages as though they were the novel's ultimate message, indeed its logical conclusion, would be to falsify them. They are the élan of its spirit and should be understood as such. Tolstoyan and Dostoevskian motifs, and also not a little of Shestov and Berdyaev, come together in Pasternak's Christianity. Yet, in the over-all equilibrium of the work, it is certainly the Tolstoyan inspiration that predominates, particularly in the expression of the religious emotion of the individual's dependence on the life of the cosmos and the noble pride that comes from this dependence.

In any case, what matters are not the 'solutions' proposed by Pasternak. What matters and what moves us most deeply are the questions. It is to see arise today, out of the thick of history, when it seemed that history itself had suppressed them forever, the great Russian questions expounded by a living Russian writer, the questions about man, about life, about good and evil. The 'accursed questions', as the Russians of the last century called them, and he who speaks for the others – the writer – must know how to confront them, must run the risk of 'damnation'.

In Boris Pasternak's poetry one can read this quatrain:

> Related to all that which exists, deciding
> To meet the future in the life of everyday
> At the end one cannot help but incur, as in a heresy,
> An incredible simplicity.

The son, like Alexander Blok, of 'Russia's terrible years', Pasternak has wholeheartedly incurred this heresy. Confronted by the great event which his book represents, one is inclined to repeat what he himself has said about the October revolution: 'Something ancestral and familiar. Something of Pushkin's absolute light, of Tolstoy's direct faithfulness to the concrete.' It is a book born out of the depths of pain and love, nourished at the very roots of human liberty. And the presage of freedom on which it majestically ends is only its final harmony.

SOURCE: *Partisan Review*, Winter 1958. Translated from the Italian by Raymond Rosenthal.

ISAAC DEUTSCHER

Pasternak and the Calendar of the Revolution (1959)

I

THE most striking characteristic of Boris Pasternak's *Doctor Zhivago* is its archaism, the archaism of the idea and of the artistic style alike. The book has been received, in the West, as part of the recent Russian revulsion against Stalinism and as its most consummate literary expression. Yet, *Doctor Zhivago* is nothing less than it is that – it is utterly unrelated to the Russia of the 1950's and to the experiences, troubles, and heart-searchings of the present Soviet generation. It is a parable about a vanished generation. Pasternak, now approaching his seventieth year – his formative period fell in the last decade before the October revolution – might have written this book in 1921 or 1922. It is as if his mind had stopped at that time, after the traumatic shock of the revolution; and as if nearly all that his country has since gone through had remained a blank. His sensitivity has remained unaffected, almost untouched, by the great and grim, yet not unhopeful drama of Russia's last three decades. The actual story of *Doctor Zhivago* ends in 1922. Pasternak brings it artificially 'up to date' in two brief and hurried postscripts, 'Conclusion' and 'Epilogue', the first covering thinly the years from 1922 to 1929, till Zhivago's death, and the second jumping straight into the 1950's. The postscripts have almost none of the better qualities of the work but show all its weaknesses and incongruities absurdly magnified.

Much of the climate and the local colour of *Doctor Zhivago* and many of its ideas can indeed be found in the poems and prose of Andrey Belyi, Zinaida Gippius, Evgenii Zamyatin, Marietta Shaginian, and other writers of the 1920's, who were once polemically described as 'internal émigrés'. They were so called because they lived, worked (and published their works) under the Soviet regime, but in some measure shared the ideas and moods of the actual anti-Bolshevik émigrés. Some, like Gippius and Zamyatin, eventually went abroad and there voiced their opposition to the revolution without inhibition. Others adjusted themselves, assumed the postures of 'fellow-travellers', and eventually became Stalin's court poets – Shaginian, for instance, was a Stalin Prize Winner. It is with the voice of that original, authentic 'internal émigré' that Pasternak has now spoken, equally unshaken in his hostility towards Bolshevism and his deep, physical and poetic, attachment to Russia. It is as if, in the course of nearly four decades, he had managed to preserve this his identity intact. His perception, his emotions, and his imagination have remained as if closed to the many deep changes that have transformed his country beyond recognition and to some of the storms that have raged over it in the meantime. This testifies to the organic strength of his character but also to an extraordinary rigidity and limitation of his sensitivity. *Doctor Zhivago* is indeed an act of resurrection. But risen from the dead, Pasternak speaks the language of the dead, not of the living.

II

Doctor Zhivago is a political novel *par excellence*; and so its appraisal must start with the analysis of its political message. The author puts the message into the mouth of his chief character, who is largely his own projection, and into the mouths of the other figures who all talk at great length about their attitude towards the revolution. They dwell on the revolution's failure, on its inability to solve any problems, on the violence it has done to the human personality, and on the disillusionment it has brought in its wake. The plot is designed to bear out this critique. Nearly all the characters are driven to misery, despair and death; and love and humanity are defeated and destroyed by the 'politics of revolution'. In the background there is Russia, shown as senselessly convulsed and tormented to no purpose, unless in mystical expiation of sin. Christianity remains the hope and refuge, a Christianity which need not be clearly defined but is recognizable in its humanitarian outlook, its humility, its acceptance of history, and its refusal to try and remake man's earthly destiny. It is from this quasi-fatalistic Christianity that finally springs Pasternak's ethereal note of reconciliation even with the revolution, the unexpectedly optimistic note on which the novel ends. It may be, the author suggests, that the great expiation has been accomplished and the deluge is over: its few survivors can already sense a 'presage of freedom in the air' and a 'silent music of happiness'; and they 'feel a peaceful joy for this holy city' of Moscow.

A message of this kind is a matter of faith and hardly lends itself to rational discussion. Nor is it likely to be fruitful artistically. With nothing but these beliefs and convictions, Pasternak's characters are from the beginning outsiders to the revolution, lacking all point of contact with it, and psychologically static. The author evidently feels this and seeks to animate them, to take them 'inside' the revolution, and invest them with something like dilemmas. He presents Doctor Zhivago as almost a revolutionary at first, or, at any rate, a man sympathetic to the revolution, who suffers disillusionment and disintegrates in despair. In the same way he tries to complicate other characters like Strelnikov, the Red commander, and Lara, Strelnikov's wife and Zhivago's mistress. In every case, however, he fails. He tried to square a circle. From Christian rejection of the October revolution it might be possible for a Russian writer to produce perhaps a new version of Chateaubriand's *Génie du Christianisme*, but not a true, coherent, and convincing image of the revolution and of the human beings who have made it or experienced it.

How does Pasternak arrive at the rejection? Is his (and Zhivago's) profession of sympathy with the origins of the revolution mere pretence? Certainly not. He is the victim of a genuine and in a sense tragic confusion. He himself reveals this when he describes Zhivago's, that is his own, state of mind shortly before October 1917: 'Here too were his loyalty to the revolution and his admiration for it, the revolution in the sense in which it was accepted by the middle classes and in which it had been understood by the students, followers of Blok, in 1905.' The revolution accepted by the middle classes in 1905, it should be recalled, had as its ideals either a Czardom reformed into a constitutional monarchy or, as an extreme, a Liberal-Radical bourgeois republic. That abortive bourgeois revolution was implicitly opposed to the proletarian revolution of 1917. Pasternak-Zhivago is unaware that his 'admiration and loyalty' to the former must necessarily bring him in conflict with the latter.

The confusion goes even deeper: the Zhivago of 1917 is as if unaware that even this his 'loyalty to the ideas of 1905' is by now only a fading memory. 'This familiar circle', Pasternak goes on, 'also contained the foretaste of new things. In it were those omens and promises which before the war, between 1912 and 1914, had appeared in Russian thought, art, and life, in the destiny of Russia as a whole and in his own, Zhivago's.' The allusive reminiscence would convey to a Russian, if he could read it, far more than it can possibly convey to a Western reader. 'Between 1912 and 1914' Russia's middle classes, the bourgeoisie, had definitely turned their backs on their own radicalism of 1905, had taken their distance from the revolutionary underground movement, and were seeking salvation exclusively in a liberalized Czardom. The mildly socialistic and radical intelligentsia, encouraged by a slight softening of the autocracy, spoke of the 'liquidation of the illusions and methods of 1905'; and the Bolsheviks were already virtually alone in upholding the tradition of revolutionary action – outside their ranks only Plekhanov and Trotsky, and their very few followers, did the same. This then is the climate of opinion which Pasternak–Zhivago recalls in 1917, reflecting that 'it would be good to go back to that climate once the war was over, to see its renewal and continuation, just as it was good to be going home'. Thus, even at this stage, on the eve of the October insurrection and well before his disillusionment had begun, Zhivago's 'loyalty and admiration for the revolution' is nothing but a transfigured and glorified nostalgia for pre-revolutionary Russia.

Latent and unconscious at the beginning, this nostalgia comes into its own and bursts to the surface later. 'I can still remember a time when we all accepted the peaceful outlook of the last century,' says Lara to Zhivago. 'It was taken for granted that you listened to reason, that it was right and natural to do what your conscience told you. . . .' she adds (as if Russia had not lived in serfdom for most of that golden age, 'the last century', and in semi-serfdom for the rest of it!). 'And then there was the jump from this calm, innocent, measured way of living to blood and tears, to mass insanity. . . . You must remember better than I do the beginning of disintegration, how everything began to break down all at once – trains and food supplies in towns, and the foundations of home life and conscious moral standards.'

'Go on,' Zhivago interjects. 'I know what you will say next. What good sense you make of it all! It's a joy to listen to you.'

Pasternak's recital of the broken pledges of October is thus based on a false premise: The October revolution had never promised to satisfy his nostalgia and to 'go back to the climate' of 1912–14, let alone to that of the nineteenth century. He rests his case on the fact that the October revolution was not a bourgeois revolution or rather that it did not content itself with a mildly reformed version of the *ancien régime*. Of all the charges that have ever been levelled against Bolshevism, this is surely the most archaic one. When it was voiced around 1921 it was still the echo of a fresh controversy. In 1958 it comes to us like a voice from the grave.

III

'Comme *La Guerre et La Paix*, le *Docteur Jivago*', writes François Mauriac, 'ne restitue pas seulement des destinées particulières, mais l'histoire politique qui naît d'elles et qui, à son tour, les infléchit et leur donne une signification.'

Mauriac naturally finds himself in the warmest sympathy with Pasternak's Christianity. But has he also based his opinion on a consideration of *Doctor Zhivago*'s merits as a novel? Even though Pasternak himself, through various imitative details of composition and style, evokes *War and Peace*, it is difficult to see how any novelist can make the comparison seriously. Tolstoy's huge canvas is alive and crowded with a magnificently full blooded, richly individualized yet organically integrated, social milieu. In *Doctor Zhivago* a mere fragment of a milieu comes only partly alive, and this only in the opening chapters – the milieu of the pre-revolutionary intelligentsia, Platonically 'faithful to the ideas of 1905' but well adjusted in fact to the *ancien régime* and leading a smug existence on the fringes of the upper and middle bourgeoisie and of the Czarist bureaucracy. After 1917 this milieu disintegrates and disperses, as it was bound to do; and – as nothing takes its place – its *membra disjecta*, as individuals, are whirled furiously into a social vacuum, from which they hark back to their lost felicity. No *histoire politique* emerges therefore from their private destinies, certainly not any *histoire politique* of the Bolshevik epoch.

Tolstoy takes the characters of *War and Peace* straight into the center of the great events of their time. He throws them right onto the stream of history, which carries them until they are overwhelmed or come on top. Pasternak places his characters in the backwoods and backwaters. They do not participate in any single important event; nor do they even witness any such event. Yet, what would *War and Peace* have been without Austerlitz and Borodino, without the fire of Moscow, without the Czar's Court and Kutuzov's headquarters, and without the retreat of the Grande Armée, all reproduced by Tolstoy's epic genius? What significance would have had the *destinées particulières* of Pierre Bezukhov and André Bolkonsky without their deep and active involvement in these events? The drama of 1917-21 was at least as great as that of 1812; and it is far more momentous in its consequences. Yet Pasternak never manages to give us a single glimpse of its main theme, of its central occurrences, and of its significant actors. It is not only that he lacks the gift of epic narration and has no eye for the historic scene. He runs away from history, just as all the time his chief characters flee from the scourge of revolution.

We barely hear in *Doctor Zhivago* a grotesquely remote echo of the stormy prelude of 1905. Then, during the World War until September 1917, Zhivago serves as an army doctor in a God-forsaken Carpathian village and a Galician townlet on the Hungarian frontier, hundreds and hundreds of miles away from the centers of the revolutionary upheaval. He returns to Moscow almost on the eve of the October insurrection and stays there during the insurrection. What he sees, experiences, and has to say about it consists of a few flat and meaningless sentences which do not add up to half a page. Throughout the rising, which in Moscow lasted much longer and was much bloodier than in Petrograd, he stays in his rooms. His child has a cold, his friends come, talk about the fighting outside, get stuck at the Zhivagos' for three days, after which they go home at last. 'Yuri had been glad of their presence during Sasha's illness and Tonya forgave them for adding to the general disorder. But they had felt obliged to repay the kindness of their hosts by entertaining them with ceaseless chatter; Yuri felt exhausted by it and was glad to see them go.' This is all we hear or learn of the upheaval: not a single person appears that participates in it. On the next page we are told abruptly that Zhivago was 'shaken and overwhelmed by the greatness of the moment and the thought of its significance for centuries to come'. We must believe the author upon his word; we have seen no one 'shaken and overwhelmed'. Zhivago did not even look at the event, so full of 'significance for centuries to come' through the window of his flat or even through the chinks of his shutters. The revolution had only added to the 'general disorder' in his household and exposed him to the 'ceaseless chatter' of his friends. What curious lack of artistic sense the author shows here, and what intellectual infantilism!

There follow a few thin and incoherent pages in which we are shown how the revolution adds further to the 'general disorder' in the household. Then, Moscow succumbs to starvation, epidemics, cold; Zhivago himself falls ill with typhus and recovers. By now the author and his hero have began to brood over the breakdown of civilized life and the calamitous deterioration of human nature. 'In the meantime the Zhivagos were tried to the limits of endurance. They had nothing and they were starving. Yuri went to see the party member he had once saved, the one who had been the victim of a robbery. This man helped him as far as he could, but the civil war was beginning and he was hardly ever in Moscow; besides, he regarded the privations people were suffering in those days as only natural, and himself went hungry, though he concealed it.' And so the Zhivagos pack up and leave for the Urals, hoping to recoup there and to enjoy some quiet well-being on what used to be their family estate.

Thus we have left behind the famished, tense, and severe Moscow of the early months of civil war, without getting even as much as a hint of the issues agitating it: war and peace, Brest Litovsk, the German threat to Petrograd, the move of Lenin's government from Petrograd to Moscow, the attempts of the counter-revolution to rally, the hopes for the spread of revolution in Europe, the uprising of the Left Social Revolutionaries, the final dissolution of the old army, the emergence of the new one, not to speak of the distribution of land among the peasants, workers' control over industry, the beginnings of socialization, the attempt on Lenin's life, the first outbreaks of the Red terror, etc., all occurring during the months of Zhivago's stay in Moscow. We get no inkling of the severe pathos of these months, of the mass enthusiasms and the soaring hopes, without which the shocks to the hopes remain meaningless. We are hardly able to guess that Moscow is already being cut off by the Whites from food and fuel bases in the south: and so famine and chaos appear as the results of an apocalyptic breakdown of moral standards.

By coincidence I have read simultaneously with *Doctor Zhivago* the manuscript of memoirs written by an old worker who, himself an anarchist, took part in the Bolshevik uprising in Moscow. Without literary pretensions, very plainly, he describes the same period with which Pasternak deals; and he too is now bitterly disillusioned with the outcome of the revolution. But what a difference between the two pictures of the same city (even the same streets!) seen at the same time. Both writers describe the famine and the sufferings. But the old anarchist draws also unforgettable scenes of streets which, as far as he could see from a crossroads, were filled with Red workers, hastily arming themselves, and even with war cripples begging for arms; and then – the same streets changed into a battlefield; and he brings alive the inspired and tense heroism of Moscow's working class, an atmosphere of which Pasternak conveys not even a whiff. Again, it is as if Tolstoy had brought Pierre Bezukhov to burning Moscow only to let him bemoan the hunger and the ruins, without letting him (and us) feel how the great and tragic conflagration illumines Russia's past and present. To Tolstoy the fire of Moscow and the cruel deeds and sufferings of 1812 are no mere atrocities – if they had been, Tolstoy would not be himself, and *War and Peace* would not be what it is. To Pasternak the revolution is primarily an atrocity.

Zhivago's resentment swells in him during his long and weary journey to the Urals. He travels in an overcrowded goods train, packed with human misery. Here are some of Pasternak's best descriptive pages. The scenes and episodes are true to life – the literature of the 1920's is full of similar descriptions. Zhivago's chief preoccupation is still with his and his family's well-being, although he tries to 'defend the revolution' in a brief and rather lifeless dialogue with a deported anti-Bolshevik politician. He is finally overcome by disgust with the new regime, and with his time at large, in the Urals, when his expectation of satiety and quietude on the old family estate is disappointed, when he is torn between loyalty to his wife and love for Lara; and when eventually the Red partisans trap him on a highway, abduct him to their forest camp, and force him to serve them as doctor.

The picture of the Forest Brotherhood is forcefully drawn. There is in it a sense of space, Siberian space, of the cruelty and mercy of nature and man, and of the primordial savagery of the fight. Still, we touch here only a remote periphery of the civil war, a forlorn and icy corner of Mother Russia. (Pasternak himself spent those years in the Urals, though not in any Forest Brotherhood.) The types or rather situations he depicts here are convincing, and at times (for instance the doings of the witch in the Forest Brotherhood) even fascinating; but they are only marginal. They represent the anarchic fringe of the Red Army which by now fights its battles against Kolchak, Denikin, Yudenich, and Wrangel – elsewhere, mostly far to the West, in European Russia. There the human element, the problems, and the situations were different from those encountered in this Forest Brotherhood, although the civil war was savage and cruel everywhere. The Forest Brotherhood, at any rate, forms, even in fiction, too slender a basis for any *histoire politique* of this period.

It is there, in the partisans' camp, that Zhivago's final 'break' with the revolution occurs. Abducted from the highway, he explodes in anger over the violation of his rights as an individual, the insult to his human dignity, and the breakdown of all moral standards. After eighteen months in captivity, during which at moments he feels almost closer to the Whites than to the Reds, he manages to escape. If this were all, one could say that the story has its psychological and artistic logic and that the author has 'taken it from life'. But Pasternak does not content himself with this. Not relying on objective narrative and portrayal, he incessantly idealizes his hero, his own projection, and leaves us in no doubt that he shares Zhivago's thoughts and emotions and all his indignation. (Nearly all his characters do the same, because the author does not manage to set up any real contrast or counter-balance to Zhivago!) Politically and artistically Pasternak thus involves himself in a self-revealing inconsistency. Zhivago, we know, had, as doctor, spent several years in the Czarist army; and all those years he behaved extremely meekly, never making any fuss over his sacred rights as individual and his offended dignity. Implicitly, he thus acknowledges the right of the *ancien régime* to press him into service – he denies that right only to the Red partisans. Yet they do exactly what the old army had done: they make the doctor look after the wounded. Unlike the Czarist army, they had not sent him call-up papers by mail but had kidnapped him – they had not yet had the time to build up a military machine which would mobilize doctors and others in a 'civilized' manner. Surely from the angle of Pasternak–Zhivago's morality this should have been an irrelevant detail: at any rate, it should not have made so great a moral difference to the idealistic and humanitarian doctor whose wounded soldiers he cured, those of the Czar, of the Whites or the Reds. Why then does he only now feel so deeply insulted in his human dignity?

The juxtaposition of these two situations in Zhivago's life is significant in other respects as well. Near the Carpathian front, that cemetery of the Czarist army, Zhivago had seen blood, suffering, death, and countless atrocities. Pasternak sparingly describes a few of these but he does not dwell on that side of Zhivago's early experience. He presents as an almost uninterrupted atrocity only that part of the story which begins with the revolution. Nostalgia for the *ancien régime* here too colors his entire vision, determines for him his horizon, and dictates even the composition of the novel.

Unintentionally, Pasternak portrays his hero, the sensitive poet and moralist, as the epitome of callousness and egotism – unintentionally, because otherwise he could hardly have so insistently identified himself with Zhivago and lavished on him all the lachrymose love with which the novel overflows. The egotism is physical as well as intellectual. Zhivago is the descendant not of Pierre Bezukhov but of Oblomov, Goncharov's character who, though not worthless, had spent all his life in bed, as symbol of the indolence and immobility of old Russia. Here is Oblomov in revolt against the inhumanity of a revolution that has dragged him out of bed. Goncharov, however, conceived Oblomov as a grand satirical figure; Pasternak makes of him a martyr and the object of an apotheosis.

Willy-nilly one thinks of a fierce and ruthless, yet historically just passage in Trotsky's *Literature and Revolution*, written in 1923, which appears to anticipate Zhivago. In truth, however, Trotsky did not anticipate him; he merely summed up a certain type that belonged to that time:

> When a certain Constitutional Democratic aesthete, having made a long journey in a stove-heated goods wagon, tells you, muttering between his teeth, how he, a most refined European, with a set of superb false teeth, the best in the world, and with a minute knowledge of Egyptian ballet techniques, was reduced by this boorish revolution to travelling with despicable lice-ridden bagmen,[1] then you feel rising up in your throat a physical nausea with his dentures, ballet techniques, and generally with all his 'culture' pilfered from Europe's market stalls; and the conviction grows upon you that the very last louse of the most uncouth of our bagmen is more important in the mechanics of history and more, so to speak, necessary than this thoroughly 'cultured' and in every respect sterile egotist.

We recognize at once the 'Constitutional Democratic aesthete' – it was to him that the 'omens and promises of 1912-1914' had been the most congenial – and we have some idea even of his long journey in a goods wagon, with despicable lice-ridden bagmen. True, his specialty now is not Egyptian ballet techniques but the old Slavonic Prayer Book; and his culture comes from native stores as well as from Europe's market stalls. Perhaps so many years after the revolution our throats at his sight are less susceptible than Trotsky's was to violent physical nausea. All the same we cannot help identifying the same sterile egotist in Zhivago the moralist and humanitarian.

[1] Meshochniki, those who travelled with their bags in search of food or trading food.

IV

With the archaism of the idea goes the archaism of the artistic style. *Doctor Zhivago* is extremely old-fashioned by any standards of the contemporary novel; and the standards by which, being what it is, it has to be judged are those of the old-fashioned realistic novel. The texture of its prose is pre-Proust, nay, pre-Maupassant. It has nothing in it of the experimental modernity of Pilniak, Babel and other Russian writers of the 1920's. Obsolescence of style is not a fault in itself. The point is that Pasternak chooses deliberately his mode of expression which is the mode proper to the *laudator temporis acti*.

In his diary Pasternak-Zhivago thus expresses his artistic programme: 'Progress in science follows the laws of repulsion – every step forward is made by reaction against the delusions and false theories prevailing at the time.... Forward steps in art are made by attraction, through the artist's admiration and desire to follow the example of the predecessors he admires most.' Nothing is further from the truth. In art as well as in science progress is achieved by a combination of 'repulsion' and 'attraction' and the tension between these two forces. Every step forward, as Hegel knew, is a continuation of tradition and at the same time a reaction against tradition. The innovator transcends the heritage of the past by rejecting some of its elements and developing others. However, Zhivago's reflections have some relevance to Pasternak's literary conservatism.

This is Pasternak's first novel, written at the age of about 65, after he had been a poet all his life. His main formative influences had been the Russian Symbolist school, which flourished early in the century, then, for a short time the pre-revolutionary Futurism, and finally, the 'Formalism' of the early 1920's. These schools enriched the idiom and refined the techniques of Russian poetry, but often they also weakened its élan and narrowed its imaginative range. Within the Symbolist and the Formalist traditions Pasternak has achieved almost perfection. His virtuosity of form has made of him Russia's most eminent translator of Shakespeare and Goethe. As far as I can judge from his poems, of which some are not easily accessible and others have remained unpublished, virtuosity rather than vigorous, inventive, and creative mastery, distinguishes Pasternak. Yet as a poet too he is curiously antiquated compared with Mayakovsky and Yessenin, his contemporaries.

What prompted him to write his first novel at so advanced an age was the feeling that his poetry, or poetry at large, could not express adequately the experience of his generation. There is a touch of greatness in this admission and in the poet's effort to transcend his limitations. However, for any writer whose gifts had, for nearly half a century, been attuned exclusively to lyrical poetry, it would, in any case, have been risky to try his hand at a realistic and political novel. Pasternak's poetic tradition has proved an insuperable obstacle to his literary metamorphosis. He has not been able to jump the gulf between lyrical symbolism and prose narrative.

This accounts for the incongruity between the various elements that make up *Doctor Zhivago*: on the one side lyrical passages, noble, richly imaginative, refined, and fastidiously polished; and on the other the core of the novel itself, flat, clumsy, labored, and embarrassingly crude. It is as if the book had been written by two hands: the virtuoso-poet of 65 and a beginning novelist of 16.

Scattered like jewels over the pages of *Doctor Zhivago* are Pasternak's exquisite descriptions of nature or rather of mood in nature which serve him as keys to the moods and destinies of his hero. The method, with a long tradition behind it, is familiar; but Pasternak excels at it. There is richness and delicacy in his images of forest, field, river, country road, sunrise and sunset, and of the season of the year. The realistically painted landscape is shot through with a mystical symbolism, which selects a bush torn by a storm or a frozen tree as omen or token. The writing on the walls is the writing on the face of nature itself. Even in these passages, which would by themselves make an impressive anthology of Pasternak's poetry in prose, his range is limited – he rarely succeeds, for instance, in the drawing of an urban scene; and not infrequently there is a note of affectation and preciosity in his manner of pressing on the reader the symbolical meanings 'hidden' in landscape or mood. All the same, Pasternak the image-maker and word-polisher shows himself at his best.

Unfortunately, a novel aspiring to the large and realistic scale cannot be built around such lyrical fragments. The author's evident attempt to do so has only shown up the perplexing contrast between his sophisticated word-mastery and his ineptitude as a novelist. His plot is, from beginning to end, a jumble of absurd and assiduously concocted coincidences, such as would have discredited a novelist even in Stendhal's days. The *deus ex machina* jumps incessantly before our eyes. Without his help the author simply does not manage to establish any connection between the characters, to bring them together, to separate them, and to evolve and resolve their conflicts. He fails in this because he does not manage to develop and bring alive the characters themselves. Even Zhivago is little more than a blurred shadow. The psychological motivation of his behavior is incoherent. The author substitutes for it exalted lyrical and symbolic allusions; and he speaks for Zhivago and on his behalf instead of letting the personality speak for itself. 'Everything in Yuri's mind was mixed up together and misplaced and everything was sharply his own – his views, his habits, and his inclinations. He was unusually impressionable and the freshness and novelty of his vision were remarkable.' 'The vigor and the originality of his poems made Yuri forgive himself what he regarded as the sin of their conception, for he believed that originality and vigour alone could give reality to a work of art....' 'Shyness and lack of simplicity [were] entirely alien to his nature.' The superlatives which the author heaps on his hero and the subtle poetic aura by which he surrounds him cannot give reality or depth to the figure. Zhivago's attitudes towards his wife and mistress, and towards his many children born of three women, are strained or never assume verisimilitude: not for a single moment does the father come alive in him (and none of his children has any individuality). Not only the author sings his hero's praises – nearly all the characters do the same. Nearly all are in love with Yuri, adore him, approve his ideas, echo his deep reflections, and nod their heads at whatever he says.

The other characters are altogether puppet-like or *papier mâché*, much though the author exerts himself to make them move of their own accord, or to make them look 'unusual', enigmatic, or romantic. Even more than in the case of Zhivago, lyrical patches, naïve and stilted dialogues, and affected superlatives have to stand for the portrayal of character and of actual relationships. This, for instance, is how the intimate concord between Lara and Zhivago is described:

> Their low-voiced talk, however unimportant, was as full of meanings as the Dialogue of Plato.
>
> Even more than by what they had in common, they were united by what separated them from the rest of the world....
>
> They loved each other greatly. Most people experience love, without noticing that there is anything remarkable about it. To them – and this made them unusual – the moments when passion visited their doomed human existence like a breath of timelessness were moments of revelation, or of ever greater understanding of life and of themselves.

In his *histoire politique* of the epoch the author makes no attempt to draw a single Bolshevik figure – the makers of the revolution are an alien and inaccessible world to him. He underlines that his revolutionaries are not party men. They are primitively picaresque types or wholly incredible eccentrics, like Klintsov-Pogorevshikh, the deaf-mute instigator of rebellions in the Czarist army, Liberius, the chieftain of the Forest Brotherhood, and the most important of them Strelnikov, Lara's husband. Of Strelnikov we learn that he 'had an unusual power [how Pasternak loves this adjective!] of clear and logical reasoning, and he was endowed with great moral purity and sense of justice; he was ardent and honorable'. From disappointment in family life – apparently his only motive – he plunges into revolution, becomes a legendary Red commander, the scourge of the Whites and of the people at large; but eventually falls foul of the Bolsheviks – we do not know why and how but presumably because of his 'moral purity and sense of justice'; and he commits suicide. A few workers appear fleetingly in pale episodes, and are either half-wits or servile post-seekers. We do not see the Whites at all, apart from one remote and evanescent apparition. One could not even guess from this grand cross-section of the epoch who were the men who made the revolution, who were those who fought the civil war on either side, and why and how they lost or won. Artistically as well as politically the epoch-making upheaval remains a vacuum.

V

Yet despite this void, and the unctuous moralizing and all the falsettos, there is in *Doctor Zhivago* a note of genuine conviction. The suggestive indictment of the revolution must make its impression on the reader who is unfamiliar with the background of the years 1917–22 but is vaguely aware of the horrors of the Stalin era. Confusing the calendar of the revolution, Pasternak projects those horrors back into the early and earliest phases of the Bolshevik rule. The anachronism runs through the entire novel. In the years 1918–21 Zhivago and Lara are already revolted by the tyranny of the monolithic regime which in fact was not formed until a decade later:

> They were both equally repelled by what was tragically typical of modern man, his shrill text-book admirations, his forced enthusiasms, and the deadly dullness conscientiously preached and practised by countless

workers in the fields of art and science in order that genius should remain extremely rare.

It was then that falsehood came into our Russian land [Zhivago and Lara agree]. The great misfortune, the root of all the evil to come was the loss of faith in the value of personal opinions. People imagined that it was out of date to follow their own moral sense, that they must sing the same tune in chorus, and live by other people's notions, the notions which are being crammed down everybody's throat.

I do not know [says Zhivago] of any teaching more self-centred and farther from the facts than Marxism. Ordinarily, people are anxious to test their theories, to learn from experience, but those who wield power are so anxious to establish the myth of their own infallibility that they turn their back on truth as squarely as they can. Politics mean nothing to me. I do not like people who are indifferent to the truth.

Zhivago–Pasternak goes on in this vein without any substantial contradiction from any other character. Yet, the 'forced enthusiasms', the deadly uniformity in art and science, the 'singing of the same tune in chorus', and the degradation of Marxism to an infallible Church – all this fits the fully-fledged Stalin era but not the years in which these words are spoken. Those were years of *Sturm und Drang*, of bold intellectual and artistic experimentation in Russia, and of almost permanent public controversy within the Bolshevik camp. Does Pasternak–Zhivago confuse the calendar of the revolution or is he confused by it? Whatever the truth, only this confusion enables him to make his case. He could not have actually argued in 1921 the way he does. Yet readers familiar only with the atmosphere of the latter day Stalinism are all too likely to believe that he could. It may be objected that the author need not concern himself with historical chronology, and that he has the right to compress or 'telescope' various periods and so reveal the evil embedded in the thing itself. Where then are the limits of the compression? And does not historical and artistic truth come out mangled? Pasternak, at any rate, establishes most carefully, almost pedantically, the chronology of the events which form the background to Zhivago's fortunes; and so he should be expected to demonstrate the 'spirit of the time', on which he dwells so much, in accordance with the time.

To be sure, the deadly uniformity in art and science, the disregard and contempt of personal opinion, the infallibility of the ruler, and so many other features of the Stalin era evolved from germs which had been present in the early phase of the revolution; but they evolved in continuous and inexorable conflict with that phase. No great artist could possibly have missed, as Pasternak has, the colossal tragedy inherent in this chain of cause and effect and in the tension between the early and the late phases of the revolution and of Bolshevism. What Pasternak does is not merely to blur the contours of the time – he pulverizes all the real aspects of the revolution and dissolves them into a bloody and repulsive fog. Art and history alike, however, will reestablish the contours and make their distinction between the revolution's creative and its irrationally destructive acts, no matter how entangled these may have been, just as, in the case of the French Revolution, posterity, with the exception of extreme reactionaries, has drawn its distinction between the storming of the Bastille, the proclamation of the Rights of Man, and the rise of the new and modern, be it only bourgeois, France, on the one hand, and the nightmares of revolution and the gods that were athirst, on the other.

Pasternak hardly ever alludes (even in his 'Conclusion' and 'Epilogue') to the great purges of the 1930's. Yet he constantly uses their black hue for his picture of the earlier period – this indeed is the only respect in which he draws for his writing on any significant social experience of the last three decades. His silence about the great holocaust of the 1930's is not accidental. This was tragedy *within* the revolution; and as such it does not concern the outsider, let alone the internal émigré. What is striking here is the contrast between Pasternak and writers like Kaverin, Galina Nikolayeva, Zorin and others, whose post-Stalinist novels and plays (unknown in the West and some of them virtually suppressed in the Soviet Union) have centered precisely on the tragedy within the revolution, the tragedy which they also see from within. In Pasternak's pages the transposed horrors of the Stalin era exist mainly as the source of his own moral self-confidence, the self-confidence he needs for his critique of the revolution at large. We have said that he might have written *Doctor Zhivago* in the early 1920's; but he could not have written it then with his present self-confidence. At that time, with the 'heroic' phase of the revolution still fresh, the internal émigré labored under the sense of his moral defeat. After all the experiences of the Stalin era, he now feels that he has morally recovered; and he flaunts his self-righteousness. This is a spurious recovery, however; and it is helped along by a *suggestio falsi*.

Pasternak traces back Zhivago's ideas and his Christianity to Alexander Blok. In Blok's *Twelve*, Christ walked at the head of armed workmen, tramps, and prostitutes, leading them, in the blood red dawn of October, towards a greater future. There was a certain artistic and even historic authenticity in this daring symbol. In it were merged the primitive Christianity and the elemental revolutionary élan of the Russia of the muzhiks who, chanting Prayer Book psalms, burned the mansions of the aristocracy. The Christ who blessed that Russia was also the Christ of primitive Christianity, the hope of the enslaved and the oppressed, St Matthew's Son of Man, who would sooner let the camel go through the eye of a needle than the rich man enter into the Kingdom of God. Pasternak's Christ turns his back on the rough mob he had led in October and parts company with them. He is the pre-revolutionary self-sufficient Russian intellectual, 'refined', futile, and full of grudge and resentment at the abomination of a proletarian revolution.

VI

Pasternak has been hailed in the West for his moral courage; and much is written about his poetry as a 'challenge to tyranny' and his stubbornly non-conformist attitude throughout the Stalin era. Let us try and disentangle facts from fiction. It is true that Pasternak has never been among Stalin's versifying sycophants. He has never bowed to the official cult and observance; and he has never surrendered his literary integrity to powerful taskmasters. This alone would have been enough to earn him respect and to make of his writing a startling phenomenon. His poetry stands out sharply against the grey background of the official literature of the last thirty years. Against that lifeless and unendurably monotonous background even the old-fashioned quality of his lyricism could appear and has appeared as a thrilling innovation. One may therefore speak of him as of a great and even heroic poet in that semi-ironical sense in which the Bible speaks of Noah as a just man 'in his generation', a generation of vice. Pasternak stands indeed head and shoulders above the poetasters of the Stalin era.

However, his courage has been of a peculiar kind – the courage of passive resistance. His poetry has been his flight from tyranny, not his challenge to it. To this he has owed his survival, in a generation in which the greatest poets, Mayakovsky and Yessenin, committed suicide, and most of the best writers and artists, Babel, Pilniak, Mandel'shtam, Kluyev, Voronsky, Meyerhold, and Eisenstein, to mention only these, were deported, imprisoned and driven to death. Stalin did not allow many of Pasternak's poems to be published; but he spared their author and, by the despot's benevolent whim, even surrounded him with care, protecting his safety and well-being. The poet did nothing to gain these favors; but Stalin knew that he had little to fear from his poetry. He sensed a threat to himself not in the archaic message of the man who harked back to pre-revolutionary times, but in the work of those writers and artists who, each in his own way, expressed the ethos, the *Sturm und Drang*, and the non-conformity of the early years of the revolution – there Stalin sensed the genuine challenge to his infallibility. With those writers and their message Pasternak has been in implicit conflict; and it would be unjust to their memory to hail him as the most heroic and authentic spokesman of his generation. Moreover, their message, even though it, too, belongs to its time and can hardly meet the needs of our day, has certainly far more relevance to the experience and the aspirations of the new Russia than have the ideas of *Doctor Zhivago*.

When all this has been said, one cannot react otherwise than with indignation and disgust to the suppression of *Doctor Zhivago* in the Soviet Union, and to the spectacle of Pasternak's condemnation. There exists no justification and no excuse for the ban on his book and the outcry against it, or for the pressure exercised on Pasternak to make him resign the Nobel award, the threat of his expulsion from the country, and the continuing witch-hunt. The Writers' Union of Moscow and its official instigators or accomplices have achieved nothing except that they have given proof of their own obtuseness and stupidity.

What are Pasternak's censors afraid of? His Christianity? But the Soviet State Publishers print in millions of copies the works of Tolstoy and Dostoyevsky, every page of which breathes a Christianity far more authentic than Pasternak's. His nostalgia for the *ancien régime*? But who, apart from a few survivors of the old intelligentsia and bourgeoisie, people of Pasternak's age, can share that nostalgia in the Soviet Union today? And even if younger people were to experience it vicariously – what possibly could the Soviet Union fear from that? It cannot and it will not go back to the past, anyhow. The work of the revolution can no longer be undone or reversed: the huge, formidable, and ever growing structure of the new Soviet society will hardly stop growing. Can perhaps a poet's eye, turned inwards and backwards, and wandering over the wastes of his memory, cast an evil spell? Zhivago still represents a powerful force, frequently felt and heard, in Poland,

Hungary, Eastern Germany, and elsewhere in Eastern Europe; but in the Soviet Union he is the survivor of a lost tribe. In the fifth decade of the revolution it is time to view him with detachment and tolerance and to let him mourn his dead.

Pasternak's censors, too, are evidently confusing the calendar of the revolution. They have broken away from the Stalin era, or have been wrenched out of it; but somehow they still imagine themselves to be living in it. They are still superstitiously seized by old and habitual fears and resort to the customary charms and exorcisms. Above all, they distrust their own, modern and educated, society which is growing mightily above their heads as well as Pasternak's.

Time does not stand still, however. Ten years ago *l'affaire Pasternak* would not have been possible. Pasternak would not have dared to write this novel, to offer it for publication in Russia, and to have it published abroad. If he had done this, Stalin's frown would have sent him to a concentration camp or to death. Despite all the present witch-hunting in Moscow, however, Pasternak's personal freedom and well-being have so far remained undisturbed; let us hope that they will remain so to the end. He might have gone abroad and in the West enjoyed fame, wealth, and honor; but he has refused to 'choose freedom' in that way. Perhaps he does indeed hear that 'silent music of happiness', of which he says, in the last sentences of *Doctor Zhivago*, that it spreads over his country, even if he does not quite understand that music. Slowly yet rapidly, painfully yet hopefully, the Soviet Union has moved into a new epoch, in which the mass of its people is seizing anew the sense of socialism. And perhaps in ten years time another *affaire Pasternak* will also be impossible, because by then the fears and the superstitions of Stalinism will have long been forgotten.

SOURCE: *Partisan Review*, Spring 1959.

IRVING HOWE

Freedom and the Ashcan of History (1959)

> Those who cannot remember the past are doomed to repeat it. (SANTAYANA)

IF one's first response to Mr Deutscher's essay is a rush of feeling which I shall keep myself from describing, one's second response is a kind of gratitude: *good, let it all come out into the open*. For Mr Deutscher is an authoritative spokesman for a political-intellectual tendency of growing importance; only babes will suppose his attack on Pasternak to involve serious literary issues: it is neither more nor less than a political act.

As long as Soviet Russia remains a powerful state, and no matter how often it displays its contempt for freedom, it will exert an attraction for Western intellectuals, particularly those 'authoritarians of the left' who have replaced the dimmed fraternal sentiments of their youth with a hard-headed valuation of industrial power. Among the French this takes the form of a rationalist dementia cut off, on principle, from the domain of fact; among the British, a gentlemanly tolerance for 'those chaps'; among Germans, a commitment to the asserted *logos* of History which moral experience seems unable to deflect; and among Americans a managerial *camaraderie* resting upon a joint esteem for the gestures of power, the wonders of technology, and bureaucratic planning (the fetishism of the plan having, in our time, replaced the fetishism of commodities).

These converging sentiments make up together what might be called a *new conciliationism* in regard to the Communist dictatorship. Among intellectuals a major symptom of this is the desire to add to the undisputed necessity for political coexistence an attitude that might be called moral coexistence. And since *Doctor Zhivago* has already provided a decisive test for many people – for men in power like Khrushchev, for men out of power like the 'revisionist' writers of Poland who recently acclaimed the book – so, through what might be called the dialectic of irritation, it has provoked Mr Deutscher into an unusual bluntness of statement. His major charge against *Doctor Zhivago* – that its devotion to individual and liberal values is 'archaic', that it 'speaks the language of the dead' (though, considering their tragic history, might it not be appropriate that Russia's greatest living poet speak their language?) – this can be understood only if one realizes that Mr Deutscher writes as a theorist who believes that the irrevocable progress of History is floating the Communist state. His assault upon Pasternak derives from a fundamental identification with the 'essence', though not necessarily with each manifestation, of that progress.

At the end of his essay, in a burst of rapture – it depends, rather amusingly, upon his simplification of a phrase from Pasternak – Mr Deutscher speaks of the 'music of the future', the music of socialism no less, of which he hears the anticipatory chords in Khrushchev's Russia. I write from another standpoint. The 'music' I hear from Russia is that of a party-state still in basic opposition to the values of democracy and socialism: a party-state that systematically silences those who would speak for freedom. The people of Russia remains a prisoner: the leash has been lengthened, the rations are improved, but the prisoner is not free. And I do not believe that the growing wealth and strength of this jail-society assures a gradual slide into freedom, though it *may* offer new opportunities for those who want freedom to struggle against the party monopoly of power.

This much understood, we may look at one or two of Mr Deutscher's ventures into criticism, not because they are significant in themselves but because they lead back to the area in which his views are significant: politics.

III

Mr Deutscher describes *Doctor Zhivago* as a 'political novel *par excellence*' and then, quite as if he were reviewing a full-scale political-social history of Communist Russia, bemoans its failure to present directly the tumultuous events of the revolutionary and post-revolutionary years. The novel does not even show us, he complains, a single *bona fide* Bolshevik. But if by a 'political novel' (especially '*par excellence!*') we mean one that focusses primarily upon a course of political happenings or upon a clash of political ideologies, then *Doctor Zhivago*, despite its occasional passages about Marxism, might better be described as an 'anti-political' novel, one that deals with the effort of a man to survive in his own being at a time when the imperious demand of politics is total.

Mr Deutscher's critical strategy lends itself to unexpected uses: he could, for example, dismiss *The Charterhouse of Parma*, since its hero Fabrice merely glances at the central event of his time, the battle of Waterloo, and then lives a dream-like and non-political existence, even though the political events of the Napoleonic era, as Stendhal makes clear, decisively shape his life. (For that matter, Mr Deutscher's complaints about the 'coincidences' in *Zhivago* would also permit him, like recent generations of students, to dismiss Thomas Hardy's great novels in which the sense of a fate beyond human control is similarly projected through the use of 'coincidence'.)

The novel Pasternak happens to have written is quite different from the one Mr Deutscher thinks he has or should have written. Pasternak largely takes for granted the sweep of historical events and the likelihood that his Russian readers will be familiar with them. (Given their 'education', it is perhaps the one thing he can take for granted.) What he wishes to impress upon his readers is the value of an independent consciousness, sometimes heroic, more often passive and helpless, yet clinging to its own terms of existence. But this, judging from his article, does not seem to interest Mr Deutscher very much.

A good many of the terrible events, however, are touched upon in the novel, either by implication or through brief presentiments – and to my mind, touched upon with great force and objectivity. One thinks of the moments when Zhivago is at the front, a witness to the disintegration of the Czarist army; or later in Moscow, discovering that in times of stress the snatched pleasure of duck and vodka, because it is not shared with other men, is no pleasure at all (is that perhaps an incident justifying the resort to Trotsky's vulgar passage about aesthetes?); or still later during the marvelously-portrayed journey to the Urals, when Zhivago argues in behalf of the revolution against one of its 'premature' critics, shares with ease and affection the trials of the ordinary people who are his companions on the train, and experiences, in his inner self, the meaning of a vast historical uprooting.

Here is Zhivago as a witness to the revolution – and one wonders whether it is this passage that prompted Mr Deutscher to his delicate comparison with the 'Constitutional Democrat aesthete':

> He realized he was a pygmy before the monstrous machine of the future; he was anxious about his future, and loved it and was secretly proud of it,

and as though for the last time, as if in farewell, he avidly looked at the streets and the clouds and the people walking in the streets, the great Russian city struggling through misfortune – and was ready to sacrifice himself for the general good, and could do nothing.

When Mr Deutscher charges Zhivago, as a representative of his class and/or generation, with yearning for a period (1912–14) when Russia's middle classes 'had definitely turned their back on their own radicalism of 1905', he neglects to add that those were also years in which, perhaps mistakenly, many Russian intellectuals felt some hopes for a *liberal* development. And when he charges Pasternak with basing his 'recital of the broken pledges of October . . . on a false premise', he is being less than just: for while it is true that the Bolshevik revolution did not promise to return to the climate of 1912–14, it is also true that in its first year or so it gave the intellectuals reason to hope that it would honor at least some of the freedoms Pasternak clearly had in mind when referring to the pre-revolutionary years. In any case, if the point of *Doctor Zhivago* were really so preposterous as a piping for the Czarist past, the dictatorship would surely not have reacted to it with so sustained and intense a fury: for what damage could it then have done, what impact could it have had? No, when the students of Moscow hailed Pasternak a few years ago, chanting a request that he read his translation of Shakespeare's sixty-sixth sonnet ('And art made tongue-tied by authority'), they saw him not as a relic of 'the dead' but as a spokesman and symbol of the freedom they desired.

It is true that Zhivago's political consciousness, never more than a fragment of that complex human consciousness toward which he strives, can at no point satisfy the strict requirements of a Leninist. One of the main themes of the novel is that the Bolshevik regime, as it rapidly became monolithic and bureaucratized, gave people like Zhivago no margin for survival. As Nicola Chiaromonte has written in a moving essay (*Dissent*, Winter 1959): 'What Pasternak has done is to show what is left of characters under conditions in which the very identity of the individual is threatened, and tends to be reduced to an inconsistent sequel of occasions and acts.'

That is why the passage Mr Deutscher singles out as 'naïve and stilted' – the passage in which Pasternak compares the conversation of Zhivago and Lara with the dialogues of Plato – acquires in context a noble and tragic character. Loyalty to the text would require readers to be told that this passage occurs in a quick transitional section which summarizes what has been and will again be shown in dramatic fullness: that Zhivago has been ill, that he has now been reunited with Lara, that they find it possible, while living on the edge of the precipice they know awaits them, to rediscover something of the value of human existence through sharing in the spirit of sacrifice and love. But to the accomplice of History, all this seems 'naïve', a residual sentiment of 'a survivor of a lost tribe'. Yes, the human tribe.

Chiaromonte's point – central for an understanding of the novel – also helps explain why Mr Deutscher's comparison between *War and Peace* and *Doctor Zhivago* betrays both literary and political insensitivity. I happen to think, unlike other critics, that Pasternak did begin his novel with an intention of composing a story of Tolstoyan breadth: hence, its least successful section, the opening series of dry vignettes. But it must have become clear to him that, if he were to write honestly, he could not compose this kind of novel about the Russia of the last decades. Pasternak began, perhaps, by desiring to capture something of the Tolstoyan freedom and spontaneity, its joy as a token of man's gratitude for existence; his characters reach for it eagerly, pathetically; but the Russia he comes to describe, whether of the War Communism years or the Stalin and post-Stalin periods, is too grey, too grim in its inhumane monolithism to permit a prolonged release of the Tolstoyan ethos. To have pretended otherwise would have been to acquiesce in a characteristic falsification of Soviet fiction.

Yet after about the first 100 pages – far from repeating, as Mr Deutscher supposes, the usual business of the old-fashioned social novel – Pasternak radically shifts his focus and begins to compose a quite different kind of novel. The very 'substance' of his imagined world, in respect to which all the other characters are observed and validated, becomes Zhivago's sense of consciousness: his sense of consciousness as it is the last refuge of freedom. Through his doomed yet exemplary struggle to maintain the life of contemplation, through his proud insistence upon the autonomy of his inner 'organic' being, Zhivago comes to represent – and even in those moments of lassitude and demoralization that so offend Mr Deutscher's spartan sensibilities – all that which in human life must remain impervious to the manipulation of the party-state and its ideology.

It is for this reason that *Doctor Zhivago* is not merely a remarkable novel in its own right but a testament for the silent and suppressed, all those who, no matter how they might reject Zhivago's ideas, share with him the yearning for the right to free reflection. It is for this reason that Zhivago, feeble broken creature that he finally becomes, still presents the 'permanent revolution' of man against the total state.

Whether Pasternak confuses 'the calendar of the Russian revolution' would therefore seem a secondary matter. (Other great Russian novels, Dostoevsky's *The Possessed* and Turgenev's *Virgin Soil*, have also been accused, perhaps with greater justice, of violating the 'calendar' of their day: a fact that in no way diminishes their value as literature or 'evidence'.) In any case, is this confusion quite so shocking as Mr Deutscher claims? Outright terrorism Pasternak shows only at the end of the novel, as in the chilling paragraph which records that Lara 'died somewhere, forgotten as a nameless number on a list that afterwards got mislaid, in one of the innumerable mixed or women's concentration camps in the north'. (A passage reflecting, perhaps, Pasternak's 'archaism?') What Pasternak portrays in the early 'twenties is the cruelty of the Civil war ('White and Red atrocities rivalled each other in savagery'), the gathering fanaticism of the triumphant Communists, the agonies of personal survival. I submit that his novel shows a greater faithfulness to the essential history of our time as it has become the crucifixion of freedom and consciousness, than all of Mr Deutscher's dialectical turnings.

III

About the literary merits of *Doctor Zhivago* there can of course be legitimate disagreement. But one would expect an intellectual to feel only the deepest sense of comradeship with Pasternak as a man, to be stirred to emotions of fraternity by the sight of this aging poet as he suffered in loneliness the assaults of the party-state. (Or should we congratulate Khrushchev for not having arranged his liquidation?) And here, despite Mr Deutscher's careful statement of opposition to the witch-hunt and the banning, I find his article lamentable. No one, not even the reader who disagrees with every word I have written, could say that Mr Deutscher's moral-political impulse is a warm solidarity with the artist absorbing the blows of the state.

Mr Deutscher chastizes 'the censors' for their 'obtuseness and stupidity'. But surely it is more than a matter of 'censors', and something far more serious than 'obtuseness'. These 'censors' did not act on their own, apart from the cues of Khrushchev and Mikoyan; the whole apparatus of the party-state – including that agent of Russia's 'not unhopeful drama', the Komsomol leader who called Pasternak a pig – threw itself into the vendetta against the writer. Mr Deutscher, faithful to his theories, must however present the matter as if it were the result of the 'obtuseness' of officials out of step with History, bureaucrats who, having perhaps mislaid the calendar of the revolution, don't understand their own true interests, which Mr Deutscher tries so patiently to explain. (One wonders, incidentally, whether the suppression of the Hungarian revolution was also due to mislaying the calendar.)

What Mr Deutscher does not face up to is the political significance of the Pasternak case. Pasternak, writing almost as if he too, at the end of the book, accepted Mr Deutscher's optimistic prognosis, offered a novel that forced the regime to decide how far the 'thaw' could go. The party-state answered by brutally suppressing the book. Does this fact support Mr Deutscher's theory about the expected gradual 'democratization' of Russian Communism, or does it indicate that, with less violent methods, the regime stands ready to suppress fundamental disagreement and criticism, and insists upon maintaining its ideological monopoly?

Mr Deutscher seems almost to plead with 'the censors': let the senile old poet mumble his memories of the dead, he can do you no harm, Tolstoy and Dostoevsky were also Christians. But the 'censors' may realize that Pasternak's version of 'Christianity', because it speaks of human freedom, *is* a danger to them; and they may feel that they can manage their dictatorship without the help of Western *Besserwissers*. Or perhaps there is truth in Herbert Marcuse's remarks about the Soviet attitude toward art:

> ... it is precisely the catastrophic element inherent in the conflict between man's essence and his existence that has been the center toward which art has gravitated.... The artistic images have preserved the determinate negation of the established reality – ultimate freedom. When Soviet esthetics attacks the principle of the 'insurmountable antagonism between essence and existence' ... it thereby attacks the principle of art itself.

May it not be then, that from *their* point of view, the 'censors' are not so obtuse? Mr Deutscher gives involuntary support to this possibility when he writes that, while a relic in Russia, 'Zhivago still represents a powerful force' in Poland and Hungary. But the Russian 'censors' know how short is the distance from Warsaw or Budapest to Moscow. And in any case, what is the logic of Mr Deutscher's statement? If Zhivago stands for nostalgia for the *ancien régime*, and if in eastern Europe he is a threat to 'the revolution', does it not follow that there may be some ground for suppressing the book, not in Russia, but in Poland and Hungary? Mr Deutscher will of course protest; but let him look to his own words before protesting too quickly.

IV

The heart of the matter is Zhivago's 'archaism' – a charge that reminds one, unhappily, of Trotsky's arrogant habit of dismissing political opponents to the 'ashcan of history'. If one believes that in their essence the Communist states embody the necessary and/or desirable future, then perhaps Zhivago is 'archaic'. But if one believes that the central issue of our time is freedom and that all the 'old' nineteenth-century problems have acquired a new value since the rise of the total state, then Zhivago speaks for the best of the past as it relates to the future. That Pasternak is a kind of 'old-fashioned' and even conservative nineteenth-century liberal I do not doubt; but if socialism is to prove something better than a cruel caricature of its own pretensions, the task of modern politics becomes that of finding a new and more humane mode of realization for the values of nineteenth-century liberalism. It becomes necessary, that is, to find a link between the values of an older generation that is represented by men like Pasternak and a younger generation that is represented by men like the Polish writer Marek Hlasko, who remains a rebel but has broken from Communism because, as he writes, life under Communism is 'a moral atrophy'.

If you have read only Mr Deutscher and not the novel itself, you might suppose Pasternak has nothing to say about such matters. Quite the contrary! It is a main concern of his book. Does, for example, the following passage betray an aesthete's 'archaism' or a profound insight into characteristic vices of totalitarianism?

> Microscopic forms of cardiac hemorrhages have become very frequent in recent years.... It's a typical modern disease. I think its causes are of a moral order. The great majority of us are required to live a life of constant, systematic duplicity. Your health is bound to be affected if, day after day, you say the opposite of what you feel.... I found it painful to listen to you, Innokentii, when you told us how you were re-educated and became

mature in jail. It was like listening to a horse describing how it broke itself in.

Or the following passage: is this a 'voice from the dead' or a humane intelligence portraying the disease of party fanaticism?

> Dudorov's pious platitudes were in the spirit of the times. But it was precisely their conformism, their transparent sanctimoniousness, that exasperated Zhivago. Men who were not free, he thought, always idealize their bondage. So it was in the Middle Ages, and later the Jesuits exploited this same human trait. Zhivago could not bear the political mysticism of the Soviet intelligentsia....

Or is the following a 'parable of a vanished generation' or a voice anticipating the democratic aspirations of tomorrow?

> To conceal the failure [of forced collectivization] people had to be cured, by every means of terrorism, of the habit of thinking and judging for themselves, and forced to see what did not exist.... This accounts for the unexampled cruelty of the Yezhov period, the promulgation of a constitution that was never meant to be applied, and the introduction of elections that violated the very principle of free choice.

If this be 'archaism', let every man who believes in freedom declare himself archaic.

v

Finally, putting aside Mr Deutscher's unfortunate venture into literary criticism, let me try to summarize what seems to me the political meaning of our disagreements. Since I have very little space left, what follows will necessarily be overly condensed, schematic and lacking in qualification.

When a modern state exerts total control over the economy, political power becomes indistinguishable from social and economic power. If, as in Russia, the Party has a monopoly of political power, it also tends to have a monopoly of social and economic power. Democracy then becomes not a 'luxury' which may be gradually expected to make its appearance, parcelled out decades after the totalitarian party has seized power. It is a *sine qua non* for any socialist or 'progressive' development, and its absence signifies that the people have been rendered helpless.

Hegel wrote that 'The lower classes have been left more or less unorganized. And yet it is of the utmost importance that they should be organized, for only in this way can they become powerful. Without organization, they are nothing but a heap, an aggregate of atoms.' This brilliant observation applies exactly to Soviet Russia: the one major industrial country in the world where the working class has never so much as known the experience of a legal strike, an elementary right won in the bourgeois world over a century ago.

The political outlook I have called 'left authoritarianism' remains committed, with all sorts of qualifications, to what it regards as an 'essential' value – the *idea* – of the Communist world. Usually this value is found in nationalized property, which is seen as an ultimate guarantor of progress. Where Marx spoke of 'the categorical imperative that all conditions must be revolutionized in which man is a debased, an abandoned, contemptible being' (how archaic this sounds!), the left authoritarians prefer to speak of the tempo of Russian industrialization or the necessary unfolding of the iron laws of History. Where socialists have traditionally declared that the possibility of a humane society rests upon the capacity of men to act autonomously and freely, ceasing to be objects and becoming subjects of history, the left authoritarians put their faith in economic processes or historical abstractions acting beyond – indeed, usually against – the desires of living men.

Those who accept, wholly or in part, the left authoritarian outlook expect an orderly development, a moderate 'democratization', from within the Communist world and *within the limits of its ethos and power*. It follows that, while sincerely deploring the Russian intervention, they deprecate the Hungarian revolution; that they regard the passion of a Zhivago for individual freedom as a sign of archaism. I think, however, that a commitment to democracy and/or socialism involves a belief in the need for a fundamental change of social relations in the Communist world, which means first and foremost, the collapse or destruction of the monopoly of power of the ruling party, such as occurred two years ago in Hungary and Poland. These contrasting perspectives involve far more than differences in theory or estimate: they involve the very heart of political and moral values.

What Pasternak's views about the future of the Communist world may be, I do not know. But I believe that if and when freedom is re-established in Russia, the people will regard him as one who, quite apart from political opinions, was faithful to the truth of their agony. And for that they will honor him.

Select Bibliography

BOOKS
(a) In English:
Robert Conquest, *Courage of Genius* (Collins & Harvill, 1961).
Donald Davie, *The Poems of Doctor Zhivago* (Manchester U.P., 1965; Barnes & Noble, 1965).
Robert Payne, *The Three Worlds of Boris Pasternak* (Robert Hale, 1961; Coward-McCann, 1961).
Dale L. Plank, *Pasternak's Lyric: A Study of Sound and Imagery* (Mouton & Co., 1966).
Mary F. and Paul Rowland, *Pasternak's Doctor Zhivago* (Southern Ill. U. P., 1967).

(b) In French:
Guy de Mallac, *Boris Pasternak* (Universitaires, 1963).
Jacqueline de Proyart, *Pasternak* (Gallimard, 1964).

(c) In Russian:
Sbornik statei, posvyashchennykh tvorchestvu Borisa Pasternaka ('Collection of articles devoted to the work of Boris Pasternak') ('Institute for the Study of the U.S.S.R., 1962). This volume contains articles by Gleb Struve, Boris Zaitsev, A. Gayev, Fedor Stepun, N. A. Poplyuiko-Anatolyeva, I. Mezhakov-Koryakin, Dmitri Obolensky, L. Rzhevsky, V. A. Aleksandrova, I. N. Bushman and Viktor Frank.

CHAPTERS OF BOOKS
(a) In English:
Maurice Bowra, 'Boris Pasternak 1917–1923', in *The Creative Experiment* (Macmillan, 1949; Grove Press, 1958) pp. 128–58.
Helen Muchnic, 'Boris Pasternak and the poems of Yuri Zhivago', in *From Gorky to Pasternak* (Methuen, 1963; Random House, 1961) pp. 341–404.
Renato Poggioli, 'Boris Pasternak...', in *The Poets of Russia 1890–1930* (Harvard U.P., 1960) pp. 321–42.

John Strachey, 'Russia', in *The Strangled Cry* (Bodley Head, 1962; Sloane, 1962) pp. 44-74.

(b) In Russian:

Mark Slonim, 'Boris Pasternak', in *Portreti sovetskikh pisatelei* (Paris, 1933) pp. 38-47.

Ivan Rozanov, 'Boris Pasternak', in *Russkiye liriki* (Moscow, 1929) pp. 103-31.

A. Selivanovsky, passage in *Ocherki po istorii russkoi sovetskoi poezii* (Moscow, 1936) pp. 183-203.

K. Zelinsky, passage in *Kriticheskiye pis'ma* (Moscow, 1934) pp. 237-57.

ARTICLES

(a) In English:

L. Abel, 'Boris Pasternak's *Doctor Zhivago*', in *Dissent* (Autumn 1959) pp. 334-341. This article is a reply to N. Chiaromonte's article – reproduced in the present volume – in *Partisan Review* (Winter 1958).

Isaiah Berlin, 'The Energy of Pasternak', in *Partisan Review* (Sept-Oct 1950) pp. 748-51.

Nicola Chiaromonte, '*Doctor Zhivago* and modern sensibility', in *Dissent* (Winter 1959) pp. 35-44. This is a reply to L. Abel's article in *Dissent* (Autumn 1959).

J. M. Cohen, 'The Poetry of Pasternak', in *Horizon* (July 1944) p. 23.

—— 'Servant to the Ages', in *Spectator* (6 April 1962) pp. 449-50.

Victor Erlich, 'The Concept of the Poet in Pasternak', in *Slavonic Review* (June 1959) pp. 325-35.

Alexander Gerschenkron, 'Notes on *Doctor Zhivago*', in *Modern Philology*, LVIII (February 1961) iii 194-200.

Stuart Hampshire, '*Dr Zhivago*. As from a lost culture', in *Encounter* (1958) LXII 3-5.

Manya Harari, 'On Translating *Dr Zhivago*', in *Encounter* (May 1959) pp. 51-3.

Max Hayward, 'Pasternak's *Dr Zhivago*', in *Encounter* (May 1958) pp. 38-48.

Angela Livingstone, '*The Childhood of Luvers*: an early story of Pasternak's', in *Southern Review* (Adelaide) (1963) I 74-84.

—— 'Pasternak's Last Poetry', in *Meanjin* (1923) IV 388-96.

—— 'Pasternak's Early Prose', in *Aumla* (November 1964) XXII 249-67.

V. Markov, 'Notes on Pasternak's *Dr Zhivago*', in *Russian Review* (1959) I 14-22.

Helen Muchnic, 'Toward an analysis of Boris Pasternak', in *Slavic and East European Journal* (1957) II 101-5.

Dmitri Obolensky, 'The Poems of Doctor Zhivago', in *Slavonic and East European Review*, XL (1961) xciv 123-45.

Renato Poggioli, 'Boris Pasternak', in *Partisan Review* (Autumn 1958) pp. 541-54.

Select Bibliography

Aleksis Rannit, 'The Rhythm of Pasternak', in *Bulletin of the New York Public Library*, LXIII (1959) xi and LXIV (1960) viii.

F. D. Reeve, '*Doctor Zhivago*: From Prose to Verse', in *Kenyon Review* (Winter 1960) pp. 123-36.

Andrei Sinyavsky, 'The Poetry of Boris Pasternak', trans. P. Tempest, in *Soviet Literature* (Moscow, 1963) II 151-9. All the material in this article was later included by Sinyavsky in the essay reproduced in the present volume.

John Strachey, 'The Strangled Cry', in *Encounter* (December 1960) pp. 23-37. Later reprinted as part of the book *The Strangled Cry* (see above under Chapters of Books).

Gleb Struve, 'Sense and Nonsense about *Dr Zhivago*', in *Studies in Russian and Polish Literature* (The Hague, 1962) pp. 229-50.

—— 'Russia's Terrible Years: *Dr Zhivago*', in *The New Leader* (17 October 1958).

Edmund Wilson, 'Doctor Life and his Guardian Angel', in *New Yorker* (15 November 1958) pp. 201-26.

—— 'Legend and Symbol in *Dr Zhivago*', in *Encounter* (June 1959) pp. 5-16, and *Nation* (25 April 1959).

C. C. Wrenn, 'Boris Pasternak', in *Oxford Slavonic Papers*, II (1951) 82-97.

(b) *In French:*

Michel Aucouturier, 'Boris Pasternak', in *Esprit* (March 1957) pp. 465-9.

—— 'Rôle de l'image dans la poésie de Pasternak', in *Revue des études slaves*, XXXVIII (1961) 45-9.

Alberto Moravia, 'Entretien avec Pasternak', in *Preuves* (July 1958) LXXXVIII 3-7.

Hélène Peltier-Zamoyska, 'L'art et la vie chez Boris Pasternak', in *Revue des études slaves*, XXXVIII (1961).

—— 'Pasternak, homme du passé?', in *Esprit* (January 1963) pp. 16-29.

Denis de Rougemont, 'Nouvelles Métamorphoses de Tristan', in *Preuves* (February 1959) XCVI 14-27, but see especially pp. 23-6.

(c) *In Russian:*

V. Aleksandrov, 'Chastnaya zhizn' ', in *Literaturny kritik* (1937) III 55-81.

Pavel Antokol'sky, 'Boris Pasternak', in *Ispytaniye vremenem* (stat'i) (Moscow, 1945) pp. 99-107.

Nikolai Aseev, 'Pis'ma o poezii', in *Krasnaya Nov'* (1922) III.

Ya. Chernyak, a review of *Sestra moya-zhizn*, in *Pechat' i Revolyutsiya*, VI (1922) 303-4.

V. S. Frank, 'Stikhi Borisa Pasternaka iz romana Doktora Zhivago', in *Opyty* (1958) IX 17-22.

—— 'Realizm chetyryokh izmereniy', in *Mosty* (1959) II 189-209.

L. Khalafov, 'O muzyke stikhov Pasternaka', in *Mosty* (1961) VIII 120-9.
Viktor Krasil'nikov, 'Boris Pasternak', in *Pechat' i revolyutsiya* (1927) V 78-91.
Mikhail Kuzmin, 'Govoryashchiye', in *Uslovnosti* (Stat'i ob iskusstve) (Petrograd, 1923) pp. 158-61.
Konstantin Loks, a review of Rasskazy, in *Krasnaya Nov'* (1925) VIII 286-7.
R. Miller-Budnitskaya, 'O 'filosofii iskusstva' Borisa Pasternaka i R. M. Rilke', in *Zvezda* (1932) V 160-8.
Marina Tsvetayeva, 'Epos i lirika sovremennoi Rossii: Vladimir Mayakovsky i Boris Pasternak', in *Novy Grad* (1933) VI 28-41.
Wladimir Weidle, introductory essays to vol. I (pp. xxxv-xliv), vol. II (pp. vii-xiii) and vol. III (pp. vii-xv) of Pasternak, *Sochineniya (Works)* (University of Michigan Press, 1961).

PUBLISHED LETTER

Novy Mir Editorial Board, 'Letter to Boris Pasternak', in Russian in *Literaturnaya Gazeta* (25 October 1958) and in English (i) as an appendix to R. Conquest, *Courage of Genius* (see above under Books) pp. 136-63, and (ii) entitled 'A Letter of Rejection', in *New York Times Book Review* (7 December 1958).

Notes on Contributors

ANNA AKHMATOVA (1888–1966). Russian poet. She belonged to the Acmeist school of poetry and was the author of *Vecher, Chetki, Belaya staya, Anno domini MCMXXI* and *Requiem*.

NIKOLAI ASEEV (1889–1963). Russian poet. He belonged to the same Futurist group as Mayakovsky and helped to found the journal *Lef* in 1923. He was the author of *Stolichnaya lirika* and *Stikhi na sluchai*.

MICHEL AUCOUTURIER is lecturer in Slavonic languages and literatures at the University of Geneva, and author of *Pasternak par lui-même*.

NICOLA CHIAROMONTE is co-editor, with Ignazio Silone, of the Italian monthly *Tempo presente* and author of *La situazione drammatica*.

ISAAC DEUTSCHER (1907–67). Historian and journalist, and author of *Stalin, a political biography, The Prophet Armed, The Prophet Unarmed* and *The Prophet Outcast*.

ILYA EHRENBURG (1891–1967). Russian journalist and novelist. He was a war-correspondent for Russian/Soviet newspapers during the First World War, the Spanish Civil War and the Second World War. He lived for many years in Western Europe and returned permanently to the Soviet Union in 1940. He was the author of *Padeniye Parizha* (*The Fall of Paris*), *Burya* (*The Storm*), *Ottepel'* (*The Thaw*) and *Lyudi, gody, zhizn'* (*People, Years, Life*).

IRVING HOWE teaches at the City University of New York and is the author of *William Faulkner* and *Politics and the Novel*.

ROMAN JAKOBSON, Russian literary historian and theoretician, linguistic scholar, and a leading member of the Moscow group of Formalists, left Russia in 1920 and became a leading authority in the Prague Linguistic Circle. He has lived in the United States for the last twenty years, teaches at Harvard and is the author of *Noveishaya russkaya poeziya*.

A. LEZHNEV (1893–1938). Russian literary critic. He belonged to the literary group Pereval (1923–32) and contributed to its journal *Krasnaya nov'*. He was the author of *Proza Pushkina*.

OSIP MANDEL'SHTAM (1891–1938). Russian poet. One of the founders of the poetic movement Acmeism. He was exiled within Russia in 1934, arrested again in 1938 and died in a prison camp. He was the author of *Kamen'*, *Tristia* and *Yegipetskaya marka* (*The Egyptian Stamp*).

ANDREI SINYAVSKY, Russian literary critic and novelist, was senior research fellow at the Gorky Institute of World Literature in Moscow until 1965, when he was sentenced to seven years' imprisonment 'for defaming his country' in works of fiction published abroad under the pseudonym Abram Tertz. At present he is in a prison camp. He is the author with A. N. Menshutin, of *Poeziya pervykh let revolyutsii 1917–1920*, and, as Tertz, of *Sud idyot* (*The Trial Begins*) and *Lyubimov* (*The Makepeace Experiment*).

MARINA TSVETAYEVA (1892–1941). Russian poet. She left Russia in 1922, lived in Prague and Paris, returned to Russia in 1939 and committed suicide there. She was the author of *Versty*, *Pereulochki*, *Posle Rossii*, *Remeslo*, *Tsar'-devitsa* and *Krysolov*.

YURI TYNYANOV (1894–1943). Russian biographical novelist, literary historian and theoretician. He was a prominent member of the Formalist school of criticism in Petrograd, and author of *Kukhlya*, *Pushkin* and *Problema poeticheskovo yazyka*.

VLADIMIR WEIDLE, Russian literary scholar and thinker, left Russia in 1924 and has lived since then in Paris where for twenty years he was Professor of the History of Christian Art at the Institute of Orthodox Theology. He is the author of *Les Abeilles d'Aristée: essai sur le destin actuel des Lettres et des Arts*, *La Russie absente et présente* (*Russia Absent and Present*) and of critical introductions to each of the first three volumes of Pasternak's *Works* published at the University of Michigan.

Index

AERIAL WAYS 113, 114, 119–20, 149, 221
Afinogenov, A. (quoted) 31–2
'AFTER THE STORM' 204
Akhmatova, Anna 41, 56–7, 69, 76
'APPROACH OF WINTER' 203
Aseev, Nikolai 25–6

Batyushkov, K. 16, 68
Baudelaire, Charles 15
Bely, Andrei 75
BLACK GOBLET, THE 187
Blok, Alexander 20–1, 23, 43, 75, 166, 175–6; *Retribution* 196–7; *The Twelve* 255–6
'BREAK, THE', 25–6, 81–3, 89–90
Brik, Osip ('Zvukovye povtory') 19
Bryusov, Valeri 14, 17–18, 76
Bukharin, Nikolai 30
Byron, George Gordon, Lord 16–17, 47

Centrifuga 14, 40
Chaplin, Charles (*A Woman of Paris*) 141
CHILDHOOD OF LUVERS, THE 93–4, 113, 119, 139, 144, 148, 178, 221
Chopin, Frédéric 173
'CONQUEROR, THE', 203
Conquest, Robert 30
Crane, Hart 23; *White Buildings* 13; *The Bridge* 25

Dal', Vladimir 112 and n
'DEATH OF THE POET' (quoted) 27–8, 179–80; (discussed) 28–9, 179, 184–5
'DEFINITION OF POETRY' 211
'DEFINITION OF THE SOUL' 211
Deutscher, Isaac 259–68 passim
DOCTOR ZHIVAGO 29, 31, 32, 33, 221, 231–8, 240–58, 259–68
Dryden, John 28, 29
Duncan, Robert (quoted) 12

Ehrenburg, Ilya 42, 43
Eliot, T. S. 15; 'Love Song of J. Alfred Prufrock' 14; *Four Quartets* 14
Erlich, Victor 22
ESSAY IN AUTOBIOGRAPHY, AN 32, (quoted) 175–6

Fet, Afanasy 70, 74–5, 133
'FIRST FROSTS' 167
Ford, Ford Madox 26–7
Formalism 19–20
'FROM AN UNPRINTABLE . . . (quoted) 90–1, (discussed) 91–2
Futurism 17, 70 n, 76, 95, 100–1, 110, 126, 135, 136, 157, 172, 174, 175

Goethe, J. W. von 88
Gogol, Nikolai 73
Gorky, Maxim 23–4, 30, 198–9; *Life of Klim Samgin* 199
'GRASS AND STONES' 204
Gumilev, Nikolai 76

'HAMLET' 228
Heine, Heinrich 41, 47

Hlasko, Marek 266

IL TRATTO DI APELLE 113, 221–6, 229
Impressionism 209–11
'IT SOUNDS STILL, LIKE THE PLAINT . . .' (quoted) 87–8, (discussed) 89

Joyce, James (*Finnegans Wake*) 12

Khlebnikov, Viktor 68 and n, 70, 75, 110, 126, 138–9, 146, 151, 182
Khomyakov, A. S. 75
'KREMLIN IN A STORM, THE' 188–9
Kuzmin, Mikhail 69; *Otherworldly Evenings* 69

Laforgue, Jules 15
LAST SUMMER, THE see Tale
Lermontov, Mikhail 22, 39, 45, 75
LETTERS FROM TULA 113, 226–8
LIEUTENANT SCHMIDT 23–4, 120–1, 193, 196, 205
'LITTLE GIRL, A' 169
LOFTY MALADY, THE 23, 120, 190, 191–2
Lomonosov, Mikhail 68
Lowell, Robert (*Life Studies*) 25

Mallarmé, Stéphane 14
Mandel'shtam, Osip 16, 18
'MARGARITA' (quoted) 116, (discussed) 13, 117
Mayakovsky, Vladimir 15, 18, 20–1, 23, 53, 75, 101, 104, 126, 137, 138, 140–1, 143, 146, 147, 148, 151, 155, 165, 166, 168, 178, 186
'MIRROR, THE' 169
Mirsky, D. S. 24–5
MY SISTER LIFE 13, 16, 22, 24, 33, 42–66, 69, 71, 130–3, 142, 156, 157, 158, 169, 187, 223
'MY SISTER LIFE' 89

Nadson, S. 75
NARRATIVE, THE see Tale

Nekrasov, Nikolai 75
NINETEEN HUNDRED AND FIVE 23–4, 25, 120–4, 191, 195, 198

Olson, Charles (*Projective Verse*) 26
ON EARLY TRAINS 32, 159, 203
'ON EARLY TRAINS' 204
OVER THE BARRIERS 20, 46 n, 147, 157, 222

Pisarev, D. I. 74
Plank, Dale 12, 13, 14, 24–5, 26, 27
Poggioli, Renato 22
Pound, Ezra 13, 23, 32–3; *Homage to Sextus Propertius* 26; *Cantos* 27
Pushkin, Alexander 69, 74; 'The Prophet' 88; 'I Recall a Miraculous Moment' 88

Reavey, George 22
Reissner, Larissa see 'To the Memory of Reissner'
'RENDING THE RAIMENT BRUSH...' see 'Margarita'
Revolution, Pasternak and 17–18, 19, 24, 54–6, 106, 155, 176, 186–90, 200, 240–58 passim, 262
Richards, I. A. (*Principles of Literary Criticism*) 12

SAFE CONDUCT 14, 15, 20–1, 22, 142, 144–6, 147, 148, 149, 150, 176
SECOND BIRTH 26, 27, 158, 216
SELECTED POEMS 96
SELECTED TRANSLATIONS 31
Severyanin, Igor 75, 130
Shakespeare, William 28, 207–8; *Hamlet* 205–6, 207
Shklovsky, Viktor 19
Sinyavsky, Andrei 25
'SLANTWISE IMAGES, THE' 128
Sologub, F. 69 and n
SPEKTORSKY 23, 120, 193–4, 199–202
'SPRING' 203
Stendhal 13
Symbolism 13–15, 17, 21, 69, 109–10, 135, 136, 137, 139, 157, 175, 225

Index

'TAKE AND BLOCK ME...' 117
TALE, A 165, 229–30
'TERRIBLE TALE, A' 203
THEMES AND VARIATIONS 75, 78, 79, 81, 84, 117, 118, 120, 158, 174
'TO THE MEMORY OF REISSNER' 213
Tolstoy, Aleksei 75
Tolstoy, Lev 93; *War and Peace* 244, 247, 263
Translation 31, 206–8
Trotsky, L. (*Literature and Revolution*) 249
Tsvetayeva, Marina 32, 166, 168, 179
TWIN IN THE CLOUDS 157, 222
Tynyanov, Yuri 12, 20
Tyutchev, Fyodor 74, 75, 85, 102–3

Valéry, Paul 14, 15

VAST EARTH, THE 203
Verlaine, Paul 14, 15, 26, 129, 181

'WAVES, THE' 185, 202–3
'WEEPING GARDEN, THE' 168–9
Weidle, Wladimir 13, 27
WHEN THE WEATHER CLEARS 33, 203
Williams, William Carlos 23

Yazykov, N. M. 67, 74, 75
YEAR 1905, THE *see* Nineteen Hundred and Five
Yeats, W. B. 16–17, 23, 29
Yesenin, Sergei 20–1, 23, 88, 132, 166

Zamyatin, Yevgeni 15
Zukofsky, Louis 13, 21, 22, 23